RECONCEIVING PART-TIME WORK

RECONCEIVING PART-TIME WORK

New Perspectives for
Older Workers and Women

Hilda Kahne

Wheaton College

ROWMAN & ALLANHELD
PUBLISHERS

ROWMAN & ALLANHELD

Published in the United States of America in 1985
by Rowman & Allanheld, Publishers
(a division of Littlefield, Adams & Company)
81 Adams Drive, Totowa, New Jersey 07512

Library of Congress Cataloging in Publication Data

Kahne, Hilda.
  Reconceiving part-time work.

Bibliography: p. 160.
  Includes index.
  1. Part-time employment — United States.   2. Aged —
Employment — United States.   3. Women — Employment —
United States.   I. Title.
HD5110.2U5K33   1985   331.3'94   85-2386
ISBN 0-8476-7376-6

85 86 87 / 10 9 8 7 6 5 4 3 2 1
Printed in the United States of America

For Merton
Whose view of the forest is never obscured
by the many trees

Contents

Tables and Figures

Preface

A number of trends in societal values and demographic and economic directions have converged in the mid-1980s to make urgent the need for thoughtful inquiry into part-time work. An awareness of these trends has led me to write this book.

First, the growing importance of paid work in the lives of both women and men is occurring at the same time that more flexibility and a greater range in gender roles and lifestyles have come into being. These changes raise questions about the allocation of time and about the work arrangements that would help to dovetail paid work with other productive activities and to time devoted to education, leisure, and family.

Second, these value changes in the use of time have been matched by a series of demographic and socio economic trends that influence in several ways the demand for and the supply of workers. For one thing, we are experiencing a graying of America. About one-fifth of our population in 1982 were aged 55 and over; that proportion may grow to one-third in the next half-century. By 2010 the longevity of persons aged 65 and over, now 19 years for women and 14 years for men, may increase by another two to three years. Long-range planning must not only assure the provision and financing of economic security for the greater numbers of older workers and retirees and for the extended length of their later lives, but must also develop options that permit these years to be spent in satisfying ways. Although at present there is strong older worker interest in one option, part-time work, older workers do not always elect to work that schedule, even when it would seem to fit their needs, partly because of the lack of status and low pay of its standard form. More appealing and broadly available reduced-hour work schedules could alter the choices older workers make about working part time.

The growing proportion of women in the labor force — 43 percent today, perhaps 47 percent by 1995 — is another significant trend. For particular periods in the lives of some women, part-time work, even when low in status and poorly paid, has been a necessity. One-fourth of all employed married women work part time. Seventy percent of persons who work part time by choice are women. For the forseeable future, with only slowly changing gender roles at best, availability of part-time work with desirable qualities is critical for women's well-being and quality of life.

Both demographic changes portend an increase in the demand for part-time work. At the same time, there is a potential increase in the supply of part-time jobs related to the expansion of occupations and industries where part-time work has been traditionally found. Also, the experience of new social programs demonstrates the possibility of part-time work in workplace settings where it has not heretofore been common.

These trends have provided the context for the book's development. But I also came to the study with a general belief in the importance of institutional change for ensuring social betterment. I believe that the specific institution of work structures must adapt if on-going changes in attitudes and activities and policies about paid work and the use of time are to result in an improved quality of life rather than an increase in stress and conflict. I have sought through this study to test whether such adaptation was possible and at what cost and benefit. I found that a new concept of part-time work was evolving in the society. Sometimes it arose from individual initiative; sometimes it was developed cooperatively by groups affected by the schedules; sometimes it was introduced unilaterally by employers or resulted from governmental policy. Whatever its origin, however, part-time work brought benefits both to individuals and to their employing organizations, and had some positive "spillover" effects for societal well-being as well.

This book contributes to an excellent, already existing literature on work structures, which sometimes creates a foundation of cases on which to base generalizations, and other times provides an overview of prevailing attitudes and experience. Although sharing some of the outlook and information provided in these earlier studies, this book differs from them in at least two important respects.

1. Since issues become clearer when viewed in specific context, I chose to focus the study on the perspectives and consequences of part-time work for older workers, aged 55 and over, and in one central chapter, on the special case of women, for whom part-time work is not only useful in later life, but is an essential option to have available throughout the course of life. The lessons of the experience, however, apply more generally than to the specific focus of the book. They could apply equally well to young women and men who seek part-time work as an accompaniment to education and training. Or they could relate to men in adult years, gradually becoming less locked into full-time work as a continuing, unremitting course of life, who want to experiment with breaks in full-time employment to enhance their careers, pursue an avocation, increase their family time, or simply take a break from the pressures of work.

2. The book distinguishes between standard, "Old Concept" part-time work, that is, work in low paid, low status jobs with few fringe benefits, and "New Concept" part-time work, which began to emerge in the late 1960s. Of several types — regular part-time work, job sharing, work sharing, phased retirement — the New Concept forms combine a common quality of fewer than 35 work hours a week paid on the basis of prorated earnings and at least

some prorated fringe benefits, with their own distinctive structure. Although not yet widespread, the forms apply to a variety of occupations in both public and private sectors. This book is primarily focused on these New Concept part-time work forms, which offer both job status and work history progression. Among other concerns, the study seeks to determine whether and where such schedules are likely to grow and what are the expected problems and benefits to be taken into account in guiding their development. Public policy encouragement could be of great help to worker and employer initiatives that seek to forge mutually advantageous reduced-hour work options for a particular labor force and workplace setting.

As it sets forth the case for an extension of New Concept part-time work, the book relies heavily on American experience. It examines expressed preference of older workers for reduced-hour schedules and the experience of both women and older workers with part-time work. It also provides an analysis of the attitudes, policies, and programs of organizations (both trade unions and firms) that relate to part-time work, and the social policies and legislation that influence the availability and provisions of the part-time work that is offered.

When I began my research I visited Sweden, hoping to discover some guidelines for improving and extending part-time work opportunities applicable to needs in the United States. What I found was a situation much like that in our own country. In both countries a high proportion of persons who work part-time schedules by choice are women (70 percent in the U.S.; about 85 percent in Sweden), and they do so because of the need simultaneously to care for family and to work. Swedish trade unions, like those in the United States, primarily focus their policies on the needs of full-time workers. They are skeptical about part-time work as a short-run goal, worrying, not without some justification, about the potential competition of part-time with full-time jobs. At present, rather than seeking to integrate a broader concept of part-time work into the customary work structures, they advocate, as do trade unions in the United States, a reduction in the standard time of a full-time work period (work day or workweek) for all workers. Nonetheless, Swedish social policy does include a national program providing for phased retirement. Because of its uniqueness and its successful functioning in an area where American experience is limited, I have included a discussion of the Swedish partial pension program.

The book is addressed to several audiences. I have tried to speak particularly to researchers—both academic and those who are program-oriented—in the hope that a better understanding of what is known can provide a useful foundation for addressing the many research questions on program and policy development that have yet to be examined. To this end, the book is heavily referenced. At the same time, I hope that unions, employers, policy makers in state and federal governments, and persons in organizations working with or thinking about the needs and interests of older workers and women will find the discussion enlightening and suggestive of the useful (and less useful) directions for moving in this "new, old field." Readers who, in another context, may find themselves in the groups for whom part-time structures are being developed, may also find the discussion helpful in formulating perspectives about the value of part-time work for themselves as individuals and the circumstances under which working such schedules would benefit them.

In this era of realism, no one expects to find a universally applicable magic formula for designing beneficial part-time work options. What may be surprising to the reader, however, is the variety of advantages that can redound to the several affected groups. My hope is that the book goes beyond spelling out "the state of the art" to provide specific indications of the values to be gained, as well as the pitfalls and problems to be avoided in developing and implementing an expanded concept of part-time work. While not guaranteeing an instant panacea, I have tried to demonstrate the strong need that exists for more concentrated, serious thinking on the part of workers, unions, management, and government about general policies and company programs that will help New Concept part-time work move from visionary concept to practical reality among the range of work structure options available. If the concept does take shape in this way, the expansion of part-time work which is certainly in the cards for the future, will be, for some, considerably more than an adaptation to need: it will be a source of progress toward an improved quality of life.

As in any evolution of ideas, the contribution of others has been critical to the development of my own thinking. The long list of acknowledgments begins with deep gratitude to President Alice Emerson and Provost Hannah Goldberg at Wheaton College, who made possible work on the book through a two-year appointment as the A. Howard Meneely Professor. The appointment provided released time from teaching and financial support, although it also created some conflict in having to isolate myself from a campus that is both enormously stimulating in its forward educational thrust and collegial in its working environment. A grant from the John Anson Kittridge Foundation made possible a 1982 trip to Sweden to explore part-time work arrangements and policies and helped to delineate the focus of the book. An appointment as Visiting Scholar at the Wellesley College Center for Research on Women provided contact with other researchers. Colleagues in the Wheaton Economics Department relieved me of departmental burdens and were always willing to listen and to react to my questions. Kathy Francis, Nancy Shepardson, and Diane Rowe prepared the tables and instructed me in the use of the computer. Liz Murtha, Maliha Chughtai, Jackie George, Ann Kohler, Sue Taylor, and especially Linda Fitzpatrick, who computerized the reference list, all have my gratitude for doing my work when they had plenty of their own to keep them occupied. The Wheaton College Computer Center was an important support.

A host of friends and professional contacts generously contributed time and expertise to development of the manuscript. Sara Rix heads my list. She, along with Steve Sandell, encouraged me to move forward on the project. Sara also introduced me to persons in her large network of research and government contacts, provided otherwise unobtainable research materials, and offered, with continuing enthusiasm and good humor, immediate, supportive, yet honest comment on every chapter. Other readers for specific chapters included Karen Arenson, Lenore Bixby, Deborah Chollet, Sally Coberly, Janet Giele, Howard Hayghe, Linda Ittner, Eric Kingson, Barbara Lazarus, Stephen McConnell, Ida Merriam, Stanley Nollen, Michael Piore, Joseph Pleck, Virginia Reno, Ruth Roemer, Bob Rosenbaum, Marjorie Rosenbaum, Gail Rosenberg, Rosalie Schofield, James Schulz, Lois Shaw, Dean Tibbs, and George Wallis. Without the contribution of their comprehensive knowledge and generosity of time, the book would be less accurate and less rich. Ann Bark of Boston and Stockholm and Marianne Pettersson Sundström and Mats Fellenius of Stockholm, among others, provided me with materials and comment about part-time work and social policies in Sweden. Judith Cohen and Shirley Radlo made sure that I had the most accurate and recent government data. In addition to generously shared written materials from a variety of sources and a first conference of the Association of Part-time Professionals, led by Diane Rothberg, a number of interviews were held with researchers, lobbyists, trade union leaders, and company representatives. Interviewees included Cynthia McCaughan, Alice Quinlan, Linda Tarr-Whelan, Joseph Perkins, Larry Smedley, Jennifer Schirmer, Ellen Wernick, Laura Walker, and John Zalusky.

Spencer Carr and the staff of Rowman & Allanheld, especially Janet Johnston, gently provided both guidance and support and taught me that publishing can be a pleasure as well as a challenge. They both improved the manuscript in a number of important ways and gracefully accepted, when necessary, my editorial stubbornness.

My family, as do families of all writers, deserves special thanks. David Kahne read what I thought was a finished manuscript. He managed not only to convince me of the benefits of one more editing round, but showed me ways to realize those benefits. David, Daniel, and Joseph, by their interest but even more by their own social values, enthusiasm, high standards, and professional commitment for their own work, kept me focused on mine. As in all good things in my life, Merton Kahne played a major role. He constantly clarified issues, expanded my thinking, and checked on the more technical details of how best to communicate and transcribe what I was trying to say. Without his perceptive overview I would long ago have become lost in some black hole of unfinished business or been buried by the consequences of following some blind alley of inquiry.

Of course, the final responsibility for whatever errors remain is mine.

RECONCEIVING PART-TIME WORK

1

Introduction

Part-time work assumes a new importance today. Partly it is so because of increasing longevity and new attitudes toward allocating time between work, family, leisure, and retirement. But changing labor force characteristics, evolving occupational and industrial trends, continuing underemployment, and technological job displacement are also helping to shake up established norms surrounding work patterns. It has become apparent that a reassessment of industrial and social policies on work scheduling is called for to respond to worker needs and interests and to meet enterprise and societal production and welfare goals. Clearly, it is time to take stock of our institutional arrangements to see how well work scheduling meshes with the interests, needs, and lifestyles of individuals in the mid-1980s and with the production efficiency of enterprises where they work.

Changing Values and Labor Market Trends

Part-time work has been around for a long time, but it has traditionally applied to a limited range of occupations and offered few opportunities for career advancement. In its traditional form, which I will designate "Old Concept" part-time work, hourly earnings are low, even if measured against equivalent full-time jobs, and fringe benefits are minimal or nonexistent. This kind of part-time work, although useful and necessary for many individuals at various times in their lives, has been held in low esteem.

In recent years, however, several simultaneous trends have stimulated an interest in what we may call "New Concept" part-time work, under which full-time earnings are prorated, fringe benefits are paid, and a career progression is possible. Changing values since the 1960s — an outgrowth of the philosophy underlying the women's movement — fostered and supported greater engagement of all adult women in paid work at a time when the proportions of younger and older men in the labor force were decreasing.[1] These developments have raised critical questions about how to reconcile the interests and needs of family lives — important to both women and men as a source of life satisfaction[2] — with the time constraints associated with full-time paid work. More and more individuals are experiencing the need and desire for flexibility in work and life patterns.[3] We no longer think, for example, of education and training as occurring only prior to labor market entry, to be followed by a period of full-time work in adult life and then retirement.[4] It is increasingly acceptable for education and training to take place at any time during adulthood, whether it is education for pleasure or profit, retraining in response to technological change, or recharting of career direction. Sometimes flexibility takes the form of a temporary "stopping out" of paid work, made easier perhaps by the fact that in 62 percent of married couples with an employed husband, the wife also works. Sometimes the preference is to combine a commitment partially to paid work and partially to non-paid activities; here the options are much more limited.

The trend in changing values has been matched by a second series of demographic and economic changes that affect the demand for and supply of workers in several ways. In the mid-1980s the U.S. economy is creating 4 million new jobs a year, and a changing industrial/occupational mix reflects a relative increase of those occupations where reduced hours synchronize well with fluctuating production or service needs. The greater demand for labor is tempered, however, by both a continuing short-run unemployment rate (hovering, in the spring of 1984, around 7.5 percent) and the threat of a growing technological unemployment. This demand is not uniformly strong throughout the economy.

At the same time, several changes are affecting the supply of labor. Although the overall labor supply is growing, particularly for groups for whom part-time work has traditionally been important, it is not keeping pace with the annual increase in demand. Moreover, as the baby-boom generation born in the 1950s moves through the adult years, there is also some shift in the age distribution of the labor force, with fewer young workers, numerically as well as proportionately. Older workers are living longer. The view is growing that older workers offer a resource of labor that must be encouraged not only to provide stimulation and income for them during the longer length of their lives, but to prevent the waste of socially valuable skills and experience.

There is increasing inquiry into the appropriate combination of retirement income and paid work that will respond to older worker preferences and at the same time serve the needs of society. Focus is increasingly directed toward alternative ways of scheduling worktime that will help to prevent the loss of the resource potential that older workers offer. An increase in part-time work is one way of responding to these several interests, an increase that is fostered by emerging new forms of reduced hours that have a broader occupational and industrial applicability than has been true in the past.

This book explores the interest and experience with a new conception of part-time work in order to understand more fully its potential and problems. It seeks to assess the degree to which New Concept part-time work is a viable work scheduling form, first, for workers in later years of life who are moving toward retirement, but ultimately for other workers as well, for whom the options have appeal.

It is a book with a message as well as a purpose, for it notes that many of the on-going currents of societal change have implications for the scheduling of work hours. At the same time, the emerging new forms of part-time work offer a variety of reduced hour alternatives with economic rewards often equivalent to those of full-time jobs. Such an environment can lead only to growth in the use of part-time work. The book is thus more than an academic exploration into an interesting topic; it is a study to guide the development of a useful work schedule arrangement that is sure to increase in importance. Institutional change in the workplace is often slow to occur. But when it does, it is important that it takes a form that maximizes the benefits for individuals and enterprises and minimizes the problems and costs.

Workweek Hours and Part-Time Work: A Brief History

There has been a long history of change in the length of the standard workweek and the average number of hours actually worked at a point in time. As early as 1887, Samuel Gompers declared, "As long as we have one person seeking work who cannot find it, the hours of work are too long,"[5] and this provided a general philosophical underpinning for the historical movement for shortening the full-time workweek. Standard weekly hours for workers on full-time schedules, which were about 60 hours in 1900, declined to approximately 50 hours in 1929. During the Depression, the 40 hour workweek was widely adopted, often to share the available work in a period of mass unemployment.[6] A standard workweek of 44 hours was written into social policy with enactment of the Fair Labor Standards Act of 1938 and was reduced to 40 hours in 1940, and pay at a time and a half penalty rate was required for hours worked beyond the weekly maximum.

Since World War II, although the average workweek hours for non-agricultural workers on full-time schedules have remained quite steady (43.8 hours in May 1969, 42.7 hours in 1983),[7] the average weekly hours worked, including part-time work, have continued a gradual decline, falling from 39.7, in May 1968, to 38.1 hours, in 1983. Reasons for this edging downward of hours include the increase of women and youth in the labor market, groups for whom reduced work hours have particular appeal because of additional time demands of family or education; the increase in the importance of those industries where part-time work has been a tradition; the effects of collective bargaining provisions and hours legislation shortening work hours of full-time workers; and sometimes unemployment levels.[8] Employed part-time workers during this period have increased at a faster rate than full-time workers. Their proportion in the non-agricultural labor force grew from 16.4 percent of employees in 1970 to 20.2 percent in 1982. Partly offsetting the diminishing effect of part-time work on average hours worked was a slight increase in the average hours of the part-time work itself.[9]

Until some recent changes, part-time work has largely reflected negative characteristics that have come to be associated with it as a work form. Part-time jobs are often located in occupations (for example, waitressing, sales, clerical) and industries (for example, service) that require relatively little skill and involve discrete tasks that are repetitive and associated with little career advancement. Entrance to and exit from such work requires little dovetailing or overlap of duties or of communication. Job status is low, earnings are poor — even in relation to a comparable full-time job, and fringe benefits are few and, in fact, often absent.

Despite these drawbacks, standard, Old Concept part-time work provides a useful work and earnings connection for several groups of workers — women, youth, older workers — when a full-time labor force attachment is not possible. It also acts as a flexible scheduling mechanism for employers in maintaining low costs for the kinds of jobs just described and for those with irregular work flows. Employers often take a narrow view of the effects that part-time work can have. Although they often see such work as a way of maintaining low labor costs, they do not commonly perceive it as a scheduling form that contributes as well to productivity, either directly or indirectly, through the increased work satisfaction that the reduced hours can engender. In its present guise, employers see part-time work as having a particular, but limited, value. Workers view it as a useful, although frequently exploitative work schedule.

Need this be so? Is it inevitable that part-time work have such a negative image? Can the concept be more broadly applied occupationally, with economic rewards more commensurate with those of equivalent full-time work, and still offer benefits to workers, employers, and society, that compensate for any additional costs? These are the questions addressed in this book.

Future Possibilities: A Focus on Older Workers

The questions asked are large ones and cannot yet be answered definitively. But the data and experience on which to base a judgment are growing. For one thing, the supply of those workers who have traditionally sought part-time work schedules is increasing. As a proportion of the civilian labor force, women are expected to grow from 43 percent today to about 46 percent by 1990.[10] The population is also gradually aging, and under attractive work circumstances this could mean some increase in the numbers of older workers and in the degree to which they seek part-time work to accompany other non-market activities.

Demand factors will also have an effect on part-time work of the future. Growth is expected in those industries and occupations where part-time work has been traditionally found. Between 1982 and 1995, service industries are expected to account for almost 75 percent of all new jobs, compared with 16.9 percent in manufacturing.[11] Professional and technical jobs, service employment, clerical work, and sales occupations will all exhibit considerable growth.[12] One in three new jobs will be in direct service areas such as medical care, personal services, and business and professional services.[13]

Accompanying these changes in the demand for and supply of labor is a quietly growing experience with a variety of forms of New Concept part-time work, a work pattern initiated by individuals or innovative companies and fostered by social policies and, at times, by researchers who have brought together in their writing information gained from case studies, with interpretive insights. The forms include job sharing (where two persons fill an equivalent full-time position), work sharing (where work hours are reduced, sometimes to enlarge opportunities and sometimes to ration available worktime in temporary periods of employment slack), and phased retirement (a combination of part-time work and partial retirement). Together with regular, New Concept part-time work, they offer rearranged work schedules that enlarge the part-time occupational and industrial range, and in so doing increase the numbers of persons for whom part-time work is seen as a viable alternative to the choices of full-time work or full retirement. They offer more flexibility of worktime, prorated earnings and fringe benefits, as well as career potential. Their increased adoption could change the image of part-time work and demonstrate that it is neither a passing fancy, nor as limited in applicability and potential as was once thought.

The focus in this book will be primarily on older women and men workers, aged 55 and over, a group constituting a growing proportion of our population (20.6 percent in March 1982 and a projected 24.4 percent in 2010). For them, part-time work can have particular appeal, as children become independent and economic requirements of maintaining a family become less. Part-time employment can combine the possibility of some income cushion for the stress arising from the job, health considerations, or general economic climate of inflation. The free time it creates can be used to further education or training or to enjoy leisure activities and the serenity that can accompany a gradual transition to retirement. But the implications of the findings will extend to other working groups, as well, especially to adult women of all ages, for whom reduced-hour work is often essential in some periods of their life span to meet the competing claims on time of home responsibilities. By highlighting issues and experience in relation to the older population, it is hoped that the result will be a greater awareness of the general applicability of part-time work to working members of society and of its potential benefits for enhancing productive efficiency as well as for improving the quality of individuals' lives.

Chapter Organization

The themes of the book will become clear in a description of the chapter organization. Chapter 2 provides an overview of demographic, labor market, and labor force characteristics and trends that help to explain the current situation and why an expanded concept of part-time work is relevant for the U.S. labor market and for older workers in the 1980s and beyond. Chapter 3 examines the prevalence and characteristics of part-time work in both its positive and negative attributes. Standard, Old Concept part-time work and New Concept forms of reduced-hour schedules are discussed and compared, including the rationale behind their introduction. Older workers, although not alone in their interest in part-time work, often have particular reasons for wanting to ease the strains of full-time work schedules. Sweden's phased retirement public policy approach is examined for the lessons it can bring to the evolution of American policies.

The book turns in Chapter 4 to the special case of women workers. Particularly pertinent to women are the difference in work experience between older women and older men and the need of many adult women of all ages to find a way to combine work and family roles that will result in fewer discontinuities in attachment to the labor market, with their negative consequences for careers, earnings, and retirement income. These are the negative consequences that New Concept part-time work could ameliorate.

Chapter 5 focuses more sharply on older worker interest in part-time work in general and on factors of economic status and health that influence and mold these preferences. Measures of economic status for aged and non-aged groups are compared and consideration given to the role that part-time work could play in contributing to economic security. A continued attachment to the paid labor market for older persons is closely related both to retirement provisions and to health. The question to be considered here is how employment and retirement decisions for persons with no more than moderate health limitations might be affected by a greater availability of part-time jobs with prorated earnings and fringe benefits.

Chapter 6 continues the exploration of the contingent factors by looking at the impact of inflation and unemployment on worker well-being and the effects of these economic conditions on older worker interest in part-time work. Because experience with inflation seems not, under present conditions, to have influenced retirement decisions in a major way, it is difficult to predict the effect that an enlarged concept of part-time work might have in extending an employment connection under inflationary conditions. On the other hand, social policy has brought about an increase in reduced-hour scheduling through state programs of work sharing in periods of temporary employment retrenchment. These programs provide important information about attitudes and experience with reduced-hour part-time work, discussed in Chapters 6, 7, 8, and 9. The role that part-time work could play in reducing the effects of long-run structural unemployment is also considered.

With respect to older workers, social policy has not been neutral toward part-time work, although, until the past few years, its effect has been felt indirectly through legislative provisions affecting the choice between work and retirement. In recent times, the influence has been more direct, with legislation facilitating development of reduced-hour schedules or providing a part-time public employment role model. Chapter 7 examines the influence of provisions of Old Age, Survivors, and Disability Insurance (OASDI), the Employee Retirement Income Security Act (ERISA), and the Age Discrimination in Employment Act (ADEA) on part-time work and describes other federal and state legislation that extends or supports development of New Concept part-time jobs.

In Chapters 8 and 9, attention turns to the industrial scene and the views and experience of unions and enterprises with respect to reduced-hour work.

Chapter 8 discusses union attitudes about and representation of part-time workers and differing perspectives among unions with respect to reduced-hour worktime adjustment. Although a few unions support and encourage part-time work in collective bargaining, for many it is seen as potentially competitive to full-time work and less useful than layoffs in countering employment fluctuations. Only public short-time compensation programs (STC), which reduce hours with compensatory benefits, engender enthusiastic union support. These union attitudes are analyzed in relation to the further development of part-time work.

The issues and experience of interest to firms provide the basis of the discussion on employer perspectives on part-time work for older workers contained in Chapter 9. Employer views and the growing forms of reduced-hour work are described, as are the cost saving and cost increasing aspects of part-time schedules. Although research evidence on dollar amounts remains sparse, it appears that labor performance and turnover costs provide the major savings, and fringe benefits the major cost addition of New Concept part-time schedules. Research indicates that age itself is a poor predictor of worker productivity; more important is the relationship between worker characteristics and job traits. Innovative thinking about job structures, work schedules, and evaluated experience provide the keys to further progress in reduced-hour jobs.

Chapter 10 summarizes what has been learned from putting part-time work under the microscope. The discussion is organized according to five major questions, which in themselves summarize the scope and developmental themes of the book.

1. What can be said about the preference for part-time work for older workers? What is the evidence of interest and of apathy and resistance to this work schedule form?
2. What are the purposes and forms of New Concept part-time work that influence its initiation? How prevalent is part-time work for older workers? What are the findings about part-time work experience and about the work experience of older workers?
3. How do legislation and social policy affect part-time work for older workers? Does the Swedish social policy experience with phased retirement offer any lessons for the United States?
4. What are the growth trends? How does part-time work fit into the scheme of things? What is its relation to economic policies and conditions?
5. Where do we go from here? What next steps would advance policy development of a new conception of part-time work?

Investigation of part-time work reveals that although the current spread of New Concept part-time work hardly qualifies as a surging revolution in institutional structures, the New Concept forms have much more to offer than is commonly realized, both for enterprises in pursuit of maximizing productive efficiency, and for workers who seek some relief in the hours of worktime. For older workers moving toward retirement with a particular interest in reducing the stress of work, the chance to maintain some income as a supplement to retirement benefits makes reduced-hour work particularly attractive. Not only does part-time work have much to offer, but viewed against the backdrop of other societal changes in values, labor force characteristics, and labor market trends, its further growth is seen as inevitable. How much better it would be if this further development is guided by informed planning, rather than undirected happenstance.

Notes

1. The trends in labor force participation rates of women and men reflect these evolving choices about paid work (Chapter 2, note 31; Tables 2.3, 4.1). There has been a continuous rise in the proportion of women in paid work in most age groups and a marked narrowing of the difference in labor force participation rates among women of varying marital status (Rones, 1982, p. 28; O'Neill and Braun, 1981, p. 4).

Over time, because of prolonged education and earlier retirement, participation rates of young and older men have been declining; for men in adult years (aged 20–54), the rates have remained relatively stable. Thus, although participation rates for men continue to be higher than for women, the difference between their rates is decreasing. These trends are expected to continue, perhaps at lower rates of change than in the past (Fullerton and Tschetter, 1983, p. 5).

2. A major national survey inquiring into aspects and satisfactions of work and family lives, was conducted by the Survey Research Center of the University of Michigan in the mid-1970s. The survey found that for men as well as for women who were involved in the three roles of marriage, work, and parenthood, family roles were far more important than work roles as a source of life satisfaction (Douvan, 1983, p. 209).

3. Americans have become used to talking about flexible hours and part-time work*weeks.* Some European employers and unions are now thinking in terms of flexible work *years,* where an agreed-upon annual number of work hours can be flexibly spaced over the course of the year. The hope is that variable work rhythms will synchronize both with individual worker interests and with variable requirements of business functioning. An "hours bank" with credits and debits maintains balance in the annual hour commitment (Clutterbuck, 1984).

4. Best and Stern, 1977, p. 3.

5. Best, 1981, pp. 2–3.

6. According to economic theory, increases in productivity can be shared with workers either as higher real wages or as fewer work hours and more leisure. In seeking to maximize "satisfaction" as real wages rise, on the one hand workers may respond to an "income effect" and choose to purchase more leisure at higher wage levels, which causes work hours to fall. At the same time, there is a "substitution effect" of work for leisure, because leisure becomes more expensive as wages rise, and this results in work hours tending to move in the opposite direction. The net effect of rising productivity on work hours depends on the relative strength of these two forces.

According to economists, workers in the nineteenth and early twentieth centuries benefited from productivity gains both through a shorter full-time workweek and through rising real wages. In recent years, the gains of productivity have been taken only in the form of rising wages while the standard full-time workweek remained at 40 hours a week. Only the average weekly work hours declined, for reasons explained in the text (Hedges and Taylor, 1980, pp. 3–11; Becker, 1965, pp. 493–517; Clark and Spengler, 1980, pp. 85–86; Mincer, 1962, pp. 63–105; *Employment and Training Report of the President,* 1979, pp. 77–80; Levitan and Belous, 1977, ch. 2.) For comment on the effect of further hours reduction, see Owen, 1982, pp. 107–31.

7. Several reasons account for the cessation of the downward trend in the standard workweek: the baby boom brought increased financial burdens which increased the preference of workers for higher wages; higher recruitment costs increased the preference of employers for paying overtime rather than increasing hiring; rising expectations in standard of living; inflationary pressures (*Employment and Training Report of the President,* 1979, pp. 78–79; Levitan and Belous, 1977, ch. 2, p. 23).

8. Hedges and Taylor, 1980, pp. 3–11; U.S. Department of Labor, BLS, 1984a, pp. 192, 193.

9. Hedges and Gallogly, 1977, p. 22; Hedges and Taylor, 1980, p. 5; U.S. Department of Labor, BLS, 1983b, pp. 56–58.

10. Fullerton and Tschetter, 1983, p. 5.

11. Personick, 1983, p. 25.

12. Morrison, 1983, p. 18.

13. Personick, 1983, p. 24.

2

Setting the Stage: Demographic and Labor Market Trends and Characteristics

Our contemporary society is an aging one. This situation not only raises fundamental social questions about friendship patterns, living arrangements, and family relationships, but economic questions about income and its connection to work and retirement. Living longer means thinking harder about how to safeguard, if possible, financial independence both before and during retirement. Living longer may change consumption and savings patterns, intergenerational income transfers, and household economic status. The implications of living longer have a special relevance for women: not only do they live longer than men, but that longevity gap is increasing over time.

Despite the widespread awareness that the population is aging, defining the "older population" is not easy to do. Statistical demarcation points for the population as a whole sometimes begin at age 45, sometimes at age 55, or even at age 60. In terms of the labor force, an "older worker" is frequently considered to be age 45 and over. The protection of the Age Discrimination in Employment Act (ADEA) begins even earlier, at age 40. In discussion of retirement issues, however, the older population is often thought of as aged 55 and over, an age when early retirement sometimes begins.[1] The "elderly population" is commonly described as being aged 65 and over, although with mandatory retirement now raised to age 70, this benchmark could change. Persons aged 75 and over are termed "aged," and those 85 years and over are called the "very old." Unless otherwise indicated, age 55 and over is used here to identify the *older* population, 55 years being about the time when labor market commitment begins to lessen. Following current custom, the *elderly* are defined as persons aged 65 and over.[2]

Given these benchmarks, what do the statistics tell us about demographic characteristics and trends?

Population Trends

Older persons constitute an increasingly significant segment of society. In March 1982 the U.S. population numbered about 232 million persons.[3] Of these, 48.3 million persons (20.6 percent) were older—that is, aged 55 and over; 11.1 percent were elderly, that is, aged 65 and over. Because of increasing longevity of the population, both proportions are higher than in the past. Although over the next 30 years the elderly population is expected to grow at about the same rate as the total population, after 2010, when the post–World War II baby boom generation begins to reach what is now conventional retirement age, the proportion of persons aged 55 and over may rise to one-fourth from its present level of one-fifth. By 2030, the older population may exceed 30 percent of the total, and the elderly population may reach 21.1 percent.[4] If these events come to pass, the median age of the population will rise from 31 to 38 years. "Growing older" will be a fact of life for increasing numbers and proportions of persons in society.

The continuing increase in the longevity gap between women and men means that their proportion within the older population will continue to grow.[5] In 1982, women were 56.9 percent of older persons and 59.8 percent of the elderly (see Table 2.1). By 2000 those proportions may increase to 57.5 percent of older persons and 60.8 percent of the elderly. Until that time, older women will both predominate and grow as a proportion of older age groups. Their particular needs require special attention in the formulation of social policy.[6]

Changing population patterns have implications for health and work. Living longer does not always mean living longer in perfect health, although not

Table 2.1. Population Projections by Age and Sex, 1982–2030 (middle series)

Year	Population 55+ Years			Population 65+ Years		
	Total	Female	Percent Female	Total	Female	Percent Female
1982	48929	27825	56.9	26833	16057	59.8
1990	52889	30347	57.4	31799	19147	60.2
2000	58815	33811	57.5	35036	21302	60.8
2010	74097	41910	56.6	39269	23773	60.5
2020	91629	51134	55.8	51386	30383	59.1
2030	98309	55193	56.1	64344	37744	58.7

Source: U.S. Department of Commerce, Bureau of the Census, *Current Population Reports*, Series P–25, nos. 949 (May 1984) and 952 (May 1984).

until age 85 do about half of the population report that chronic illness inter-feres with an ability to carry on a major activity.[7] Nor does it mean that all older persons are similar in their interests, or choices, or abilities with regard to activities. Population trends raise questions about how to care for increas-ing numbers of the very old and also about what activities can or should be available to older and elderly persons generally—activities that not only might add interest to their lives, but could use their talents to benefit society as a whole.[8] As has been noted, work *or* retirement need not be the only op-tions available; part-time work in combination with partial retirement may be another alternative.

Income of the Older Population

So long as older workers work full time in the labor force, their income is similar to that of the rest of the population of the same race and sex.[9] But among the significant sources of income for individuals at or beyond age 65, unlike those who are non-aged, are social security and private pensions. In-come sources differ also in relative importance for women and men. Over 90 percent of older men and women received social security benefits or rail-road retirement annuities in 1981. Overall, social security accounted for 37 percent of total money income received by elderly persons; earnings, 25 percent; property income of rents, dividends, and interest, 23 percent; pri-vate and other pensions, 13 percent; and other income, 2 percent. One-fifth of the elderly received virtually all their income from social security.[10] In-come is supplemented very unevenly by asset ownership, which is usually positively associated with income level.[11] Except for home ownership, which is often not easily convertible into cash, inflationary pressures have seriously eroded the value of financial assets of the elderly.[12] For most elderly with property or private pension income, the amount of such cash income is no more than $1000 to $2000 a year.[13]

Elderly men aged 65 and over are more likely than elderly women (18.8 per-cent versus 9.3 percent in 1981) to receive some wage and salary income. Women aged 65 and over, on the other hand, are more likely to have public assistance or supplementary security income (9.4 percent versus 4.9 percent in 1981).[14] Private pensions are also more frequently received by elderly men than elderly women.[15]

In addition to a different emphasis in income sources from those of the non-aged, elderly families and individuals commonly have a lower cash in-come than the average income of non-aged groups, for many much lower.[16] Despite the fact that income of the elderly has risen since the late 1960s, espe-cially since the 1972 amendments to the Social Security Act tied benefits to cost of living changes and raised the proportion that social security contrib-uted to cash income, that growth has not been sufficient to restore the relative position of elderly to non-elderly cash income that prevailed in the 1950s. A study by Duffy and associates found that the relative cash income level of the elderly in the late 1970s was only about 54 percent of non-elderly income, compared with about 60 percent in the early 1950s.[17] There was a slight improvement in the relative status of the elderly in the late 1970s, but further relative decline in the elderly cash income position was projected for the 1980s due to (1) a slowing down of the rate of growth in real government transfer payments to the elderly, (2) a continuing decline in their labor force participation, and (3) demographic changes increasing the proportion of the elderly in the total population and the proportion of very old in the elderly group—conditions that would further depress the ratio.[18] In 1981, the median cash income of men aged 60–64 was about three-fourths that of men 15 years younger, but almost double that of men aged 65 and over. For women, the decline in income began at age 50, and income levels were much lower.[19] Parnes and Less found that median real family income in 1980, for a national sample of married retirees, was about one-half the income they received in the year prior to retirement.[20]

For the elderly who are in poverty, the situation is worse than merely being at a relative disadvantage.[21] Although the poverty rate of the elderly has declined, from 15.2 percent in 1979 to 14.1 percent in 1983,[22] there are still 3.8 million elderly Americans, or one in seven, in poverty. Elderly women are more likely than elderly men to be poor (17.5 percent versus 10.4 percent; elderly widows are particularly at risk.)[23] Black poverty rates are four to five times as high as those for comparably aged white men and women. About one-half of poor, elderly persons live alone.[24]

Much more than part-time work is needed to solve the problems of the elderly poor. But for the group of elderly whose standard of living, including non-cash benefits, reaches the Bureau of Labor Statistics intermediate budget standard recommended for use in delineating income adequacy,[25] part-time work rather than full retirement could make a real difference in providing a satisfactory income level. According to this standard, only 42 percent of elderly singles and 64 percent of elderly families have an adequate income.[26] In thinking about part-time work as a means of alleviating this problem, it is important to note that the lowest poverty rates in 1981 were reported for older persons who had some wage and salary income.[27]

Labor Force and Labor Market Trends of Older Workers

When the focus shifts from that of the older population to that of the older labor force, a host of new issues arises. Some relate to the place of the worker in the spectrum of aging. At "younger older ages," continuity of work rather than retirement may be the goal; for this employed group, particularly those in unionized, stable firms with seniority provisions, age may not be an issue of concern. At later ages, or when jobs are scarce, the situation becomes more complex and decisions are often more painful. Work *or* retirement may no longer be a voluntary choice based on the value of retirement benefits, but may be determined by factors of employment conditions, health status, or subtle forms of age discrimination. Despite passage of the Age Discrimination in Employment Act in 1967, older workers still experience more difficulty than younger workers in finding a new job following a layoff;[28] moreover, the new job, once found, may have lower occupational status and earnings than the former one.[29] The need for income adequacy and for the security resulting from social interaction with working colleagues adds to the complexity of adjustment in this major turning point of life. Older workers in making choices respond to what is possible — usually full-time work or retirement. It is much more difficult to express a preference for what *might be* a choice if it were available — part-time work with prorated earnings and fringe benefits, for example.

LABOR FORCE TRENDS

Some understanding of the characteristics and trends of the labor force attachment of older workers, as well as the way future labor market and demographic developments may affect their work participation, is a necessary background for considering additional work schedule options for older workers. In 1982, the U.S. civilian labor force was estimated to be 110.2 million persons — 62.5 million men and 47.8 million women. Of this labor force, 13.7 percent were older Americans. Only 2.7 percent were elderly, and 58.9 percent of these were between the ages of 65 and 69.[30]

Population trends influence labor force trends in a major way, but of course are not exactly parallel. Moreover, future labor force projections do not exactly mirror past trends but must take into account changing tendencies of groups to be in the labor force. One set of projections by the Department of Labor, for example, assumes that early retirement trends will continue.[31] The diminished growth in labor supply in the early 1980s, which was partly caused by a slowing down of the rate of increase of adult women in the labor force, compounded by reductions in the pool of new, young entrants and perhaps by an increase in discouraged workers leaving the labor force, seems to be affecting the situation for older workers. Demand is apparently increasing in some areas for older workers to perform jobs — often part time and low level — formerly filled by young women and men.[32] Labor experts are puzzled by this recent slower labor supply growth trend and what it portends for labor recruitment and employment of older workers in the future. It could mean an increased demand for employment of older workers.

Overall, most researchers expect that the total civilian labor force in the future will grow much more slowly than in the past. Between 1982 and 1995, nearly two-thirds of labor force growth will be due to women's entry or re-entry to work, especially women in the prime working ages of 25 to 45. That percentage will be equal to that of the 1950s and 1960s and somewhat higher than for the 1970s, when large numbers of young men were also entering the workforce. If the tendency to early retirement among older male workers, aged 55 and over, continues and there is relative stability in the expected numbers of older working females, there will be both a decline in the size of the older workforce and an increase in the proportion which older women aged 55 and over will be of all workers in that age group (see Table 2.2).[33]

Although the number of older males in the population aged 55 and over will increase somewhat between 1982 and 1995, this effect will be counter-

Table 2.2.   Older and Elderly Civilian Labor Force and Middle Growth
             Population, by Sex and Age, 1982 and 1995 (labor force in
             thousands)

Labor Group	1982	1995
Workers, 16 years and over		
Total	110,205	131,387
Total, aged 55 and over	15,092	14,047
55-64	12,062	10,982
65 and over	3,030	3,065
Men		
Total	62,450	69,970
Total, aged 55 and over	9,019	8,039
55-64	7,174	6,311
65 and over	1,845	1,728
Women		
Total	47,755	61,417
Total, aged 55 and over	6,073	6,008
55-64	4,888	4,671
65 and over	1,185	1,337
Women as a percent of labor force		
Total	43.3	46.7
Total, aged 55 and over	40.2	42.8
55-64	40.5	42.5
65 and over	39.1	43.6

Source: Derived from Fullerton, H.N., and J. Tschetter, "The 1995 Labor Force:
A Second Look," Monthly Labor Review 106, no. 11 (November 1983): 5.

acted by the effects of the greater growth of prime age working males (that is, the baby boom generation now in their prime years), and by the decrease in the number of older working males, aged 55 and over. Male workers aged 55–64 are expected to be a somewhat smaller percentage of the total male labor force than ten years earlier (9.0 percent in 1995; 11.5 percent in 1982). Elderly male workers are projected to be 2.5 percent in 1995, compared with 3.0 percent in 1982.

The proportion of older (aged 55–64), and elderly (aged 65 and over) women in the female labor force will similarly be affected by trends in the several factors affecting numbers of working women. The older female population is projected to grow. But the effect of the strong continuing entry into the labor force of prime age women will dominate the effect of the relatively constant number of older and elderly working women. By 1995, there will be a slight rise in the proportion of older women who work and a slight fall in the proportion of elderly women who do so. The combined effect is expected to result in a decrease in the proportion of older women workers aged 55–64 to all women workers (from 10.2 percent in 1982 to 7.6 percent in 1995) as well as a roughly constant proportion of elderly to all women workers (2.5 percent to 2.2 percent).

Thus, it is important to know both the percentage of the male and female labor force who are older and elderly workers, and the proportion of older and elderly persons who choose to engage in paid work, which affects that percentage. These proportions and their trends, reflected in the labor force participation rates (that is, the proportion of men and women aged 55 and over who are in the civilian labor force),[34] have been different for older women and older men. It is decisions about labor force participation that ultimately determine not only the number of older and elderly employed workers, but the size of the non-employed elderly population, which affects the financial costs of social security benefit payments.

LABOR FORCE PARTICIPATION RATES

Although the proportion that men and women aged 55 and over were of the civilian labor force were not far apart in 1982 (8.2 percent and 5.5 percent), the level and the trends of their labor force participation rates have been quite different (see Table 1.3, Figure 2.1). The labor force participation rate of men aged 55–64 and 65 and over have both declined since the 1950s. In 1982, the labor force participation rate was only 70.2 percent for men aged 55–64

Table 2.3. Labor Force Participation Rates by Age for Women and Men, Selected Years 1952–1982 (percent of civilian noninstitutional population in the civilian labor force)

	Year	All 16 and Over	Young 16–19	Adult 20–44	Adult 45–54	Older 55–64	Elderly 65 and Over
Women							
	1952	34.7	42.2	39.1	40.1	28.7	9.1
	1962	37.9	39.0	41.8	50.0	38.7	9.9
	1972	43.9	45.8	52.2	53.9	42.1	9.3
	1982	52.6	51.4	68.4	61.6	41.8	7.9
Men							
	1952	86.3	61.3	96.2	96.2	87.5	42.6
	1962	82.0	53.8	95.4	95.6	86.2	30.3
	1972	78.9	58.1	92.9	93.2	80.5	24.4
	1982	76.6	56.7	92.5	91.2	70.2	17.8

Source: U.S. Department of Labor, Bureau of Labor Statistics, Handbook of Labor Statistics, Bulletin 2175, December 1983, pp. 16–17; U.S. Department of Labor, New England Regional Office, Bureau of Labor Statistics. Some of data derived from Department of Labor, Bureau of Labor Statistics Current Population Survey: A Databook, Vol. 1, Bulletin 2096, 1982.

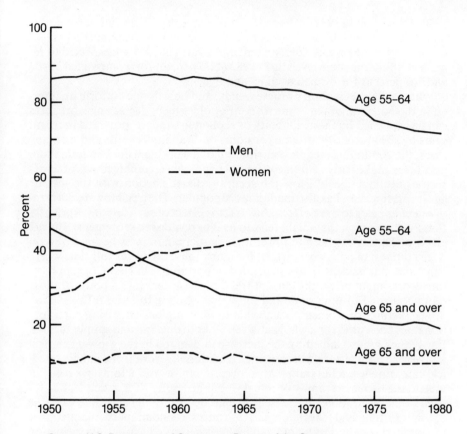

Source: U.S. Department of Commerce, Bureau of the Census, "America in Transition: An Aging Society," Current Population Reports, Series P-23, No. 128. September 1983, p. 22.

Figure 2.1
Labor Force Participation of Persons Aged 55 to 64 and 65 and over, by Sex, 1950-1980.

(86.9 percent in 1950) and 17.8 percent for those aged 65 or more (45.8 percent in 1950).[35] That downward trend is expected to continue, although perhaps at a slower pace, in the future.[36] The labor force participation rate is projected to fall to 64.5 percent in 1995 for men aged 55–64, and to 13.3 percent for men aged 65 and over (see Table 4.2).

In contrast, the labor force participation rate of older women aged 55–64 has increased over time, although less than for younger women. It rose from 27.0 percent in 1950 to a high of 43.1 percent in 1969 and then remained fairly stable throughout the 1970s, fluctuating between 41 and 43 percent. The rate for 1982 was 41.8 percent. For women aged 65 and over, although the rate decreased between 1950 and 1982, the decrease has been small (9.7 percent in

1950; 7.9 percent in 1982).[37] Even for women over age 70, the labor force participation rate, which was 6 percent in 1950, fell only to just under 5 percent in 1981.[38] For older and elderly women, the rates in 1995 are expected to remain at about the same levels as in 1982 (42.5 percent for women aged 55–64 and 7.0 percent for women aged 65 and over).[39]

What is the explanation of these trends, and how do they inform an interest in the potential of part-time work? For older men, decreasing work rates can be explained by the availability of economic support, provided in recent years by social security, private pensions, or disability benefits and, in many cases, the continuing income contribution of a working wife. Economic support helps make early retirement feasible and, when combined with factors such as declining health, low job security, dissatisfaction with the job, or leisure preferences, has also made it more popular. The trend toward early retirement appears to have offset, thus far, the effect of such factors as price inflation or recession that might tend to lead to postponed retirement. The net effect of all this has been to lower male participation rates because of a reduced interest in paid work, which for many jobs still means full-time work. What remains unclear is how expanded opportunities in New Concept part-time work might affect the current trend of these decisions — both for those now choosing full-time work and those now electing to retire fully.

The picture for women is somewhat more complex. The rising participation rates for women as a whole also reflect both demand and supply factors. Partly they are explained by the increase in demand in the growing clerical and service occupations where women traditionally work (for example, medical care, finance, retail trade). Moreover, a number of factors have contributed to the increased supply of female labor generally — for example, heightened career aspirations, decreased time needed for home and child care due to lower fertility and to technological advances, economic need, maintenance of a desired standard of living, and higher levels of education. Participation rates of older women have been positively affected by these same expanding employment opportunities in traditional female occupations and by many of these supply-side factors.

The relatively stable participation rates of elderly women may reflect not unchanging attitudes in response to the increased demand for female labor, but rather the resolution of two strong opposing forces.[40] On the one hand, there has been for women, as for men, an improvement in the level of social security benefits; although because women still receive lower wages and have longer periods out of the labor force to care for family and children,[41] benefits are not as high as those of men. At the same time that higher retirement benefits tend to lead to fewer work hours, demand and supply factors that have caused women's work participation to rise (including that of older women) tend to result in a contrary tendency of more work hours. This latter effect of more work hours is reinforced by high and rising divorce rates, the still low level — despite improvement — of women's social security benefits, the low coverage and low benefits women receive under private pension plans either as workers or as dependents or survivors,[42] and the decreasing real value of widows' benefits over time (adjusted for cost of living increases but not for productivity growth, which benefits the working population).[43]

As the current generation of women with strong labor market attachment ages, it is expected that their labor force participation will remain high.[44] The influence of changed attitudes about women's lifetime attachment to the paid workforce, combined with a growing societal value that emphasizes economic independence for women as well as for men and the lower levels of their alternative retirement income, will be likely to foster a continued interest in work in later years. Such interests will tend to extend the appeal of part-time work, already reflected in work rhythms, that grows out of the stress that results from trying to combine the duties associated with both paid work and family responsibilities.[45] These are some of the reasons why part-time work, if more readily available, will be of interest to older women workers.

OCCUPATIONAL AND INDUSTRIAL TRENDS

Where do older workers work? Is there likely to be an expansion of work opportunities for them in the decade ahead?

Up to the age of 65 the distribution of older men among industries is similar to that of younger men. The proportion who work in manufacturing industries is 31.3 percent, in miscellaneous services 20–21 percent, and in trade 15.8 percent. But after age 65 there is a change. Only 17.3 percent of elderly men work in manufacturing, while 30.3 percent work in miscellaneous services (including business and repair, personal services other than private household, and in education, welfare, and religious organizations), and almost one-fourth (23.0 percent) work in wholesale and retail trade. Occupations with the highest proportions of elderly employed males include managerial and administrative positions, farmers and managers, service workers, and sales workers.[46]

The distribution of women is more concentrated in a few occupations.[47] In 1981, for example, 71.4 percent of all employed women aged 20–54 worked in three occupational categories: professional and technical work; clerical work; and service occupations. If sales occupations, which are of greater importance among the elderly, are counted also, the proportion rises to 77.4 percent. Women's concentration in these occupations does not change as women age. But there is a shift in their relative importance. Professional occupations decrease in importance for older women (19.2 percent of employed women aged 20–54 work here; 12.7 percent of women aged 55 and over) as does clerical work (35.4 percent of employed women aged 20–54 work here; 30.3 percent of women aged 55 and over). There is a growth of the percentage of mature women compared with younger women in sales (6.0 percent of younger; 8.2 percent of older) and service occupations (16.9 percent of younger; 23.6 percent of older). Two thirds of women aged 65 and over are employed in sales, clerical, or service occupations.[48]

Future Labor Market Trends: Older Workers and Part-Time Work

As noted in Chapter 1, during the period 1982–1995, it is expected that almost 75 percent of the new jobs created will be in service industries (including direct services, retail and wholesale trade, and finance, insurance, and real estate), compared with a growth of 16.9 percent in manufacturing and a decline in agricultural employment.[49] In terms of occupations, the greatest employment growth will be experienced by service workers and by workers in professional and technical categories. These include scientists, engineers, technicians, medical and health service workers, computer specialists, and technologically trained clerical workers, to name a few.[50] Industries and occupations in which older workers are employed are projected to show strong growth.[51] Because of this, if other things remain the same, there should be an expansion of employment opportunities for older workers, including an increase in the number of part-time jobs. In 1980, about 20 percent of all employees in professional and technical occupations and in clerical jobs worked part time. These were mostly women. But because of the shifting demographic complexion of the labor force mix—a large proportion of middle-aged workers, including women, for example—there may be increased competition for these jobs.[52] It is not known for certain how this competition will be played out. What is clear is that if the jobs materialize and older workers wish to extend their working lives—either in full-time or part-time work—rather than to retire, their competitive position will be strengthened if their skills have been enhanced and up-dated in response to the rapidly changing technological scene. It could be that even if workers have the needed skills, unless work structures and attitudes about paid work relative to retirement change significantly, there will be a considerable increase in the numbers of non-employed older workers.[53]

The challenge facing society with respect to its older workers is really twofold: how to respond to the work needs and interests of those who wish to work, and how to ensure a satisfactory level of retirement for the increasing numbers of non-employed individuals who choose to retire. Once more, the question is raised whether part-time work can make a positive contribution to meeting the needs of this two-pronged problem.

Given the present circumstances and structure of work and the levels of retirement benefits, the trend among the male labor force continues to be toward early retirement. Among women, retirement benefit levels are lower and less available. This, added to other factors favoring increased work participation, gives older working women a more stable outlook with respect to work participation. The trend of paid work interest among women, including an interest in part-time work, will undoubtedly continue. For men, the choice between work or retirement may depend on the work environment and schedules available. In the next decade, some of the areas of occupational and industrial growth will be where older workers have traditionally been employed. But whether they will be able to compete successfully for these jobs with other groups of growing importance in the labor force remains to be seen.[54]

Employment expansion will take place in the next ten years in a number of occupations and industries that traditionally have offered part-time employment. Chapter 3 looks at the structures and conditions of existing part-time work as further preparation for thinking about workplace improvements.

Notes

1. Taeuber, 1983, p. 1.
2. An alternative convention for thinking about the aging process distinguishes among the *young* old (age 55–64), *middle* old (age 65–74), and the *old* old (age 75 and over). Between 1980 and 2030, the young old are expected to increase slightly (9.6 percent to 11.2 percent of population); the middle old are projected to increase more than one and a half times (6.9 percent to 11.3 percent); and the old old may increase even more (3.4 percent to 6.9 percent for those aged 75–84, and 1.0 percent to 2.9 percent for those aged 85 and over) (Taeuber, 1983, p. 3).
3. Unless otherwise indicated, data in this section are drawn from Morrison, 1983, pp. 13–19, and Taeuber, 1983, pp. 1–28.
4. Taeuber, 1983, p. 3.
5. Life expectancy at birth in 1980 for women was 78.2 years and for men, 70.8 years. At age 65, women can expect to live 18.7 more years and men, 14.3 years. By 2010, women's life expectancy at birth is projected to be nearly 82 years, compared with 73 years for men. At age 65 they can expect to live 22 additional years, 6 years longer than men. Morrison, 1983, p. 14; U.S. Department of Commerce, 1982.
6. The Census projections assume that from now on, elderly men and women will experience similar mortality improvements. This causes the sex ratio (number of men per 100 women) of elderly age groups, age 65–74 and 75–84, to rise. Despite this, and because of the effect of the continuing-to-fall sex ratio of the old-old, ages 85 and over, the overall sex ratio of the elderly is projected to decline until 2000, after which it will rise somewhat. See U.S. Department of Commerce, Bureau of the Census, Current Population Reports, Series P-25, nos. 311 (1965), 519 (April 1974), 917 (July 1982), 929 (May 1983), and 952 (May 1984).
7. U.S. Department of Health and Human Services, 1981.
8. This issue raises a number of important questions about activities and living arrangements and care of elderly persons. Whereas initially this appears to be an issue with not much relevance for part-time work, in fact it is extremely relevant because care of elderly relatives places a large time constraint on those persons providing the care — largely women, who seek to combine work and family roles. Time constraints increase the desirability of part-time work as a work schedule arrangement (see Chapter 4, pp. 53–54).
9. Taeuber, 1983, p. 7.
10. Ibid., pp. 9–10.
11. Sherman, 1976a.
12. Duffy, Barrington, Flanagan, and Olson, 1980.
13. Taeuber, 1983, pp. 9–10.
14. U.S. Department of Commerce, 1983a, pp. 172, 174.
15. Schulz, 1978.
16. Although cash income of the elderly is lower than that of the non-elderly (because of non-cash benefits, adjustments made for family size, fewer direct taxes paid, and other factors), statistically, elderly income is beginning on average to look more like that of the rest of the population (Chapter 5, pp. 67–68; Schulz, 1985, ch. 2; Danziger, et al., 1984, pp. 175–96).
17. Duffy, et al., 1980.
18. Ibid., pp. III–18–21.
19. Taeuber, 1983, p. 7.
20. Parnes and Less, 1983, pp. 56 ff.
21. The official U.S. Census poverty threshold, below which households are classified as poor, is based on the assumption that the poor spend about one third of their income on food. The poverty line consists of three times what the Department of Agriculture estimates to be a minimum food consumption requirement. Adjustments are made for different sized families, and for price changes. The poverty level in 1982 was defined as $5,836 annual income for an elderly couple, $4,626 for an elderly individual, and $9,862 annual income for a four person family (U.S. Dept. of Commerce, 1984a, p. 94).
22. U.S. Department of Commerce, 1983b, p. 7; ibid., 1984a, p. 94; *New York Times,* October 9, p. A31.

23. U.S. Department of Commerce, 1979; ibid., 1983b; Taeuber, 1983, p. 11.

24. Taeuber, 1983, p. 11; U.S. Department of Commerce, 1983b, pp. 42–43.

25. Beginning in the 1960s, and continuing until 1982, the Department of Labor published three hypothetical annual family budgets (lower, intermediate, and higher) for an urban family of four, with a 38 year old employed husband, a non-working wife, and two children. These were based on judgments of scientists about levels of living and data from general expenditure studies of the 1960s, updated each year by changes in the Consumer Price Index. For autumn 1981, the last year of publication, the income necessary to maintain a "modest but adequate" standard of living for the urban family of four was $15,323 and the estimate for an "intermediate" standard of living was $25,407 (U.S. Department of Labor, BLS, 1967; U.S. Department of Labor, BLS, News Release, April, 16, 1982).

26. Borzilleri, 1980.

27. Taeuber, 1983, p. 11.

28. Rones, 1983, p. 10.

29. Parnes, Gagan, and King, 1981.

30. Fullerton and Tschetter, 1983, p. 5; Morrison, 1983, p. 15.

31. This "middle growth" scenario also assumes that the proportion of women aged 20 to 44 in the labor force will accelerate through the mid-1980s and then taper off, and that the decline in that proportion for older age groups will be more moderate than in the past. The rates for other groups are expected to continue their current trend (Fullerton and Tschetter, 1983, pp. 3–4).

32. Fullerton and Tschetter, 1983, pp. 3–10; U.S. Congressional Budget Office, 1982b, p. 10; *Wall Street Journal,* January 4, 1984, pp. 1 ff.

33. Fullerton and Tschetter, 1983, pp. 3–6.

34. The labor force participation rate is the percent of a given population group that is in the labor force. The labor force is defined as the sum of the employed plus the unemployed. Persons who are neither working nor looking for work are classified as "not in the labor force."

35. U.S. Department of Labor, BLS, 1983b, pp. 16–17; Taeuber, 1983, p. 22.

36. In 1983, the figures declined only slightly. The proportion of employed men aged 55–64 was 69.4 percent and the percentage of men aged 65 and over was 17.4 percent (*Wall Street Journal,* April 24, 1984).

37. U.S. Department of Labor, BLS, 1983b, p. 17.

38. Taeuber, 1983, p. 23.

39. Fullerton and Tschetter, 1983, p. 5.

40. Rones, 1980, p. 14.

41. Kahne, 1981.

42. Schulz, 1978.

43. Kahne, 1981.

44. Rones, 1982, p. 29; U.S. Congressional Budget Office, 1982a, p. 8.

45. Pleck, Staines, and Lang, 1980, pp. 29–31.

46. U.S. Department of Labor, Bureau of Labor Statistics, unpublished data, 1983.

47. Beller, 1982.

48. U.S. Department of Labor, BLS, 1982b, Table B-18.

49. Personick, 1983, pp. 24–25.

50. Silvestri, Lukasiewiez, and Einstein, 1983, pp. 37–49.

51. Morrison, 1983, pp. 18–19.

52. Ibid., p. 19.

53. Ibid., p. 16.

54. Ibid., p. 19.

3

The Concepts of Part-Time Work: The Old and the New

Part-time work, despite its long history as a work schedule arrangement, is not yet widespread. About one-fifth of all non-agricultural employees work on part-time weekly schedules,[1] a proportion that has remained constant over the past ten years. But interest in an expanded part-time concept has developed recently as new forms of reduced hours have emerged in response to a variety of worker and industrial needs. What do we mean by part-time work? In what occupations and industries is it found? What are its potential benefits and deficiencies? What are the characteristics of part-time workers? This base of information is needed to evaluate the concept of part-time work in its present standard Old Concept form, and to think about the potential benefits of the forms of New Concept part-time work that are slowly becoming a part of the workplace environment.

Standard Old Concept Part-Time Work

DEFINITION

The U.S. Department of Labor defines part-time workers as employees who work from 1 to 34 hours during a "reference week." Those who work, or usually work, 35 hours a week or more are full-time workers.[2] Part-time workers include those who prefer and usually work fewer than 35 hours a week and those who are customarily full-time workers, but who are temporarily working part time for economic reasons (for example, slack work, material shortage, plant or machinery repairs, inability to find full-time work). These two categories distinguish involuntary (or economic) part-time workers from voluntary part-time workers. The number of involuntary part-time workers, which varies with the economic climate, includes a disproportionate concentration of unskilled, less educated and young workers. Involuntary part-time employees are "work sharers," but not because they wish to be. In the work force, the proportion of voluntary part-time workers — those who choose to work fewer than 35 hours per week — has changed very little since the early 1970s.[3] Changes in work hour patterns suggest that it may be appropriate to reconsider this definition of part-time work. Average weekly hours worked have been declining over time (see Chapter 1) and vary by industry.[4] For over 6 percent of employees in non-agricultural industries, work hours of less than 35 are considered to be full-time for the job; for others, work of more than 35 hours is viewed as part time. In fact, when the 35-hour base was chosen, it was expected that the cut-off point might be changed as the length of the standard workweek was altered.[5] As of 1984, however, both the length of the standard workweek and the definition of part-time work remain as they were in the 1940s.

CHARACTERISTICS

In 1982, 18.3 million non-agricultural employees worked part time, an increase of 11.6 million in 1970. These part-time workers represent 20.2 percent of non-agricultural employees in the United States. Almost 70 percent of all part-time workers are voluntary part-timers (12.5 million); the rest (5.9 million) work part time because of market conditions beyond their control.[6] About one-half of all part-time workers work between 15 and 29 hours a week; one-fourth work 30–34 hours; the rest work fewer than 15 hours. This distribution is similar across industries. Recent data on part-time work among non-agricultural employees are shown in Tables 3.1 to 3.3.

Since 1955, part-time workers as a proportion of all workers have doubled. Until the early 1970s, most of the increase was due to an increase in voluntary part-time work. Since then, voluntary part-time workers have remained at

Table 3.1. Non-Agricultural Workers on Full-Time and Part-Time Schedules, Selected Years 1970–1982

	Total	percent[a]	Full-Time	percent	Part-Time	percent	Voluntary Part-Time	percent	Involuntary Part-Time	percent
1970	70,732	100	59,141	83.6	11,591	16.4	9,392	13.3	2,199	3.1
1975	77,381	100	63,145	81.6	14,236	18.4	10,694	13.8	3,542	4.6
1980	90,208	100	73,590	81.6	16,618	18.4	12,555	13.9	4,063	4.5
1982	90,552	100	72,245	79.8	18,307	20.2	12,455	13.8	5,852	6.5

[a]Percentages may not always equal 100 percent because of rounding.

Note: Workers shown in thousands.

Source: Derived from U.S. Department of Labor, Bureau of Labor Statistics, *Handbook of Labor Statistics*, December 1983, pp. 57–58.

Table 3.2. Non-Agricultural Voluntary and Involuntary Part-Time Workers,
Selected Years 1970–1982

	Total	percent[a]	Voluntary	percent	Involuntary	percent
1970	11,591	100	9,392	81.0	2,199	19.0
1975	14,236	100	10,694	75.1	3,542	24.9
1980	16,618	100	12,555	75.5	4,063	24.4
1982	18,307	100	12,455	68.0	5,852	32.0

[a]Percentages may not always total 100 percent because of rounding.

Note: Workers shown in thousands.
Source: Derived from U.S. Department of Labor, Bureau of Labor Statistics,
Handbook of Labor Statistics, December 1983, pp. 57–58.

Table 3.3. Non-Agricultural Women and Men Voluntary Part-Time Workers,
Selected Years 1970–1982

	Total	percent[a]	Women	percent	Men	percent
1970	9,392	100	6,368	67.8	3,024	32.2
1975	10,694	100	7,347	68.7	3,347	31.3
1980	12,555	100	8,726	69.5	3,829	30.5
1982	12,455	100	8,806	70.7	3,649	29.3

[a]Percentages may not always total 100 because of rounding.

Note: Workers shown in thousands.
Source: Derived from U.S. Department of Labor, Bureau of Labor Statistics,
Handbook of Labor Statistics, December 1983, pp. 57–58.

about 14 percent of the non-agricultural labor force, while the numbers of involuntary part-time workers have more than doubled. In the 1981–82 recession, for example, there were more than 6 million involuntary part-time workers.

Paid part-time work is more common in some industries and occupations than in others.[7] It is concentrated in trade and service industries, and in service, sales, and clerical occupations (see Figs. 3.1–3.4). In 1982, service and wholesale and retail trade industries, which accounted for 44 percent of all employment, included almost 75 percent of all voluntary part-time workers; less than 5 percent of voluntary part-time workers were in manufacturing.[8] More than three-fourths of all voluntary part-time employees were in white collar professional and technical, clerical, sales, and non-domestic service

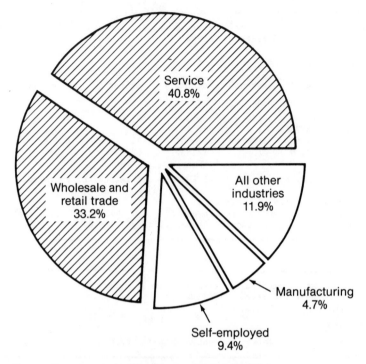

Source: Department of Labor, Bureau of Labor Statistics

Figure 3.1
Voluntary Part-Time Workers, by
Industry, 1982 Annual Averages.

occupations, occupations which represented only 57 percent of all employed workers in 1982.[9] In contrast, blue collar workers contributed less than 15 percent to the total of voluntary part-time workers. Among female part-time workers, about 70 percent work in sales, clerical, and non-domestic service occupations.[10] Even if part-time work continues to reflect only past patterns, opportunities are likely to grow because the fastest-growing industrial and occupational sectors are expected to be those in which part-time work has been a tradition.

Part-time work, even with its present disadvantageous economic rewards, fills a work scheduling need for youth, women, and older workers. Young persons often work part time as an accompaniment to going to school. About half of employed teenagers are voluntary part-time workers; 23.1 percent of part-time workers, compared with 3.0 percent of full-time workers, are aged 16 to 19 (Fig. 3.5). One-fourth of all employed women work part time; only 10 percent of men do so. In 1982, women made up about 70 percent of all voluntary part-time workers but only about 40 percent of full-time workers (Fig. 3.5). About three-quarters of all part-time women workers work part time by choice; only about one-half of men do so. The reason for these differences is readily apparent. With the increasing movement of women into the labor force, part-time work provides time relief in coping with dual responsibilities of paid work and household and family care activities (see Chapter 4). The marital status of part-time workers reflects these circumstances (Fig. 3.6). Almost one-fourth (23.9 percent) of all married working women are on voluntary part-time schedules, compared with 3.3 percent of all married employed males. In 1982, among all voluntary part-time women workers, 59.3 percent were married, and another 11.5 percent were divorced, separated, or widowed. The proportion was reversed for men—63.2 percent of voluntary male workers were single.

At the same time, part-time work is increasingly common for older men

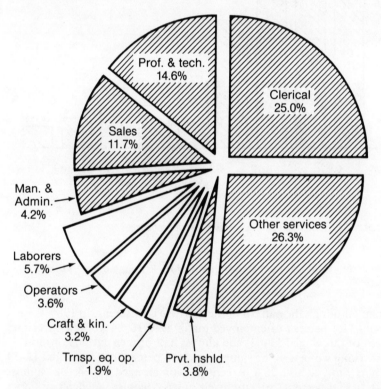

Note: White collar occupations include professional and technical, sales, managers and administrators (except farm), clerical workers. Blue Collar occupations include laborers, operatives (except transport), craft and kindred workers. Service occupations include transport equipment operatives, private household, other service workers.

Source: Department of Labor, Bureau of Labor Statistics

Figure 3.2
Voluntary Part-Time Workers, by Occupation, 1982 Annual Averages.

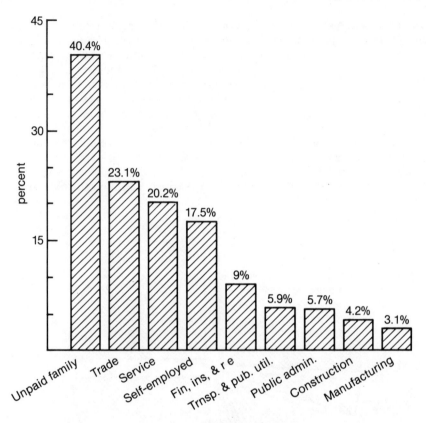

Figure 3.3
Voluntary Part-Time Workers as a Percent of All Employed, by Industry,
1982 Annual Averages.

and women, although the pattern of the increase is different. In 1980, for example, only 11.4 percent of employed males aged 16–54 worked part time,
8.2 percent of those aged 55–64, and almost half of men aged 65 or more.[11]
Among working women in the same year, 28.3 percent of those aged 16–54
worked part time, as did 26.6 percent of women aged 55–64. But almost
three-fifths (58.4 percent) of employed elderly women aged 65 or more
worked part time.[12] For employed women, as for employed men at or beyond
normal retirement age, the proportion of part-time workers jumped sharply.
Older women workers aged 55 and over are more heavily represented in part-
time than in full-time work.[13]
    Some further perspective on part-time work for older workers is provided
by looking at a national study of partial retirement of older, white, wage-
earning men.[14] The men, aged 58–63 when the study began, were surveyed at

two-year intervals into retirement and back into partial employment, often in occupations and industries that were different from those of their previous employment. The study found that partial retirement was quite widespread, especially for men not subject to mandatory retirement. More than one-third of the elderly male employees in the sample, aged 65–69, worked part time and were partially retired in at least one of the four years of the study. They more commonly worked in non-agricultural service occupations and in fi-

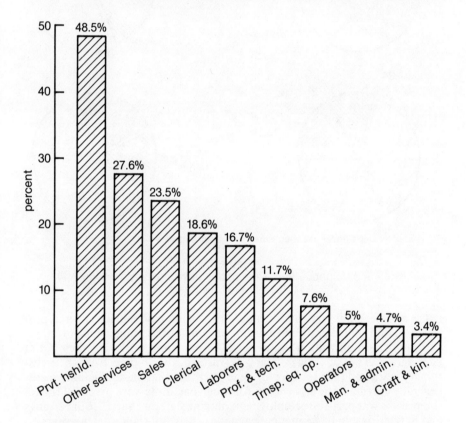

Note: White collar occupations include professional and technical, sales, managers and administrators (except farm), clerical workers. Blue Collar occupations include laborers, operatives (except transport), craft and kindred workers. Service occupations include transport equipment operatives, private household, other service workers.

Source: Department of Labor, Bureau of Labor Statistics

Figure 3.4
Voluntary Part-Time Workers as a Percent of All Employed, by Occupation, 1982 Annual Averages.

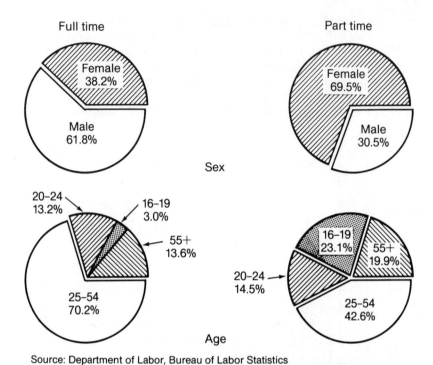

Full time   Part time

Female 38.2%
Male 61.8%

Female 69.5%
Male 30.5%

Sex

20–24 13.2%
16–19 3.0%
55+ 13.6%
25–54 70.2%

16–19 23.1%
55+ 19.9%
20–24 14.5%
25–54 42.6%

Age

Source: Department of Labor, Bureau of Labor Statistics

Figure 3.5
Full- and Voluntary Part-Time Status of Workers by Sex and Age,
1982 Annual Averages.

nance and personal service jobs, not in the higher paid managerial and professional and skilled craft occupations or in manufacturing, transportation,
and public administration industries. The part-time work that they did at
later ages was not at their regular job. Instead, they retired from their customary work and then took a part-time job in another place of employment,
generally at reduced hourly wages. Although part-time work preceded full retirement, it was part-time employment obtained at some sacrifice in earnings
and in relationship to former colleagues of their full-time working years.

The limited comparative data that is available regarding earnings for full-
and part-time work indicates lower wage rates for part-time than full-time
workers. It also indicates little difference by sex for median annual (and
weekly) earnings of part-time workers, although there is a continuing differential between men and women in full-time annual (and weekly) earnings.[15]
In 1982, the average part-time hourly wage rate was $3.88, compared with a
full-time wage rate of $6.44. This wage differential is partly attributable to
the location of part-time jobs in lower paid sectors, where there is less investment in labor training. But it also reflects the fact that some employers pay a
lower hourly rate to part-time than to full-time workers for equivalent

work.[16] Such part-time work is often characterized by a rapid labor turnover, which further contributes to the low wage level. With respect to sex differentials, the similarity in median part-time annual earnings of women and men who worked a full year ($4,848 for men and $4,959 for women in 1982) reflects the fact that men part-time workers, unlike women, are largely young or elderly — groups averaging lower earnings than men in the middle years. Among full-time workers, median annual earnings (and weekly earnings) continue to show a large differential by sex, related to a number of factors (see Chapter 4). In 1982 full-time earnings for men were $21,077, compared with $13,014 for women.[17]

In Old Concept part-time work, fringe benefits are often low or, frequently, absent altogether. A 1977 national survey of 387 companies with part-time employment reported that about 80 percent offered vacation benefits to part-time workers, but only 59 percent offered retirement benefits, and no more than roughly half paid sick leave or life insurance or health insurance benefits. These specific benefits were offered to full-time workers by 85–99 percent of the surveyed companies.[18]

Since the time of that survey, the introduction of new forms of reduced-hour scheduling has undoubtedly been accompanied by some extension of fringe benefits. But the kinds offered, and their costs, still constitute a problem in structuring of part-time work (see Chapter 9).

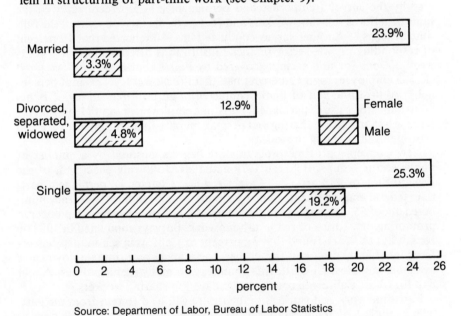

Source: Department of Labor, Bureau of Labor Statistics

Figure 3.6
Voluntary Part-Time Status of Workers by Sex and Marital Status,
1982 Annual Averages.

New Concept Part-Time Work

Because of its time-freeing quality, even under present restrictive conditions, a number of groups in society continue to find part-time work useful. By the year 2000, voluntary part-time employment, even in this traditional form, could increase from 14 percent to 20 percent of the labor force.[19] It is less clear how the concept and value of part-time work will be affected by new forms of reduced-hour scheduling, which began to appear in the late 1960s. The forms all fit the general definition of part-time work — weekly hours of work below 35 a week generally (since 1979, 16–32 hours for federal employees).[20] But each has additional distinctive qualities that distinguish it. Because of these new structures, there has been a growing diversity in the kinds of work and groups of workers to which the label "part time" applies. Data do not yet give a complete picture of the numbers of New Concept part-time workers or of the circumstances of firms where the new concept operates. But several surveys herald their growing prevalence and popularity in both public and private sectors.

A recent nationwide survey of more than 400 public and private sector organizations found one-quarter of the organizations with some job sharing, one-quarter with phased retirement arrangements, and about two-thirds with some permanent part-time employment. Of all reduced-hour employees covered by the survey (temporary and permanent), 11.5 percent received the same benefits as full-time workers and 46.1 percent received some of the full-time benefits.[21] Another survey conducted in 1980 reported that 19 percent of responding private sector financial institutions offered shortened workweek options for non-exempt (covered by Fair Labor Standards Act) and clerical employees, and 12 percent had them for lower level exempt personnel.[22] Almost one-half of banks contacted in an informal survey of Banc-Ohio indicated a use of permanent part-time employment, and 11 percent offered job sharing. Job sharing and permanent part-time employment are also growing in the nursing profession.[23]

New Concept part-time programs are being sponsored by a number of public sector groups. Between 1978 and 1981, following enactment of the Federal Employees Part-Time Career Act (see Chapter 7), permanent part-time federal employees increased by almost 10,000. In mid-1982, they numbered about 55,000 employees. The state of California has been a pioneer in promoting new forms of reduced-hour work. Surveys conducted in 1982 by New Ways to Work found that 37 percent of California school districts offered job sharing programs for teachers; permanent part-time employment is available in almost all California counties and many municipalities. About one-fourth of California counties also have job sharing workers.[24]

Part-time work and workers in the future will be different from the past. The evolution of reduced-hour work schedule arrangements will now be guided by a broader base of experience than was formerly possible. What are the distinguishing features of each of these several new forms of reduced worktime?

REGULAR, NEW CONCEPT PART-TIME WORK

Regular, New Concept part-time work differs from standard, Old Concept part-time work in two major respects. The structure of the part-time job is viewed as permanent and having career potential, rather than temporary and intermittent in its nature, and fringe benefits are generally included in the earnings package. Reflecting the change, a recent survey of 310 firms found that 80 percent of respondents offered fringe benefits, often pro-rated, to permanent part-time employees. In many companies, an employee must work more than 20 hours a week to qualify for these fringe benefits.[25]

Regular, New Concept part-time jobs, now found in both public and private sectors of the labor market, came into existence not only because of a wish on the part of workers for a shorter work-time commitment, but because employers viewed the traits of some work tasks as being particularly appropriate to such a structure. Early studies had suggested a number of work traits amenable to part time—jobs with discrete tasks "with a clear beginning and end," those with repetitive functions or stress, and those requiring a minimum of supervision or start-up or shut-down costs. In terms of work rhythms, these studies indicated that jobs best suited to part time were those where a periodic or cyclical demand for goods or services existed over the course of the day or week, where business hours extended beyond the normal work day, and where stockpiling of production was difficult. It is not difficult to think of jobs that have at least one of these characteristics—nursing, retail sales work, routine clerical duties, and restaurant work are examples. Work requiring a continuous work flow, such as assembly line production, or supervisory functions, or considerable interaction with colleagues, or extensive training, were deemed not to be suitable for part-time employment. The studies implied that a number of job traits and work unit characteristics constrained an efficient application of part-time scheduling.

The findings of these early studies were tested in a small fieldwork study conducted in 1976.[26] The investigators found that part-time and full-time work did not always differ on all of these traits. Only the trait of discreteness of task had the expected part-time emphasis; the trait of presence of supervisory functions had the expected full-time emphasis. Other traits such as routine or repetitive work, or lack of teamwork, were either not present in part-time jobs or did not significantly differ from those found in full-time jobs. Although less common than in full-time work, more than half of all part-time jobs had a continuous work flow. Training and "internal communication" were also found in more than 40 percent of the part-time jobs. Variability of demand in the service provided was not always a quality of the part-time work, although a non-standard work load, requiring more or less than an 8-hour day or 40-hour week, was more often present with users than with non-users of part-time workers. The findings of the study are particularly interesting in view of the broader application of part-time work now evolving. They suggest that although some work traits may be particularly compatible with part-time work, these traits are less necessary to efficient functioning of part-time work than has conventionally been thought to be true. New Concept, regular part-time work exemplifies this, in the broad range of occupations where it is being applied.

JOB SHARING

Job sharing, a variant form of regular New Concept part-time work, began to emerge in the late 1960s in response to an interest in part-time work with career opportunities.[27] It is most often described as the conversion of a full-time position to two part-time positions, often at the request of one or two individuals in a job, or a pair of candidates for a job. Job pairing is a version of this, where each part-time employee is responsible for the whole job and not just the individual halves.

Often the individual who requests job sharing is responsible for dividing the responsibilities, locating a partner, and ensuring the fulfillment of duties. Sometimes jobs are divided horizontally in time, with each partner performing similar tasks — for example, social workers or computer programmers working a half-day, or split or alternate weeks, or even a half-year. Sometimes organizations benefit by combining people with complimentary skills — a librarian and school teacher to fill an editing position, for example, or an engineer and a researcher working together on a project to renovate a medical school laboratory.[28] Earnings need not be equal, nor need the tasks be. But they are usually comparable to those of a full-time job.

Fringe benefits are frequently retained in the conversion from a full-time to a shared job and are often pro-rated. They are more evident in shared jobs created in recent years than in those forged earlier. Although the numbers of job sharers are growing and the qualities that lend themselves to job sharing are becoming more refined, job sharing is still largely described in the literature by case studies and anecdotal reporting. Although job sharing is commonly applicable to no more than a few jobs in one setting, organizations as well as individuals are beginning to perceive the potential benefits of the structure and at times seek to fill an opening on a job-sharing basis.

For individuals, obvious benefits flow from the freeing of time constraints to meet family responsibilities or to acquire education or training, while retaining skills and seniority, perhaps, and a line of career progress. For older workers, job sharing permits a gradual reduction in the stress of time demands of paid work in order to increase other activities in moving toward retirement or to respond to health needs, while offering a dignified way of continuing income and attachment to the labor market. Organizations, too, have become aware of the advantages of job sharing. They include enlarging the pool of applicants for openings that occur, ensuring continuity of work, combining skills of several individuals in the performance of a particular job, retaining valued older employees, and enhancing employee morale, and hence job performance, as a result of careful pairing of older and younger workers to foster an interchange of learning between them about values, skills, and commitment. There are also some costs (fringe benefits) and some problems (retirement, promotion, job evaluation) to be resolved.

Although not widespread, job sharing has strong potential. If workers and employers provide mutual support, if they design jobs carefully, if they clearly delineate schedules and responsibilities and accountability, and if job sharers match well and learn to work well and flexibly together, job sharing can offer a part-time option with mutual benefit and with broad occupational potential, in particular work circumstances and periods in individual lives.

WORK SHARING

Work sharing is a concept that has a long and troubled history.[29] Unlike job sharing, which often responds to supply-side factors such as a desire on an employee's part to conserve time for home responsibilities or non-work interests, work sharing responds to demand-side stimuli for a group.[30] It provides a mechanism for lessening the impact of a temporary employment retrenchment by cutting back the number of hours or days worked, or by rotating weeks worked and weeks not worked according to a predetermined formula. In so doing, layoffs are avoided and labor market attachment, fringe benefits (total or prorated), and sometimes income are preserved for all employees. At the same time, employers are able to institute cost-saving measures, including, perhaps, reorganization of the production process. Although such programs do not require that income reimbursement be made for lost worktime—and many do not—recent state laws effective in California, Arizona, Oregon, Washington, Florida, Maryland, and Illinois make a social policy connection with income reimbursement. Sharing a limited amount of work combined with partial unemployment insurance, called short-time compensation, instituted as an alternative to layoffs, is increasingly seen as a desirable goal for future social policy.

Work sharing in this latter configuration is no substitute for public monetary or fiscal measures to raise the general level of economic activity or for other supportive employment policies. But with compensation, work sharing can be an important supplementary policy for dealing with economic downturns, ensuring continuity of some wages and fringe benefits, and providing a way of maintaining consumer demand at the same time that it minimizes disruption to the employment schedule and maintains work skills.

There is no precise figure on the number of workers who are work sharers. But a rough idea of the number and characteristics of workers whose part-time employment results from shared work hours in an economic downturn can be derived from data on involuntary part-time workers who either work part time because of slack work, material shortages, or plant or equipment repair, or because they cannot find a full-time job.[31] Involuntary part-time workers would not work part time if they had a choice. But they do provide silent testimony to the fact that work hours of fewer than 40 a week are possible in a wide range of occupations.

In 1982, when unemployment averaged 10.7 million workers (9.7 percent of civilian employed workers), there were 6.2 million involuntary part-time workers (6.1 percent of civilian employed workers). Of this latter group, 52.9 percent (3.3 million) were involuntary part-time workers due to slack work loads; 42.1 percent worked part time because they could find only a part-time job; and 5 percent were economic part-timers for miscellaneous reasons. Among all involuntary part-time workers, there was a disproportionate representation of teenagers, women, blacks, and other minorities.[32] Those who work part time due to slack work tend to be prime age, male, and minority workers in blue collar industries. These groups would benefit the most from an expansion of short-time compensation programs.

PHASED RETIREMENT

Phased retirement — a reduction in working hours for those nearing retirement age — is directed specifically to an older age group. The form itself is not a new one — in a few companies such a program has been in effect since the 1940s. But it is quite limited in the United States, both in terms of the numbers of plans and numbers of participants. An analysis of a national sample of workers indicates that the prevalent pattern of work in the United States is full time, followed by a sudden transition to full retirement. The pattern applies to both men and women, although the movement out of the labor force starts earlier for women, and the proportion who move to part time is slightly higher. Except for those retiring after age 68, only about 15 percent worked part time in the year before retirement. Almost 85 percent worked 35 weekly hours or more during that year.[33] As noted earlier, one study suggests that a surprising proportion of men return to partial employment *after* retirement, but this work is not at their customary jobs, nor at their accustomed earnings levels. Partial retirement in this sense is different from phasing into retirement in one's customary job.

Phased retirement programs are individualized company programs, tailored to reflect company personnel policy with respect to long-service, older employees. Companies view phased retirement as an acknowledgement of the contribution of their long-term employees and as a policy to ease the trauma of moving from an active earning life to more leisurely, non-earning activities. A few companies seek through such programs to encourage early retirement; others hope that phased retirement will be a way to retain the expertise of skilled and knowledgeable workers by extending the period of paid work. Some companies use the phased retirement period to train a replacement for the potential retiree.

There seems to be no constraint on occupations that can become subject to phased retirement. Plans in existence cover supervisory and professional persons, as well as those at assembly and clerical work levels. Age (often a minimum age of 55 or 60) and sometimes also a minimum number of years of experience with the company (10–15 years is common) serve as eligibility prerequisites. Time away from work, often beginning one or two years prior to retirement, can be in the form of a reduced workweek or work year. The hours of reduced working time, sometimes compensated and sometimes not, often have an incremental monthly or yearly increase as workers approach retirement, giving the employee more time to plan other activities and to adjust to the unstructured time that will become available. Fringe benefits are often paid on a pro-rated basis. A few companies bolster retirement contributions or benefits that would otherwise be reduced because of the lower earnings near the retirement date.[34]

The Towle Silver Company, for example, a small manufacturer of sterling flatware, offers to a potential annuitant with 30 years of service forty paid days off during four months prior to retirement, one day a week during the first month, two days during the second month, and so on. By the fourth month, the employee experiences more non-work than worktime.[35] New England Mutual Life Insurance Company, with more than 4000 employees, gives all employees with 10 years of service two additional paid vacation weeks in their 62nd year, three additional weeks in their 63rd year, and four additional paid weeks in their 64th year. These weeks of paid leave are not deferrable, although regular vacation weeks are. Another example, Varian Associates, a high-tech firm of 14,000 employees with 27 plants in seven states and nine countries, provides a reduced workweek option at proportionately reduced salaries to workers over age 60 and with five years of service who are within two years of planned retirement.[36] They may reduce their workweek to four days the first year and three days the second year with other variations possible, as long as a minimum 20-hour workweek is maintained. Fringe benefits are continued, some on a pro-rated basis. Voluntary contributions can be made to the retirement account so that retirement income does not suffer as a result of the somewhat lowered earnings during the transition period.

Why have reduced-hour programs not become more widespread or more fully enrolled? Reasons for the scarcity of employer-initiated phased retirement programs, discussed further in Chapter 9, relate partly to lack of successfully operating role model plans, partly to an absence of knowledge about potential benefits for the firm, and partly, perhaps, to a lack of conviction that reduced-hour programs facilitate enterprise goals.

Several reasons also affect employee attitudes. For some, the high inflation of the past few years, which has colored the thinking of all Americans with concern about the declining value of income, may have led to a decision not to sever gradually a labor market attachment. As a hedge against the future, some individuals may have chosen to extend the length of their full-time work life rather than phase down their hours, reducing earnings and possibly compromising retirement income. This inclination could have been reinforced by the extension of mandatory retirement from age 65 to 70, although studies indicate that that effect is probably not great. In 1980, only 3 percent of male retirees were forced to retire because of mandatory retirement plans. Researchers predict that extension of the mandatory retirement age will change retirement figures very little.[37] For other employees, the paid leave of phased retirement is viewed more as a vacation extension than as a retirement preview.[38] Some employees may also lack knowledge of the benefits of the programs, or fear that in the current troubled times, participating in a phased retirement plan may give a negative signal about "commitment" that will affect their employment security.[39] A further problem for those who have begun to receive social security benefits arises from the fact that because of the "earnings test," social security benefits will be reduced if partial employment earnings exceed a stated amount.[40] Whatever the reason, participation in an available plan is not high. The recent survey of part-time work by the Andrus Gerontology Center found that only 20 percent of workers eligible to participate in phased retirement programs actually did so.[41]

Despite this worker resistance, or lack of enthusiasm for phased retirement programs, employers expect the number of plans to grow. And despite some hesitancy about participating in them, older workers continue to express a strong preference for having part-time options available. The estimated 16.7 percent of retired persons returning to the labor force in 1980 following retirement[42] suggests that there could be interest in a broader availability of phased retirement programs. Spreading of information and extending reduced-hour opportunities could increase the prevalence of part-time scheduling with advantage both to firms and to older workers who are now either fully at work or fully retired.

PHASED RETIREMENT IN SWEDEN

Although most of the discussion of this book is directed to the American experience because of the difference in workplace conditions and traditions between Europe and the United States,[43] an exception will be made in the case of phased retirement in Sweden. The Swedish nationally legislated partial pension program, available since 1976, offers a contrast in approach to that of the individualized company experience of the United States and provides some interesting information about programmatic experience that may be of use for our own evolving system.

In fact, there are two kinds of pensions in Sweden that permit the dovetailing of partial retirement and part-time work. The first is the disability pension paid to persons unable to work up to the time of the general retirement age of 65 because they are permanently occupationally disabled from medically verifiable causes. The disability pension can also be paid to persons aged 60–64 who have experienced prolonged unemployment (more than 22 months), or whose job is sufficiently demanding that it is difficult to keep pace with the work. In recent years, the fact of advancing age in a difficult job, without confirming medical evidence, has been a sufficient ground for establishing eligibilty for a pension.[44] Disability pensions are payable for total disability or partial disability, compensated at two-thirds or one-half the benefit amount; in the latter cases the partial disability benefit is combined with part-time employment. Slightly more than one-third of all disability benefits are paid to persons aged 60–64. In 1981, about 20–25 percent of all

Swedes aged 60–64 received disability pensions, with 15 percent of the recipients combining partial pensions and part-time work. Professor Wadensjö of the University of Stockholm estimates that a worker earning an average wage receives about 88 percent of prior after-tax income from such a pension, with a higher proportion received at lower earnings levels. Collectively bargained disability pensions often supplement the government payment. Although in some cases the amount of the disability pension is higher than a partial pension described below, and the number of recipients has grown because of liberalized provisions and more prolonged unemployment, the benefit is not as well received as are other pensions, perhaps because of the implication that the individual can no longer perform the duties of the job.[45]

The second way of combining retirement with part-time work is through the partial pension program. This national social policy evolved slowly in Sweden. Partial pensions were first proposed by the Swedish Metal Workers Union in 1973, as a way of easing the transition of their members from full-time heavy work to full-time retirement.[46] Study by a special commission led to cautious support for the concept but with some reservations about the practicality of its application and the effect it might have on the labor market and on productivity. Both the Commission and the Swedish Employer's Confederation (SAF) recommended implementation through collective bargaining where experimentation and flexibility in approach was more possible. But the view of the Metal Workers Union, supported by the national blue collar trade union organization (LO), prevailed. The Partial Pension Insurance Act became law, effective July 1, 1976.[47] Although its purpose was not to solve the unemployment problem but rather to provide for a gradual transition to retirement, it has had some effect on providing an easier transition to generally lower employment levels, when that became necessary.[48]

The Partial Pension Insurance Act is an important link in Sweden's flexible retirement structure. Enacted at the same time that the retirement age was lowered from 67 to 65, it provides benefits to employed and self-employed persons aged 60–64, who have been gainfully at work for five out of the preceding twelve months and for 10 years after age 45, and who choose to reduce their work hours after reaching age 60. Benefits are paid if employers agree to provide part-time work and if work is reduced by at least 5 hours weekly, while averaging at least 17 hours of weekly work. Most workers reduce their work by half and alternate weeks on and off the job.[49] Since January 1, 1981, benefits are 50 percent of foregone gross earnings (65 percent prior to this date). They are adjusted for changes in living costs but only partly so, because of the exclusion of energy costs and indirect taxes from the adjusted living costs index. At age 65, the partial pension ceases and workers enter the regular pension program with no reduction in their retirement pay. The program is financed by a 0.5 percent tax on gross wages and salaries and on incomes of the self-employed.

About one-half of the 480,000 Swedes aged 60–64 are in the labor force (61 percent in the United States in 1980). Men constitute 74 percent of the older labor force, aged 60–64 (60 percent in the United States in December 1983). Roughly 40 percent of non–self-employed Swedes, aged 60–64 meet the work-related requirements. About 70 percent of those who qualify for partial pensions each year are males. Of those eligible, about 28 percent — 14 percent of the Swedish population aged 60–64 — elect to participate in the program (33 percent of wage and salary earners and only about 5 percent of self-employed because of the required sharp reduction in working hours.)[50] Partial pensions are more likely to be paid in those industries where the proportion of older workers is high — manufacturing, accounting, clerical and commercial sectors. The combined after-tax part-time pension plus part-time earnings are about 80 percent of previous full-time earnings for most workers. Unlike disability pensions, only a small proportion of workers receive supplementary benefits (16 percent) over and above the government pension.

How successful has phased retirement been in Sweden? Although the number of partial pension participants in a company workforce is often small, employees who participate in the program perceive advantages arising both from income maintenance and from a less stressful work rhythm during the transition to retirement.

Employers have not had a problem, in large companies especially, in adjusting the hours of work of most jobs; except for senior staff positions, most persons are able to remain on their regular job.[51] Small firms have somewhat more difficulty in scheduling part-time work.[52] Employers find that the program facilitates necessary employment adjustments and lowers labor costs with a minimum of trauma for affected older individuals.[53] Whether employer support for the program will continue during periods of tight labor markets remains to be seen. Many see a favorable effect for production because of a greater output per work hour of part-time employees.[54]

Overall, it is felt that the partial retirement program offers an important employment/retirement option for workers prior to age 65.[55] Partial pensions have probably also lessened the growing tendency of complete labor market withdrawal for older persons. On the other hand, the lower compensation rate payable since 1981 has had a restraining effect on the demand for partial pensions. Moreover, although sickness absence and disability pensions have declined for persons aged 60–64, it is not clear that this is due to an improved health status — because of the partial retirement — rather than the greater tendency of older persons to forego health insurance benefits when receiving pensions. Work conditions, other than a reduction of work hours, have been little changed by partial retirement; job content has continued as it was.

All in all, partial retirement and part-time employment, whether in the form of partial pensions or partial disability benefits, have made an extended, part-time labor force attachment possible for numbers of workers who otherwise would have had to continue in full-time employment or to retire completely. Because of the emphasis on freedom of choice in these decisions, they reflect an individual time allocation preference. Although helpful in making employment adjustments in organizations when new hiring does not compensate for the reduced work hours of older and retiring workers, the existence of partial retirement has by no means solved the shortage of employment opportunities that affects both younger and older workers. Other social measures must address this issue. In Sweden, as in the United States, economic constraints pose difficult choices. It comes as no surprise that partial retirement (and part-time work) is not a total solution to labor market employment problems. That the partial pension and partial disability programs serve some labor market and enterprise needs, and at the same time ease employee transition to retirement, are benefits enough to give the programs value.

Summary and Future

Whether we look at the future characteristics of the labor force or at the direction of industrial and occupational trends, indications are that part-time work will grow in importance in the future, even at the present low rates of earnings and limited range of occupational choices of standard part-time work. The proportion of women in the labor force is expected to continue to rise. Older workers may also increase in number, although they are projected to be a somewhat smaller proportion of the labor force, because of the strong effect of the aging baby boom generation, who will be in their prime years, ages 25 to 54, and of women's continuing rising work rates generally. The labor force participation rates of older and elderly women are projected to fall only slightly, if at all. The trend in paid work orientation for them continues to be stronger than for older and elderly men.

Service and retail and wholesale trade industries and professional and technical, sales, clerical and service occupations — all areas where older persons are strongly represented and part-time work is traditional — are also expected to experience labor force growth.

What is not clear is whether these jobs will be filled by older workers or whether the increasing numbers of women, particularly in the middle age groups, and prime age males will successfully compete to fill these jobs.[56] The answers to these questions will depend partly on economic conditions and employer hiring preferences, partly on levels of retirement income, and partly on the up-dating of worker skills and training and their expressed preferences for engaging in paid work. But it will also depend on the work schedules of paid work and the availability of new, more desirable forms of part-time work scheduling.

Old Concept part-time work, although a necessary work scheduling form for some groups in society at some periods of their lives, is also considered by many to be demeaning and exploitative. Emerging new forms, not yet widespread, indicate a far greater potential in the range of jobs to which part time can be applied, and the economic rewards, including fringe benefits, that can be paid. New Concept reduced-hour work scheduling could benefit a number of working groups, including older workers, who seek to extend their attachment to the labor market or wish to phase gradually into retirement. The Swedish experience suggests that there are potential benefits from part-time work, not only for individual employees, but also for enterprise and society

in general. There also exist economic constraints that limit what the programs can accomplish.

Chapters 5 and 6 will continue discussion of the contribution that New
Concept part-time work can make, by looking at some explanatory factors —
both micro and macro — affecting the preference for reduced-hour work
among older workers. But first, Chapter 4 considers the close connection between women's work and life experience and the value of a part-time work
schedule option for them.

Notes

1. Discussion in this book focuses on issues relating to part-time weekly work, but another
type of reduced-hour schedule should be noted — that of part-year work — largely experienced
because of unemployment or school attendance or home responsibilities. In 1983, about three-
fifths of part-time workers and more than one-fourth of full-time workers were part-year
employees who worked less than 50 weeks. Part-year work, like part-time work, more common
among employed women than men, also responds to the need for time relief in paid work
activities (U.S. Department of Labor, BLS, 1984d, and Press Release, June 26, 1984).

2. The Department of Labor publishes two series on part-time work. The first relates to all
wage and salary workers at work in non-agricultural industries. Annual figures are derived from
data of the monthly *Current Population Survey,* which records information on working hours
during the week that includes the 12th of the month (the "reference week"). Full-time workers
include persons who worked 35 hours or more and those who usually work full time but worked
part time in the reference week because of illness, bad weather, holidays, personal business or
other temporary non-economic reasons. Voluntary part-time workers worked less than 35 hours
a week and did so by choice. Economic part-time workers worked less than 35 hours a week
involuntarily because of slack work, job changing in the week, repair of plant or equipment,
material shortage, inability to find full-time work, and so on (U.S. Department of Labor, BLS,
1983b, pp. 56–58). No adjustment is made for those workers, now classified as part time, for
whom less than 35 weekly work hours constitutes a full-time schedule. Part-time workers do not
include full-time workers who work a part year (Hedges and Gallogly, 1977, pp. 21–28).

Data is also reported in a second series for all members of the civilian labor force, including
agricultural workers, self-employed, and unpaid family workers. Those with a job but not at
work are distributed proportionately among the full- and part-time employed categories. The
data on which Figures 3.1–3.6 are based come from this series (See also U.S. Department of
Labor, BLS, 1984a, pp. 164, 192–95). Although the distinction between the two series is
important conceptually, there is relatively little difference between them in the proportion part-
time workers are of all workers (see table below).

Full-Time and Part-Time Workers 1982

	Total Employed	Full-Time Schedules	Part-Time for Economic Reasons	Voluntary Part-Time
All workers (000's)	99,526	79,118	6,169	14,239
Percent	100.00	79.5	6.2	14.3
Nonagricultural wage and salary workers at work	90,552	72,245	5,852	12,455
Percent	100.00	79.8	6.5	13.8

Source: U.S. Department of Labor. Bureau of Labor Statistics Communication.

3. Hedges and Gallogly, 1977, pp. 21–28; Bednarzik, 1975, pp. 12–18; Terry, 1971, pp. 70–74.

4. U.S. Department of Labor, BLS, 1984a, p. 193.

5. Hedges and Gallogly, 1977.

6. U.S. Department of Labor, BLS, 1983b, pp. 57–58.

7. Data in this section, unless otherwise indicated, come from Plewes (1983) and relate to all workers in the civilian labor force.

8. Personick, 1983, p. 26.

9. Silvestri, Lukasiewicz, and Einstein, 1983, pp. 38–39.

10. Barrett, 1983, p. 3.

11. U.S. Congressional Budget Office, 1982b, p. 9.

12. Ibid.

13. Plewes, 1983.

14. Gustman and Steinmeier, 1982, 1983a and c, 1984.

15. Plewes, 1983; Mellor, 1984.

16. Plewes, 1983, p. 5.

17. Barrett, 1984; U.S. Department of Commerce, 1983c, p. 17; Mellor, 1984, p. 26.

18. Nollen, 1982, p. 104.

19. Barrett, 1983.

20. Hedges and Gallogly, 1977; Whittaker, 1980, p. 1.

21. Paul, 1983b, pp. 6, 9, 27–28.

22. Olmsted, 1983, p. 489.

23. Ibid.

24. Ibid.

25. Ibid., pp. 489, 491.

26. Nollen, Eddy, and Martin, 1978, pp. 85–91.

27. Meier, 1978, 1982, and Nollen, 1982, contain excellent, comprehensive analyses of job sharing. This section draws from their work.

28. Nollen, 1982, p. 197.

29. Nemirow, 1984b, pp. 34–37; Chapter 8.

30. A comprehensive discussion of work sharing and analysis of issues and policy alternatives is found in Best, 1981. An excellent overview and series of case studies is McCarthy and Rosenberg, 1981.

31. Not all involuntary workers work part time because of poor economic conditions. Some of those who "can only find part-time jobs" are involuntary part-time workers because they lack skills or experience or are a high turnover risk (Bednarzik, 1983, pp. 6–7).

32. Bednarzik, 1983, p. 6.

33. Jondrow, Brechling, and Marcus, 1983, pp. 3–7.

34. McCarthy and Rosenberg, 1981, pp. 175–85, 233–54.

35. Ibid., p. 177; Jacobson, 1980, p. 14.

36. McCarthy and Rosenberg, 1981, pp. 233–38.

37. A 1981 Department of Labor study estimated that if mandatory retirement was totally eliminated, in the year 2000, only 195,000 additional male workers aged 60–70 would remain in the labor force. This would represent 5 percent of the 60–70 year old male labor force and only about 0.2 percent of the total work force in that year (U.S. Congressional Budget Office, 1982a, p. 44). Urban Institute, 1983, p. 3).

Several reasons have been suggested for the small effect that raising the mandatory retirement age has for men: many workers are not subject to mandatory retirement rules; many workers, although subject to such rules, take an early retirement and are thus not affected by them; some retire for health reasons although the reason given may be mandatory retirement; some men retire and then find other jobs. See Schulz, 1985, pp. 59–60, 62; Rones, 1978, p. 9; Parnes and Less, 1983, p. 32.

38. McCarthy and Rosenberg, 1981, p. 243.

39. Perkins, personal communication, 1984.

40. National Commission on Social Security Reform, 1983, p. 17; Chapter 7, note 5.

41. Paul, 1983b.

42. Parnes and Less, 1983, p. 25.

43. For a comprehensive and excellent analysis and series of case studies of phased retirement in five European countries see Swank, 1982.

44. Older Swedish workers, aged 45–54, have a lower unemployment rate than younger workers, but once unemployed, their unemployment duration is longer (that is, they have more difficulty in finding another job). The unemployment rate for workers, aged 60–64 has been higher than that of workers in other age groups. Several measures of social policy address the difficulties older workers face in finding employment. Workers over age 45 must be given 6 months notice prior to a dismissal. Although labor market retraining and relocation is not used much for older workers, the liberal conditions for receipt of a disability pension for older workers who become unemployed near retirement age provides them with an alternative to embarking on a difficult job search. Partial disability and retirement pensions represent other options available to older workers.

Most workers retire at age 65, especially so if they become unemployed near retirement age. The labor force participation rate for men after age 65 is 14 percent and for women, 4 percent (17.8 percent and 7.9 percent in the U.S.) (Ginsburg, 1983, pp. 25–26, 162, 193–94; Crona, 1981, p. 3; Ginsburg, 1982, pp. 22–27).

45. Crona, 1981, p. 4; Fellenius, 1984; Packard, 1982, pp. 14–15; Ginsburg, 1983, pp. 194–95.

46. Research studies in Sweden describe the anxiety and depression that can be associated with retirement. For references, see Crona, 1981, p. 6.

47. Swank, 1982, pp. 157–58.

48. For a discussion of the experience of one firm in reducing its workforce without extensive layoffs, see case study of L. M. Ericsson (Swank, 1982, pp. 163, 179–85).

49. Ibid., pp. 161, 182; Packard, 1982, p. 21.

50. Crona, 1981, p. 9; Packard, 1982, p. 20; Ginsburg, 1983, p. 195.

51. Crona, 1981, p. 10; Swank, 1982, pp. 161, 180, 184.

52. For a discussion of the use of job sharing and job rotation in structuring part-time work, see case study of Volvo (Swank, 1982, pp. 164–75).

53. Crona, 1981, p. 18.

54. Packard, 1982, p. 21.

55. Fellenius, 1984.

56. Morrison, 1983, pp. 18–19.

4

The Special Case of Women Workers: Distinctive Work Patterns and Needs

Part-time work has a special applicability to the lives of working women. This is not because it is the preferred work schedule for *all* women at some phase in their lives, such as the period of raising young children. Nor is it necessarily the form best suited to *some* working women, such as middle class women, for the *entire* span of their attachment to the labor market. But part-time employment can provide a critically important work schedule option for many women at particular periods of time. Unlike men's experience, where part-time work is still largely associated either with education or training during youth, or with work just prior to or following retirement, women's need for part-time work, whether deriving from individual preferences or imposed social roles, can occur throughout their working lives.

Women's interest in part-time work reflects several factors. Caretaking for elders, child rearing, and other socially determined responsibilities, need for income, and preference made possible by other income earners in the family, combine to lead about one-fourth of all employed married and single women to work part time by choice.[1] Only 13 percent of divorced women do so. Studies show that this employment has not been initiated by full-time workers who convert to part-time schedules, but by women who enter the labor market following a period of work and child rearing in the home.[2] Since the 1940s, about 40 percent of the dramatic increase in the number of working women has been in part-time employment.[3]

Despite the fact that 70 percent of voluntary part-time workers are women, it is not a work form receiving women's enthusiastic support. About 70 percent of female part-time workers are in sales, clerical and non-domestic service occupations, reinforcing the occupational segregation that women experience in their full-time work. Female part-time hourly earnings, only about 75 percent of full-time hourly earnings, reflect the low economic status of part-time jobs. Most part-time jobs still provide few fringe benefits and little job training and upward mobility. It is little wonder that part-time work in its Old Concept form is considered by many women to be demeaning.[4] Its effect has been to reinforce women's disadvantaged position in the labor market with respect to occupational opportunities and rewards. With the exception of freeing up time, it offers little in the way of a beneficial alternative to a full-time job with periodic work interruptions.

This chapter examines the labor market experience of women that relates to their distinctive work/life patterns, the circumstances or phases of women's lives that lead to such an interest in part-time work, and the personal and monetary consequences that result when working these alternative work patterns. The chapter concludes with comments about New Concept part-time work as an improved adaptive response, with respect both to women's work roles and to their general labor market experience.

Distinctive Experience of Older Women in the Labor Market

Two characteristics have marked women's economic activities since World War II. On the one hand, women's labor force participation rates have grown dramatically at the same time that work participation of men has been falling. Since 1960, the rates have increased particularly for married women and married women with young children, influenced by factors that affected both the demand for and supply of women workers (Table 4.1) (see Chapter 2 for a discussion of influencing factors). The labor force participation rate of all women rose from 34.7 percent in 1952 to 52.6 percent in 1982, while that of men fell from 86.3 percent to 76.6 percent (see Table 2.3). In the same pe-

Table 4.1. Labor Force Participation Rates of Married Women, Husband Present, by Presence and Age of Own Children, Selected Years 1952–1983 (percent of civilian noninstitutional population in the civilian labor force)

| | All Women | | Married Women | | |
	16 years and over	Married	With no Children Under 18 years	With Children Under 18 Years Total	Under 6 Years
1952	34.7	25.3	30.9	20.7	13.9
1962	37.9	32.7	36.1	30.3	21.3
1972	43.9	41.5	42.7	40.5	30.1
1982	52.6	51.2	46.2	56.3	48.7
1983	52.9	51.8	46.6	57.2	49.9

Note: Data were collected in April 1952 and in March of other years.

Source: U.S. Department of Labor, Bureau of Labor Statistics, Handbook of Labor Statistics, Bulletin 2175, December 1983, p. 17; Elizabeth Waldman, "Labor Force Statistics From a Family Perspective," Monthly Labor Review 106, no. 12 (December 1983): 18; U.S. Department of Labor, Bureau of Labor Statistics, "Employment in Perspective: Working Women," Fourth Quarter/Annual Summary, 1983, Report 702, p. 2.

riod, the labor force participation rate of married women doubled, and that of married women with children under age 6 more than tripled. The result has been a decrease in the disparity of paid work participation between women and men and an increasing similarity of experience among all groups of women, whether or not they are married or have children.

On the other hand, there has been little change in women's occupational segregation and in the disadvantaged status of their earnings. During the 1970s, there were some improvements in occupational distribution, particularly for new labor market entrants and for white collar occupations.[5] But women's occupational experience continues to be markedly different from that of men.[6] Median weekly earnings of full-time, year-round women workers, which hovered between 60–63 percent of men's earnings between 1967 and 1980, have since risen slightly, to 65.6 percent in 1983. It is not yet clear, however, whether the change marks an improving trend in women's earnings or is due to an economic situation that has adversely affected earnings where men generally work.[7]

Although much has been written about occupational segregation and wage differentiation between women and men generally, little attention has been paid to the distinctive, and often disadvantageous labor market experience of older women in relation to that of older men.[8] Because this situation has implications for the value of part-time work for them, the next few pages will spell out in more detail the difference in their work experience that is referred to in Chapter 2. At present, women comprise 40.2 percent of the labor force aged 55 and over. By 1995, the size of the older labor force is projected to decline somewhat, but there is expected to be a slight increase in the proportion of the older workforce that is female (42.8 percent by 1995).

LABOR FORCE PARTICIPATION RATES

The overall constancy of the labor force participation rate between 1950 (56.7 percent) and 1982 (55.1 percent), for individuals aged 55–64, results from the interplay of two different trends for women and men (Table 4.2; see also Fig. 2.1). The labor force participation of older men aged 55–64 declined gradually between 1950 and 1970, and then fell sharply (12.8 percentage points) between 1970 and 1982. For older women aged 55-64, the participation rate rose 14.1 percentage points between 1950 and 1965 and has remained relatively constant since then. Both changes have been attributed to an improved outlook for security in retirement, reflected in increased early retirement of older men and a slowed pace of labor force entry of older women.[9] Projections for 1995 forecast a continuation of these trends.

For elderly workers, labor force participation has declined by more than half between 1950 (26.7 percent) and 1982 (11.9 percent), almost entirely as a result of the sharp drop in male participation rates. The increased numbers of women in the labor force have corresponded roughly to the increase in the female population, so that their labor force participation rate has fallen only slightly. According to official projections, these trends, too, are likely to be unchanged.

Table 4.2. Labor Force Participation Rates for Older and Elderly Women and
            Men, Selected Years 1950-1995 (percent of civilian noninstitutional
            population in the civilian labor force)

	All Workers		Women		Men	
	Aged 55-64	Aged 65 and Over	Aged 55-65	Aged 65 and Over	Aged 55-64	Aged 65 and Over
1950	56.7	26.7	27.0	9.7	86.9	45.8
1960	60.9	20.8	37.2	10.8	86.8	33.1
1970	61.8	17.0	43.0	9.7	83.0	26.8
1980	55.7	12.2	41.5	8.1	72.3	19.1
1982	55.1	11.9	41.8	7.9	70.2	17.8
1983	54.5	11.7	41.5	7.8	69.4	17.4
1995[a]	52.8	9.5	42.5	7.0	64.5	13.3

[a]Projected.

Source: U.S. Department of Labor, Bureau of Labor Statistics. Shown in U.S. Senate,
Special Committee on Aging, "Aging and the Work Force: Human Resource Strategies,"
August 1982, pp. 8-9; Handbook of Labor Statistics, Bulletin 2175, December 1983,
p. 17; Fullerton and Tschetter, 1983; U.S. Department of Labor, Bureau of Labor
Statistics.

Thus, although older and elderly men continue to have higher participation rates than comparable groups of women, the trend of their labor market attachment has been steadily declining. Women's interest has risen significantly in the older age group and has fallen only slightly for elderly women.

OCCUPATIONAL DISTRIBUTION

The jobs that older men and women hold differ in ways that reflect the occupational segregation that exists in society as a whole. Among individuals aged 45 and over, a higher proportion of women than men work in white collar jobs (because of the high proportion of women who are clerical workers), and a smaller proportion are in high paying skilled craft work. The percent of older men in typically well paying managerial work is twice that of women, whereas the percent of older women in low paid service occupations is almost three times that of older men. Although a similar proportion of older women and men are sales persons, the kinds and rewards of their sales work differ. Men more often are corporate sales representatives; women are retail sales clerks, with considerably lower earnings.[10]

Two-fifths of women aged 65 and over are employed in sales and service occupations.[11] Among elderly men, more than one-third work in miscellaneous services (including business and repair, personal services other than private household, and in education, welfare, and religious organizations). Twenty-six percent work in wholesale and retail trade.[12] Although there is some occupational overlap among older and elderly men and women workers, there are also considerable differences in their jobs and in their tasks in similar titled occupations. The jobs of women at later ages are apt to be lower status and lower earning than those of comparable groups of men.

Affirmative action legislation has not yet had much of an effect on occupational segregation of older women workers. Despite the slight decrease in employment segregation noted for all women during the 1970s (p. 47), a study concentrating on a national sample of middle aged women between 1967 and 1977 found that the proportion of women in atypical semiskilled occupations actually decreased.[13] Overall, there was little desegregation in the occupational distribution of mid-life women.[14] One can speculate that the lack of change in occupational segregation of middle-aged women becomes even more marked as aging progresses because of a greater likelihood of subtle age discrimination and more personal uncertainty about working in a nontraditional environment. Continued occupational segregation of older working women could mean not only less flexibiliy and mobility in their paid work, but a negative effect on earnings as well.[15]

EARNINGS

Not only are older women concentrated in fewer occupations than are older men, but their earnings are also less than those of older men. As noted earlier, historically, the ratio of women's to men's earnings has changed little over time. Several factors, in addition to occupational segregation, contribute to this situation.[16] These include fewer years of work experience because of competing needs of caring for family, shorter job tenure with present employer, less opportunity for continuing education or on-the-job training, and discrimination.[17]

After age 45, median weekly earnings of both women and men fall. In middle and later adult years the ratio of women's to men's median full-time weekly earnings is about 60 percent. For elderly men, earnings fall more than for elderly women, so that the ratio rises to 70 percent. That does not, however, change the condition of women's lower earnings nor reduce the depressing effect that age has on them.[18] Moreover, the recent trend of improvement in the overall earnings ratio is not reflected in the ratio at later ages. The ratio of female/male earnings at ages 55 to 64 and 65 and over is lower than it was in 1975.[19] Low earnings coupled with work discontinuities, discussed below, not only increase the possibility of poverty,[20] but further differentiate elderly women from elderly men by their receipt of a lower retirement income.

UNEMPLOYMENT

In 1982, for the first time since government data collection on unemployment was initiated in 1940, the unemployment rate for women was lower than that for men, and this continued to be true in 1983 (9.9 percent for men; 9.2 percent for women).[21] The turnabout reflects the fact that variables fostering higher female rates (more labor turnover and shorter seniority) have been more than compensated for in recent years by the greater unemployment in blue collar factory operative jobs where men are located than in the while collar and service occupations where women work.[22] If similar industry/occupational jobless rates are compared, the rates for women are generally higher than for men. Measured rates also ignore the unemployment of discouraged workers who want a job but have left the labor force because they believe that no employment is available. This effect is greater for women,[23] who comprise about three-fifths of the discouraged workers.

Unemployment rates for older workers follow a similar pattern. In December 1983, for example, the unemployment rate for women aged 55–64 was 4.5 percent, compared with a male rate of 5.6 percent. For women 65 and over, the rate was 3.2 percent, compared with 3.7 percent for elderly men. But this does not reflect a comparison of unemployment in similar occupations, nor does it take account of the older, unemployed, discouraged workers. Unemployment duration, greater at later ages, is somewhat less for older women than for older men.[24]

These few comparisons highlight some major differences in paid work experience of women and men at later ages. The trend of work participation of older women continues to increase and that of elderly women is declining only slightly, as work participation of older and elderly men follows a falling trend. Yet, because of occupational segregation, a segregation that is not diminishing for women in mid-life, flexibility and mobility of employment are constrained. Earnings and incomes of later age women continue to be lower than those of older and elderly men, although the disparity in earnings is less at later ages. Although women currently have a lower overall measured unemployment rate than men, comparison of similar occupations and inclusion of discouraged workers as unemployed might reveal a different pattern.

Part-time work cannot resolve fundamental labor market problems that place older women at an economic disadvantage. Nor will it provide sufficient income for those women whose economic status is at or below the poverty level. But the fact that the proportion of part-time workers rises at later ages indicates an interest of older workers in this work schedule, even in regular low paid part-time jobs.[25] An expanded availability of New Concept part-time work would be a welcome option for buttressing economic security for many mature women where full-time work is either burdensome, not possible, or less preferred in later years. More than this, its availability in a broader range of occupations and at prorated remuneration would mark an important advance in reducing women's occupational segregation and raising the level of their hourly earnings.

Unique Patterns of Women's Work Histories

For later life, the value of New Concept part-time work for women is broader than that of reduced work hours. Because of women's primary responsibility for household and family care, their paid work adds a further pressure to the time demands of family work.[26] Sometimes both tasks are accomplished by lengthening the daily working hours. Often, during periods of greatest family need, and despite the attendant problems of re-entry and the negative consequences for career and retirement income, women withdraw from the labor market for some period of time.[27] Part-time work offers an additional alternative that, even in its Old Concept form, provides a benefit of time, while preserving work continuity and ensuring the flow of some income. This section discusses paid work patterns of women and reviews the nature and implications of family demands in three kinds of family situations, and then considers the contribution New Concept part-time work could make in providing an employment bridge in these transition periods of heavy family demands.

WORK DISCONTINUITIES

Both women's dual roles and the cohort (age group) to which they belong affect their work history patterns; these patterns differ from the full-time, continuous work pattern more often followed by men. In a 1976 national study of 5,000 families, Corcoran found that not only did white men after leaving school work more continuously than white women, but the spells of nonwork they had were likely to be one-time short interruptions concentrated at the start of their working careers.[28] Black women were less likely than either white women or men to have interrupted work once it began. Their work pattern was similar to that of white men — continuous and full time. The experience of black men also paralleled that of white men except that work interruptions were less likely and, when they occurred, were for a shorter period. In contrast to these other groups, about two-thirds of white employed women experienced one or more interruptions of work.

Further, women used their time off less often than men to improve their workplace skills and hence earnings. More than half of all men who interrupted work did so to acquire job-related training skills; only about 20 percent of women gave this reason for their work discontinuity. The periods of work interruption for women were more likely to be related to marriage and raising a family.

Other research confirms the prevalence of employment discontinuities or part-time work patterns for women and the role played by both family and cohort in their occurrence. One study of the paths of a five-year work history between 1972 and 1976 of married women and women heading households found a variety of work attachment patterns, with no one typical mode.[29] Being married and having young children increased the likelihood of having spent some time out of the labor force during the five-year period. Being older or in poorer health or with less education also increased the possibility of non-work or part-time work for at least some of the period. Thus, a number of factors were found to influence many women's intermittent work patterns.

Shaw also explored the reasons for non-work periods in women's lives.[30] The study, which looked at an eleven-year work history of married women aged 30–44 in 1967 and 40–54 in 1977, reported that only 30 percent of white married women and about 45 percent of black married women worked as much as 75 percent of the weeks during the period. Family responsibilities were an important cause of a period of non-work, as was health, especially among black women. Poor business conditions or low educational levels also affected work continuity, especially among those who were not previously well established in the labor market.

Discontinuities in paid work are not without cost, both in relation to earnings from work and to income in retirement. Traditional economic theory attributes the differential in male/female earnings to differences in human capital investment. In that view, discontinuities rationally chosen by women who elect to "invest" in home and family rather than in market work mean less investment in skill acquisition and a depreciation and obsolescence of that which has been attained.[31] Women's earnings are lower than men's, the argument runs, because of women's preference for allocating time to home affairs and their consequent lower productivity in the market.

Recent research questions this association of women's lower earnings with work discontinuities,[32] noting that the timing and length of the discontinuity itself, after adjustment has been made for the effect of lost work experience, only negligibly affect earnings. Although re-entry wages are somewhat lower than those prior to the work interruption, the gap narrows quickly because of rapid wage growth after re-entry. The wage penalty for "rusty skills" as a result of work discontinuities is small.

On the other hand, other research findings indicate that less work experience, sometimes affected by work discontinuities and sometimes by part-time work, as well as less on-the-job training, do account for a significant portion of the wage gap between women and men.[33] In one study, 29 percent of the gap between white women and white men and 17 percent of the gap between black women and white men were explained by differences in work experience. Women's earnings were negatively affected when work in the home was substituted for market experience.

Performance of home duties in place of market work can also mean a sacrifice in retirement income. Eligibility and vesting of private pensions, frequently based on a period of uninterrupted service with an employer, can be jeopardized by work discontinuities. In social security, the lack of any earnings credits for time spent out of the labor market means a lowering of average earnings on which social security benefits are based.[34] Women in retirement pay a heavy price for the market discontinuities they experience during their working years in order to cover work demands in the home.

As an increasing proportion of women work continuous full-time schedules, discontinuities will become a less important part of women's work histories,[35] but they will not disappear as long as children (although fewer) are born and family life (however the family is defined) continues. Re-entry problems for women—finding a job, updating of education and skills, and coping with family stress that may accompany a greater or different sharing of family responsibilities—will persist,[36] unless an alternative way is found to ensure a continuity of work attachment at a less than full-time intensity during demanding periods of family needs.

FAMILY RESPONSIBILITIES

Family responsibilities and the need to adapt work schedules differ among women because of individual preferences about allocation of duties, and also because family needs vary. Three situations are described below.

Caregiving for the Elderly

One of the results of high fertility rates of the pre–World War I period and of increases in life expectancy is that the elderly population, and especially the *old* old (aged 85 and over), are the fastest growing groups in society. The number of elderly persons is projected to double between 1980 and 2020 (51.4 million in 2020). The very old are expected to triple in numbers (7.3 million by 2020).[37] It is this group, about 70 percent of whom today are women, who may need care, whether it be within families, in institutions, or within a formal structure of home-based support.

Caregiving, which includes any type of non-financial helping activity, ranging from provision of incidental chores to essential tasks required to maintain the person at home, can become necessary at any age. But those likely to be in greatest need of care are the *old* old, who are widowed, or have low incomes, or live with a relative other than a spouse.[38] Elderly women are much less likely to be married and more likely to live alone than are elderly men. Their life expectancy at age 65 is now about 4.5 years longer than that of men, and the discrepancy in longevity continues to grow. By 1990, women who live to age 65 may live another twenty years; men another fifteen years.

Who are the caregivers to the elderly? Family members (primarily spouses and daughters) are both the preferred and the major caregivers today.[39] Caregivers tend to be female and are often older themselves. Although there is presently no national data base for precisely determining the number of caregivers for the elderly, it is estimated that about one in ten middle-aged women (aged 40–59) have responsibilities toward other relatives.[40] In a 1980 national study of primary caregivers of moderately to severely impaired elderly persons living in the household of the caretaker, 70 percent of caregivers were found to be women,[41] and 89.1 percent of male caregivers and 78.4 percent of female caregivers were age 50 or over. Households contributing to the support of an elderly relative, where the male household head was under age 65 and the wife was in the labor force, with no other adult woman present, were more likely to purchase institutional care than families where the wife did not work or where there was another woman in the household.

The likelihood is that the size of the needy elderly population, many of whom will be women, will grow. About two-thirds of male and almost half of female caregivers under age 65 also have paid jobs.[42] Unless flexible and reduced-hour work arrangements become more possible, the stress of family caretaking of the elderly will become more pronounced. A lack of adaptive work schedules could result not only in more stress for the increasing numbers of women (and men) who combine work and family roles in this way,

but also in a demand for more available institutional care at greater family
and societal cost.

Female Family Households

Women who head families, members of the fastest growing family form in
the United States today, carry a double burden.[43] They are responsible for
the economic maintenance of family members, and at the same time they
must provide for family care, which includes rearing of children. It is a difficult dual role to perform, especially when their training, labor market status,
and family support system is less than that of other family groups.

Families maintained by women, 15.9 percent of all families in March 1983
(9.8 million), increased four times as fast as all families between 1970 and
1983.[44] A major factor in their rapid growth has been the large number of
marriages of the baby boom generation and subsequent high divorce rate,
which by 1980 was equivalent to one divorce for every two marriages. Also
contributing to their growth, particularly since the 1970s, has been a sharp
rise in childbearing among single women, especially teenagers and those in
their early twenties.[45]

The marital characteristics of female family heads are changing. In March
1983, 55.4 percent of female family heads were separated or divorced, while
26.0 percent were widowed and 18.5 percent were never married. By contrast, in 1970, 42.8 percent of women maintaining families were widowed,
about 46.2 percent were separated or divorced, and only 11 percent were
never married. Female family heads have other distinctive traits. They tend
to be younger than family heads in other marital groups. They have less education and are more likely to be represented in minority than in white families. About 40 percent of black families compared with 12 percent of white
families are maintained by women. A greater proportion have children at
home (61.5 percent) than in the past (one-third in 1950). Almost one-fourth
(23.3 percent) have children under the age of 6. All in all, they are disadvantaged and heavily burdened.

A higher proportion of female family heads (59.6 percent) than married
women (51.8 percent) were in the labor force in March 1983, a proportion
dominated by the strong labor force participation rates of divorced female
family heads (78.2 percent). Widows were the one group with less than a
50 percent participation rate; only one-third of them were in the labor force.
But because of their lower educational achievement, women who head families work in less skilled and lower paid occupations. They often work as typ-
ists, cashiers, office and hotel cleaners, waitresses, and nurses aides.[46] Their
median weekly earnings in the first quarter of 1983 were $256, compared with
$400 for husbands or male family heads.

Adding to their problems is the fact that despite their low labor market rewards, female family heads receive less other economic support than do
heads in other family forms. Only 30 percent live in multiple-earner families,
compared with 56 percent of all married couple families. Their unemployment rates are higher than those of husbands or wives.[47] When unemployed,

only about 20 percent of families have another employed family member to assist with family maintenance. In contrast, in 1983, almost 80 percent of unemployed wives and 55 percent of unemployed husbands had the support of another working family member.[48]

As disadvantaged as the situation is for all women maintaining families, it is even more so for black female family heads who have more children, less education, lower labor force participation, lower median earnings, higher unemployment rates, and less support from other family members than do white women.

With such a situation, it does not come as a surprise that in 1983, more than one in three families maintained by women were below the poverty level (1 in 13 in other families) and that 46.6 percent of families in poverty were those maintained by women.[49] Women family heads constitute a category contributing to a frightening new societal problem—the "feminization of poverty." They are a pervasive, although not a persistent, group in need. There is a large flow of women in and out of the status of being a female family head, and a similar flow in and out of poverty, which is more influenced by changes in family composition than in labor force participation.[50] Nearly three-fifths of those employed work full time, but even with full-time work, 6.2 percent were still below the poverty level in 1983.[51]

Families maintained by women, although now growing at a slower rate than in the past, have become a permanent and common marital form,[52] in which perhaps one out of two children will live for a period during their youth.[53] Such families are "money poor,"[54] because of both low earnings and lack of child support assistance. In 1978, about half of women with children and an absent father were supposed to receive child support payments (4.2 million). Of these, about one-fourth received only partial payment and almost 30 percent received nothing at all.[55] Women with children born out of wedlock—20 percent of all woman-headed families with children—almost never receive father-supported payments.[56] In addition, female family heads are "time poor,"[57] having little support in coping with the heavy time and energy demands of combined work and family roles.

Part-time work cannot provide a total solution for those families whose economic status is already marginal. But it can permit paid work accompanied by some free time for acquiring education and training and knowledge about how to cope in an increasingly complex labor market. Although its role may be a transitional one, the new conception of part-time work, when combined with some family care support during a training period, could contribute in a major way to raising the economic status of this now seriously disadvantaged group.[58]

Dual Worker Families

Female family heads are the fastest growing family form but married couple families continue to be the most prevalent.[59] In 1983, 80.8 percent of all families were married couple families. In 62 percent of married couple families in 1981, both the husband and wife were employed, up from 50.1 percent in

1970 and 40 percent in 1960.[60] Whether due to increased job opportunities or a change in social attitudes about the value of work for women, or to maintain a given standard of living, or because of financial need or a threat to its adequacy raised by inflation or recession, more wives are employed than are not. Despite the pressures that come with combining paid work and family care, 46 percent of employed wives work full time.

Working wives contribute substantially to family income. Average income for married couples in 1981 when only the husband worked was $22,300. Income was $28,560 when both husband and wife had jobs, and $34,560 when both spouses worked full time and year-round. Wives contributed about 30 percent to family income overall, and 38 percent when they worked full time year-round. In 16 percent of married couple families, the wife's earnings was higher than that of her husband.[61]

Despite the gain in greater family income, there are also costs involved, caused by the way paid work impinges on family existence and the stress and conflict that come with performing two roles and meshing schedules of family members to ensure that household and family care needs are met.[62] Although employed wives still carry the major responsibility for taking care of home needs, for both spouses paid work can have an effect on the quality of family life, although not always to the same degree or related to the same causal factors.[63]

Role overload of working women. In the 1960s, noting the long hours of combined paid labor market work and unpaid home work that accompanied women's increasing labor force participation, social scientists described a "role overload" that working wives faced relative to their working husbands, defined as the total hours spent in combined market and family work. According to this measure, wives worked an average of 1.5 to 2.5 hours more a day than husbands.[64] Despite the fact that marriages did not become more symmetrical, nor was there an adaptation in the scheduling of paid work, by the mid-1970s role overload in this sense seems to have disappeared.[65] Its disappearance was due partly to a decline in the hours spent by employed women in family care as a result of an increased use of labor-saving household technological improvements (such as microwave ovens and home freezers), a decrease in routine housekeeping maintenance, and a reduction in the hours spent in child care, perhaps because of smaller-sized families. Partly it resulted from an increase in time spent on family tasks by husbands.[66] A recent study notes, for example, that whereas husbands contributed 20 percent of the amount of time spent by the wife in family work in 1965, that percentage had risen to 30 percent by 1981.[67]

But although role overload for wives in terms of total family and market hours worked has disappeared, and although the proportionate contribution of husbands in family work has grown, wives still carry the major responsibility for family care.[68] Not only do employed wives continue to do the bulk of family work, but they frequently do the less pleasurable tasks,[69] carry on several of them simultaneously,[70] and assume a greater level of responsibility in their performance,[71] all of which may contribute to a greater strain of family care for women than for men.

Child care of preschool children. The fact that in 1984, 52.1 percent of all mothers with children under age six were in the labor force, and 48.2 percent of all children under age six had working mothers makes child care an issue of major importance in thinking about the stress of paid work for family well-being. Two-thirds of working mothers with young children work full time. Yet, because of the limited availability of adequate institutional day care at reasonable cost, care arrangements cover a wide variety of formal and informal methods. These differ in use according to a number of factors — family income, occupation, education, race, marital status of the mother, and full- or part-time employment.[72]

In contrast to the non-parental child care arrangements used by female family heads (note 58), a June 1982 survey indicates that in 27.3 percent of married families with a working wife, care of preschool children was provided either by the father in the child's home, or by the mother while working.[73] The proportion of parental care was 20 percent for fully employed mothers and twice that for mothers employed part time. Parental care was more likely in families where the mother had less education and the parents had blue collar jobs, presumably because in these circumstances there was less income to purchase private group care and because occupational shift and night work were more possible.

Married working mothers were more likely to care for their young children while working than mothers in other marital statuses. Mothers who did so often worked at home. They were less likely to use group care. Black working mothers, a larger proportion of whom were unmarried, more commonly than whites used group care and care by relatives.

Among currently married women, 15-17 percent of fathers — a similar proportion for blacks as for whites — were the principal caretakers of the preschool child when the wife worked. But the fact that among fully employed wives, 34 percent of the husbands who were listed as principle caretakers were unemployed, compared with 15 percent of husbands with part-time employed wives, suggests that child care was not their principal activity. Multiple kinds of child care arrangements were more likely to be used when the father was the principal caretaker than in other kinds of child care arrangements.

Although there is no way to assess the level of family stress associated with care of young children when mothers work, it is clear that its provision is not easy. For many married couple working families, care continues to reside within the family unit, rather than in non-family group arrangements. Private group care appears to be used most by families who can afford it — professional workers and families with incomes of $25,000 and over.

Family stress in relation to care of young children has two components. On the one hand, maximizing family well-being requires that evaluation be made of the qualities and costs and time commitments associated with the variety of public and private group care arrangements, as compared with benefits and complexities of parental care. Too little data is available to do this. At the same time, there is a tension in family well-being, if choice is not available. And on this issue, it is known that there exists a shortage of adequate group care arrangements at reasonable cost. One recent survey noted that about one-fifth of married mothers and over two-fifths of mothers in other marital categories who were not in the labor force would look for work if child care for their pre-school children were available at reasonable cost.[74] Because of the projected childbearing of the baby boom generation, and an expected continued rise in work participation of women, it has been estimated that between 1980 and 1990 there will be a 57 percent increase of preschool children among families headed by working women. There may be a 36 percent increase of young children in married couple families with a working mother.[75] The need for child care services for preschool children at reasonable cost or for alternatives such as part-time work to facilitate a combining of child care with paid work will become increasingly urgent if the levels of stress in accommodating the work/family needs are not to increase. The fact that since 1981, federal funds for child care have been drastically cut does not bode well for the future.

Work schedules and family well-being. What can be said about the effect of work schedules on work/family interaction? Staines and Pleck studied the effect of a variety of work schedules on family stress and family well-being, looking particularly at the interactive effects of parents' work schedules among dual earner couples.[76] Among all families, they found that nonstandard patterns of days worked, such as weekend work, and of hours worked, exemplified by night shifts, were scheduled with negative effects for the quality of family life. Negative effects were reflected in less time for child care, more conflict in adjusting work and family schedules, and lower levels of family satisfaction. Long hours of weekly work meant reduced time in family roles, especially in housework, and more conflict between jobs and family.

Among dual earner families, except for shift work, husbands were more likely than wives to have stressful work schedules that interfered with family life. In these families, regular weekend work significantly and negatively affected time spent in child care and in housework of husbands, but not of wives. Shift work was predictive of higher levels of housework for both husbands and wives and more conflict between work and family life for husbands. On the other hand, longer hours worked had a significantly stronger negative effect on time in family activities, including both child care and house work, for wives than for husbands and also increased conflict between work and family life for wives, but not for husbands. For wives, the quality of family life was generally more responsive to the number of hours worked; for husbands, it was more responsive to shift and patterns of days worked. The negative effects of work schedules on family life were less severe if individuals had some flexibility in scheduling of work.

Two additional findings of particular interest for this discussion grew out of an innovative exploration by Staines and Pleck of the work schedule/family interactive effects for 500 two-earner couples. First, 12.2 percent of dual-earner couples included some shift work in their schedule, the proportion being highest for the subgroup of parents of preschool children.[77] To test a hypothesis that shift work presents an alternative child care arrangement to formal institutional care for working parents,[78] Staines and Pleck looked at a subgroup of two-earner couples with the youngest child under five. Among 83 couples with formal child care arrangements, 15.7 percent worked different shifts. The proportion rose to 27.8 percent for the 36 couples with no formal day care arrangements, providing suggestive evidence in support of the hypothesis. Shift work may make wives' employment possible, particularly in blue collar occupations in which it is more prevalent.[79] It is not necessarily a desirable choice from a family perspective, however, since it is also a work pattern reflecting a work schedule conflict and contributing to a decrease in the level of family satisfaction.

Second, the study showed differing responses of husbands and wives to several work schedule arrangements. Although working long hours was generally predictive of a decrease of time spent in housework and an increase in conflict between work and family life, the effect was significantly greater for wives than for husbands. Husbands experienced a greater work schedule conflict when wives worked evening or night shifts than wives did with husbands' non-day shift work, perhaps because husbands' shift work permits them to help with daytime household chores. On the other hand, wives experienced more conflict about work schedule when the husband worked weekends than husbands did with such work of the wife, perhaps because husbands' weekend work interferes with their child care assistance.

In sum, particular work schedules, including long hours of work, do affect family time and family stress, frequently differently for husbands and wives in two-earner couples. The Staines and Pleck analysis raises important questions about work schedules that society, as well as partners in a marriage, cannot afford to ignore.

New Concept Part Time: An Alternative Option

We are living in a new era where paid work is more and more central to women's lives and their sense of identity and well being.[80] Women marry later, have fewer children, and have them later than was true 30 years ago.[81] Their labor force participation rates continue to rise, although more slowly than in the past. Participation rates are becoming more similar among women, regardless of their race or marital status, and also more like those of men. A growing minority of households are maintained by women; in two-earner households, women contribute substantially to family income. Work interruptions over the course of their work history, although not disappearing, are fewer and shorter than in the past. Nonetheless, women continue to bear the major responsibility for household and family care.

The growing prevalence of combined paid work and family roles among women (and some men) heightens an awareness of the effects that paid work and its scheduling have on the well-being of family. Integration of these facets of life often brings stress for both women and men, although experienced differently and as a result of different causes. Understanding the implications of alternative adaptive responses to the burdens of these dual roles and, when possible, improving on them is important not only for women, but for all members of the family group who are affected by the working and living arrangements.

Sometimes dual-role commitments are met by adding full-time paid work to work in the home or by varying the pattern of work hours through shift work. Both are achieved at a cost of additional stress and work/family conflict. Sometimes the adaptive coping mechanism is to interrupt paid work by leaving the labor market for a period. Here, time available for family needs is improved, but earnings sacrifices may be involved because of less work experience and job tenure. Retirement income may also be affected because of lower earnings and interrupted labor market attachment.

Part-time work offers another way of accommodating the realities of a multiple role society. It is an option of importance not only for women (and men) and their partners, involved in working out the meshing of dual roles, but also for the increasing numbers of young children and elders for whom a balance of family care and institutional support is a critical necessity. Part-time work can provide a useful transitional support for responding to heavy family demands or acquiring new skills. At the same time, such schedules are given added importance by the needs of older women with disadvantaged economic status and work experience. For them, part-time work could supplement inadequate other income, while providing the stimulation and collegiality offered by a work environment.

Old Concept part-time work responds to these pressures of time or need, but it does not do so in a way that gives equivalent labor market status to that of full-time work. It creates a situation that is demeaning both of the work contribution of these workers and of the concept of part-time work. Moreover, it reinforces the occupational segregation of women and intensifies their low earnings status.

The new conception of part time presents a valuable alternative, not only to standard part-time work, but to full-time work and the economic disadvantages associated with its work discontinuities. It could provide a major thrust in lessening occupational segregation and low earnings and in changing the negative image associated with women's productive contributions. Extension of the availability of such work schedules would help those older women who continue to need some earnings to buttress their economic position immediately, as well as in retirement. More than this, it would offer a transition or life phase option for all adults — men, as well as women — who, by choice or necessity, fulfill both family and work roles. The greater availability of New Concept part-time work, by making institutional structures more responsive to life rhythms, could represent a major step forward toward achievement of an improved quality of life.

Notes

1. U.S. Department of Labor, BLS, 1984a, p. 194; Chapter 3, Fig. 3.6.
2. Barrett, 1983. In a study of part-time work in Sweden, 85 percent of which is female, Marianne Pettersson Sundström, 1981 also concluded that the strong growth of part-time work in the 1970s reflected a movement of young mothers of newborns into the workforce, rather than movement of full-time women workers to part-time work.
3. Plewes, 1983.
4. For a criticism of part-time work for women seen as an expression of social policy that fosters a secondary, flexible low paid labor force as necessary for economic growth, see Schirmer, 1982a, and b.
5. Beller with Han, 1984.
6. About one-fourth of all women's employment is concentrated among just 22 of the 500 Census occupational categories; men's employment is largely divided among the others. In 1980, more than 32 million persons were employed in industries whose employees were at least 80 percent female or 80 percent male (U.S. Department of Labor, BLS, 1984b, p. 1).
7. Kahne, 1975, 1978; Ferber, 1982. See also Beller, 1982; Lloyd and Niemi, 1979; Reskin, 1984a; Shack-Marquez, 1984; Shaw, 1983a; Steinberg and Haignere, 1984; Treiman and Hartmann, 1981; U.S. Department of Labor, BLS, 1982a; Mellor, 1984, pp. 26–27.
8. Kahne, forthcoming.
9. U.S. Senate, 1982, pp. 8–9.
10. Mellor, 1984, p. 19.
11. U.S. Department of Labor, BLS, 1982b, Table B-18.
12. Rones, 1978, pp. 7–8.
13. In this study, middle-aged women were 30 to 44 years old at the time of the first interview in 1967 and 40 to 54 years of age at the time of the final interview. An "atypical occupation" was defined as one where women comprised a smaller proportion of an occupation than they did of the entire labor force.

The degree of occupational segregation is affected both by the integration of men and women in the occupation and by the growth rates of occupations that are heavily dominated by women or men. The failure of middle-aged women to reflect a decrease in overall occupational segregation may partially relate to the fact that employment growth has occurred in occupations —such as service—that are heavily female.
14. Daymont and Statham, 1983, p. 66.
15. Lloyd and Niemi, 1979; Stevenson, 1978.
16. Duncan with Corcoran, 1984.
17. A new strategy of "comparable worth" or "pay equity" now supplements affirmative action policy (Treiman and Hartmann, 1981; Steinberg and Haignere, 1984) as a mechanism for redressing discrimination. The concept of comparable worth maintains that women's earnings are low not necessarily because of intentional individual discrimination, but because the work that women do is undervalued by society. A policy of comparable worth would raise earnings in occupations where women traditionally work, by evaluating and comparing required job skills (for example, dexterity, responsibility, supervisory talents) in male and female occupations and raising women's earnings to match those of men at similar skill levels.
18. Mellor, 1984, pp. 19, 26.
19. In 1975, women's usual weekly earnings were 62.0 percent of men's earnings. The ratio was 63.1 percent for women aged 55–64 and 74.7 percent for those aged 65 and over. In 1982, although the overall ratio had risen to 65.0 percent, it was only 60.1 percent for older women and 70.2 percent for those who were elderly (U.S. Department of Labor, Women's Bureau, 1976; Mellor, 1984, p. 19).
20. Grad, 1984, p. 7. In 1983 about 17 percent of elderly women compared with 10 percent of aged men had incomes below the poverty line (U.S. Department of Commerce, 1984e, p. 25).
21. *Economic Report of the President,* 1984, p. 254.
22. Urquhart and Hewson, 1983.
23. Rones, 1984, p. 27.
24. U.S. Department of Labor, BLS, 1984a, pp. 19, 33.

25. In 1980, 28.3 percent of working women aged 16–54 worked part time, 26.6 percent of those aged 55–64 and 58.4 percent of employed women aged 65 or more (U.S. Congressional Budget Office, 1982b, p. 9).

26. The discussion in this section is presented in terms of women's experience because women are the persons primarily responsible for family care. The reasoning, however, applies equally to men who perform the homemaker role.

27. U.S. Department of Commerce, 1984c.

28. Corcoran, 1978.

29. Moen, 1982a.

30. Shaw, 1983b.

31. Mincer and Polachek, 1974; Kahne, 1978; Polachek, 1975, 1981.

32. Corcoran, Duncan, and Ponza, 1984.

33. Duncan and Corcoran, 1984, find that skill differences related to work experience account for about one third of the wage gap between white women and white men and one fourth that between black women and white men. Broader based, better paid part-time work options might reduce some of this wage discrepancy, but not all. They also conclude that socialization and discriminatory factors continue to play a major role in explaining the male/female earnings gap.

34. Kahne, 1981.

35. Oppenheimer, 1982; Mallan, 1982.

36. Appelbaum, 1981; Yohalem, 1980; Cook, 1977.

37. U.S. Department of Commerce, 1983e.

38. New York State, 1983, p. 5.

39. Gurland, et al., 1978.

40. Soldo, 1980a.

41. Soldo, 1980b.

42. Ibid., p. 13.

43. Unless otherwise indicated, data in this section come from Johnson and Waldman, 1983. In 1983, there were also 2.1 million families maintained by men alone. Their labor market experience is less disadvantaged than that of women family heads, but many of the time pressures facing them are similar.

44. Waldman, 1983, p. 17.

45. U.S. Commission on Civil Rights, 1983, pp. 9–10.

46. Sarri, 1984.

47. Klein, 1983, p. 22.

48. Norwood, 1984, p. 2; Klein, 1983, p. 24.

49. U.S. Department of Commerce, 1984e, p. 27.

50. U.S. Commission on Civil Rights, 1983, p. 11.

51. U.S. Department of Commerce, 1984e, p. 28.

52. Schorr and Moen, 1984.

53. Masnick and Bane, 1980.

54. Brown, 1980.

55. U.S. Department of Commerce, 1981, pp. 1–2.

56. U.S. Congress, Joint Economic Committee, 1984, p. 59.

57. Brown, 1980.

58. Non-parent relatives and a variety of public and private group care provide the major child care arrangements for employed women without spouse. Grandparents are especially important providers of child care for unmarried women. For further discussion of resources and policies, see Kamerman, 1983; U.S. Department of Commerce, November, 1983f; U.S. Commission on Civil Rights, 1981. See also pp. 57 ff.

59. An excellent conceptual framework of the linkages between work and family in two-worker families and identification of issues is Moen, 1982b, pp. 13–43. See also Hayghe, 1981 and 1983, for annotated bibliography and further discussion of dual worker family characteristics.

60. U.S. Department of Commerce, 1984b, p. 2.

61. Ibid., p. 2.

62. The stress associated with time constraints or schedule conflicts is focused on here. Additional social and psychological dilemmas faced by working couples have also been described in Rapoport and Rapoport, 1976. and in Moen, 1982b.

63. A 1977 survey (Pleck, Staines, and Lang, 1980) provides some indication of the effect of paid work on stress in family life. Workers who were currently married (although not ncessarily living in two-earner families) and those living with a child under age 18 were asked how much their job and family life interfered with each other. About the same percent of employed wives and female family heads (35 percent) and employed husbands (34 percent) reported moderate or severe conflict in work/family interference. But the proportion of employed wives with employed husbands experiencing this conflict (38.1 percent) was greater than the proportion of employed husbands with employed wives (31.5 percent). Parents, particularly those with preschool children, experienced conflict more than others.

Members of two-earner families perceived the conflict in different ways. Husbands were more likely to report excessive work time as a problem; wives more often noted work-schedule incompatibility, with work-related fatigue and irritation negatively affecting family life.

64. Pleck, 1983. This chapter provides an excellent interpretive review of the research literature on husband's work and family roles.

65. Pleck, Lang, and Rustad, 1980.

66. Pleck, 1980.

67. Juster, forthcoming.

68. Pleck, 1983, pp. 263, 268–71.

69. Hochschild, 1983.

70. Lein, 1984.

71. Moen, 1982a, pp. 26–28.

72. For a description of after-school arrangements for school age children, see Seligson, Genser, Gannett, and Gray, 1983. See Kamerman, 1983, for discussion of preschool programs and federal policies relating to child care.

73. U.S. Department of Commerce, 1983f.

74. Ibid., p. 18.

75. U.S. House of Representatives, 1983, p. 5.

76. Staines and Pleck, 1983. Four non-standard work schedules were included in the study: non-standard days worked (weekend work); non-standard hours worked (shift work); non-standard number of weekly work hours; flexible daily work schedules, which respond in some way to worker preference. Three effects on the quality of family life were examined: interference between work and family life; levels of family satisfaction; time spent in child care and housework.

77. In another recent study of shift work (Presser and Cain, 1983) among dual earner couples with children, in which both spouses worked full time, it was found that more than one-third included a spouse who did not work a regular day shift. The most common pattern was an evening shift for the husband and a day shift for the wife. In 10 percent of these couples there was no spouse overlap in the hours of employment, which meant that children in these families spent their non-day hours with only one parent.

78. Lein, et al., 1974.

79. U.S. Department of Commerce, 1983f, p. 8.

80. Baruch, Barnett, and Rivers, 1984.

81. U.S. Department of Commerce, 1983d, p. 2.

5

Older Worker Interest in Part-Time Work: Preferences of Individuals

The early chapters provide an overview of the changing labor market and industrial scene that has sóme relevance for thinking about the potential of part-time work for older workers and for all women. They also describe the nature of existing, standard part-time provisions and indicate the variety of emerging New Concept forms that open up the possibility of a greater prevalence and a rising status for reduced-hour work schedules. What must now be considered is the degree of interest of older workers in part-time work and the personal and general factors that influence the choices that are made.

Preference for Part-Time Work

The appeal of part-time work is not limited by age or sex. It is useful for some workers in adult years because of its potential for reducing financial pressures when non-market obligations preclude the possibility of working full time. It is important for others who approach retirement in straightened economic circumstances with less than adequate retirement income, in poor health, or with financial need because of illness in the family. It also provides a gift of time for individuals nearing retirement whose incomes are adequate or financial needs are reduced because children have become financially independent and who now wish to pursue other activities while maintaining the stimulation and contribution associated with their paid work. The benefits offered by part-time work vary over an individual's life span and among differently situated individuals. Often seen as an interim phase for women during times of heavy family demands, part-time work can be a temporary activity for men, as well, who are going to school, or in or after the middle years when it serves non-job interests, career transitions, or training needs. In the years that are close to retirement, part-time work can ease the transition to permanent departure from the labor market for both women and men, sometimes reflecting individual preference, and sometimes enterprise interests in preserving skills, reducing labor costs attributable to senior employees, or in having some certainty about personnel commitments for purposes of long-range planning.[1]

For older workers, the decision process is initiated by weighing the advantages and disadvantages of work *or* retirement.[2] Once the decision to work has been made, the choice to work part time or full time depends on influencing factors that begin with circumstances of individual resources and needs (both economic and those related to health) (Chapter 5) and extend to the impact on that interest, both of general economic conditions of unemployment and inflation (Chapter 6) and of social policy (Chapter 7). The decision involves not only choice in the light of available full-time and part-time jobs and working conditions, but what that choice might be if New Concept part-time opportunities prevailed. The more accurately the inquiry specifies and reflects these factors, the more complete will be the understanding of the preference and potential of part-time work.

Opinion polls, often used to reflect the strength of individual preferences about work scheduling, are subject to a number of problems. Technical difficulties associated with survey analysis generally and with projections of choices for some years hence and for hypothetical work arrangements complicate the collection of accurate data.[3] An absence of clearly defined terms in the inquiry, such as "retirement" or "part time," as well as problems of controlling sample size and characteristics and response rates, affect the accuracy of the findings as a general statement. The phrasing of questions is not, or cannot always be, sufficiently precise to delineate all alternatives for a range of existing and possible individual circumstances and work conditions. In a transition period such as the present, when the meaning of the concept of part-time work is itself undergoing change, what is meant by part-time work (whether present or potential), may vary among individuals or across surveys. Retirement/work preferences change as aging proceeds through adulthood and color the responses made. These limitations of opinion polls help to explain why there exists some discrepancy between high levels of expressed preference for part-time work among older workers and the lower degree of participation in available programs. Despite the discrepancies, however, opinion surveys are useful as a first approximation of attitudes about part-time work and preferences for it under the specified circumstances of the inquiry.

Several surveys of recent years all lead to a similar conclusion that older workers in a wide range of occupations have a strong interest in working part time beyond their normal retirement age. A well-publicized Louis Harris survey, for example, of a national sample of persons taken between June 15 and July 31, 1981, reveals that 73 percent of elderly respondents (and about the same proportion of adults aged 18–54), would like to have the option of working part time when they retire. Among these groups with a part-time preference, 52 percent of workers aged 55–64, and 82 percent of elderly workers would choose to stay in the same job. The preference for part-time work after retirement is particularly strong among workers with incomes below $10,000 annually. It is slightly stronger for blacks than for whites and for men than for women.[4]

In answer to a similar question in that survey, 80 percent of older workers responded that greater availability of part-time work would be of "some help" or "a great deal of help" if they wanted to work after retirement. Again, there was a strong association of interest in part-time work with persons in low income, low status occupations, and persons with little or no pension or asset income. Among qualities leading to an interest in part-time work, economic need ranks high.[5]

Part-time work and job sharing were viewed with particular favor by respondents aged 55 and over: More than 70 percent thought that these work schedules would be helpful to them if they worked after retirement. By contrast, 44 percent of respondents thought more full-time jobs would be useful and 39 percent expressed a preference for a greater availability of a compressed four-day workweek. Among currently employed persons aged 55–64, 37 percent preferred a gradual phasing into retirement, with an accompanying decrease in pay, to full-time work until total retirement (49 percent). College educated older blacks and older women showed a stronger preference for phasing into retirement than their counterparts of non-college graduates, non-blacks, and older men.[6] Job interest seems to join the need for income as a reason for preferring to phase gradually into retirement.

The findings of other inquiries lend support to the view that interest in part-time work is not limited to low income groups. A survey of managers found that 60 percent preferred phased retirement to an abrupt move to total retirement "even if it means accepting a job with less authority and responsibility."[7] Travelers Insurance Company found that 15 percent of its surveyed employees aged 55–60 expected to work beyond age 65, a percentage that rose to 43 percent as employees neared that age. Eighty-five percent of respondents preferred part-time jobs.[8] The greater tendency for partial retirement among self-employed workers than wage and salary earners[9] may reflect the greater ability of self-employed workers to control the number of hours they work. That finding suggests that were it available, other wage and salary earners might welcome a more flexible and reduced-hour scheduling of work.[10]

Explanatory Factors in the Preference for Part-Time Work

ECONOMIC STATUS

The preference polls establish that part-time work for older workers is perceived, especially by those in disadvantaged economic status, as a desirable work option for later years. Because of this, and the fact that economic status differs between aged and non-aged groups, the economic position of older persons merits more detailed examination. According to some measures, the position of older workers has improved over time and the proportion of elderly persons in poverty has declined. Even so, income declines with age and the replacement ratio of retirement income to pre-retirement earnings can result in a considerable decrease from the pre-retirement standard of living.

One's perception of the economic status of the elderly is affected both by whether the measure of comparison is absolute or relative to that of the non-aged population, and whether it is based on money income or also includes non-cash benefits. This section looks at some of the issues in terms of their bearing on the value of New Concept part-time work as a source to supplement income in later life.[11]

Levels of Income of Older Population

Not only does money income decline with age, but there is considerable disparity in income levels among different household groups. In 1982, for example, median money income for households ($20,171 for all households) increased with the age of the householder (principal wage earner) until ages 45 to 54, when it was $27,985. It then declined to $22,075 among householders aged 55–64 and to $11,041 among householders aged 65 and over. A similar pattern, although at lower income levels, and less for women than for men, applied to unrelated individuals and non-family householders.[12]

The Harris Poll reported a similar decline of money income with age. Median household income, which was $22,400 in 1980 among the 18–54 years age group, fell to $6,000 for persons aged 80 and over. For persons aged 65 and over it was more than 50 percent higher for those who remained in paid work ($14,200) that it was for those who retired ($8,700). Elderly blacks and Hispanics over age 65 had incomes about half those of whites and were less likely to own their own homes.[13] Imputing a value for the return from owner-occupied housing and adding an income value for Medicare and Medicaid improves the income position of the elderly but does not cancel out the decline of income with age.[14]

Relative Income of the Elderly Population

Studies have also looked at the income of the elderly population in relation to that of the non-aged. Danziger, Van der Gaag, Smolensky, and Taussig, in a 1982 analysis of the economic status of households headed by persons aged 65 and over, estimated that in 1980 the mean money income ($12,226) was 63 percent of mean money income for all families and unrelated individuals ($19,500). Although money income of the elderly is still below that of the general population, it has improved in absolute terms between 1966 and 1981, and the proportion of elderly persons in poverty has declined more than that of all households.

Using 1973 data, which showed the relative money income of the elderly to be 48.6 percent that of the non-elderly, the researchers made additional adjustments to derive a more comparable relationship to that of the non-elderly. Adjusting the figure to take account of the contribution to family income from durable goods (older persons are more likely to own their own homes), federal personal income tax provisions (tax exemption of social security income, higher personal income tax exemptions for elderly, and a retirement tax credit), and especially household size and composition (households headed by persons aged 35–54 are twice as large on average as those headed by persons aged 65 and over), they estimated the relative economic status of elderly households to be raised to 85.3 percent that of the rest of society. Adjustments of weights taking into account the numbers and ages of household members further increased the relative position of the elderly to 90.0 percent that of the non-elderly.

No comparable estimates have been made covering the past ten years. Because of the indexing of social security benefits, however, effective in 1975, and the disproportionate receipt of a variety of non-cash benefits by the elderly (including Medicare, Medicaid, and food stamps), the researchers conclude that the current relative position of the elderly, at least until the social welfare cuts effective in 1982, has been on a par with that of the total population.[15] (See Table 5.1)

In an independent study, Hurd and Shoven examined the relative financial position of elderly persons in the 1970s, using as a measure the usual sources of money income plus an imputed value for owner-occupied housing, and an income value of medicare and medicaid — both more important for elderly than non-elderly households.[16] Based on these assumptions and data, although there was found to be an increase in the income of elderly relative to non-elderly households between 1970 and 1978 (52 percent to 58 percent), there was not an equivalence in income levels between the two groups.

Assets of the Elderly Population

Although often viewed as a principal source of income for the elderly, (see *New York Times,* October 9, 1984), in fact, asset ownership is only sometimes a major supplement to other income sources. Home ownership, for example, the most common asset form, was present in 1975 for about two-thirds of a national survey sample of the elderly population. Savings accounts, the second most common asset form, were held by almost three-fifths of the sample. On the other hand, fewer than one-fifth of the households owned bonds or stocks in 1975.[17]

Not only the ownership, but the value of assets is unevenly distributed in the elderly population and tends to be higher at higher income levels,[18] lending support where there is also other income. Even when present, for many the amount is not large. About 40 percent of non-married elderly women and men and 13 percent of elderly married couples had total assets of less than $3,000 in 1975.[19] For some, assets make possible the contemplation of partial retirement (and part-time work) earlier than would otherwise be possible, or permit total retirement when that is desired. For many individuals, however, asset income is not substantial enough to be considered an income source contributing to economic well-being. Nor are assets such as homes easily convertible to the purchase of needed consumer goods.

Replacement Rate of Retirement Income

Although the incidence of poverty (Chapter 2, note 21) among the elderly has decreased dramatically in recent years (35.2 percent of elderly in poverty

Table 5.1.   Relative Economic Status of the Elderly, 1973:   Adjustments to
             Money Income,

Income Concept/Weighting Concept for Recipient Units	Relative Economic Status of Elderly[a] (Percent)	Change in Relative Status Due to Adjustment (Percent of Total Change)
Household weights		
1. Reported money income	48.6	---
2. Adjusted for durables	52.2	8.7
3. Less direct taxes	56.2	9.7
4. Adjusted for household size and composition	85.3	70.3
Person weights		
5. Each person counted once instead of each household	88.0	6.5
6. Adjusted for classification of persons by their own age	90.0	4.8
7. Total	90.0	100.0

[a]Defined as the mean value of the income concept for the elderly divided
by the mean for the nonelderly.

Note: The adjustments are cumulative. For example, the number in line 4
is based on adjusting reported case income of households for durables,
afer subtracting taxes paid and dividing by the equivalence scales.

Source: Danziger, S., J. van der Gaag, E. Smolensky, and M. Taussig,
"Implications of the Relative Economic Status of the Elderly for Transfer
Policy," in Retirement and Economic Behavior, eds. Henry J. Aaron and Gary
Burtless, Washington, D.C.: Brookings Institution, 1984, p. 179.

in 1959; 14.1 percent in 1983) and since the mid-60s has declined more than
for other groups in society,[20] poverty among the elderly is not a problem that
has disappeared.[21] In 1982, there were 3.8 million aged poor. For this group,
part-time work does not represent a solution to the problem of disadvantaged
economic status, although it could play a supportive role when combined
with other social policies, such as skill training in assisting a person to function more effectively in the labor market. For persons not in poverty who are
nearing retirement, the benefits of reducing stress associated with full-time
work could more than compensate for the costs of foregone income. Others
entering retirement are finding that retirement income falls short of pre-
retirement income levels. For both of these groups, especially, part-time
work could provide a useful income supplement together with a workplace
attachment that is a valued source of social contact.

It has been estimated that because of reduced expenses and lower taxes,
retiring couples in 1981 required 52–86 percent of pre-retirement earnings
(depending on gross pre-retirement income) to maintain the pre-retirement

standard of living.[22] But replacement ratios of pensions to pre-retirement income often fall short of these proportions. In one study of hypothetical male and female workers with 30-year uninterrupted work histories and average earnings, median replacement rates for private pensions and social security, based on 1979 data, were estimated to be 55 percent for men and 72 percent for women.[23] Only 6 percent of the male workers were found to receive the replacement rate calculated as necessary to maintain living standards. Including a spousal social security benefit raised the proportion of male workers maintaining living standards to 59 percent.

Analysis of data from a national sample of retired men indicated that the replacement rate of public and private pensions to pre-retirement earnings in terms of 1980 dollars averaged 47 percent, but with much variation around the average.[24] Only for individuals with annual earnings of $10,000 or less was the replacement rate adequate to maintain the pre-retirement standard of living. What these two differently derived estimates of replacement rates say is that public and private pensions do not generally provide sufficient income to maintain pre-retirement living standards. In fact, even with the additional income and pensions of wives and other family members added to retiree earnings, median total family income in the 1980 study, in real terms, was only about one-half of what it had been in the last full pre-retirement year.[25] New Concept part-time work could provide a desired option for many of these persons for maintaining or improving living standards in later life at the same time that it permits the enjoyment of some relaxation in non-market activities.

Economic Status and Part-Time Work

Short of an actual experience with New Concept part-time work arrangements as an integral part of the work history, and in an environment that respects the work motivation and commitment of part-time workers, there is no sure way to predict the preference of older workers for such a schedule. If available, some persons might choose to convert to part-time work prior to the age when they normally retire, while others might postpone retirement and continue to work part-time into their 70s. But there are several indications that in either mode it would be a popular work arrangement and, for some, a link to an improved standard of living in later life. At the same time, valuable resources that older workers offer would not be lost through full retirement, at early or normal retirement ages. The drain on social welfare programs would also be reduced by the voluntary choice to stay connected to the labor market. One authority in the field maintains that preservation of a pre-retirement standard of living and financial solvency of national pension plans will make an extension of part-time work essential.[26]

Labor force participation rates have already shown that part-time work, even with its present disadvantaged characteristics, rises sharply for both women and men after age 65. Research studies document that for men, partial retirement — that is, retirement from one's customary job and re-employment in a lower status occupation at lower pay — is quite common. Opinion polls relating to part-time work generally indicate a strong expressed preference for having such an option, especially by those at the lower end of the income scale, but also by older workers who are college graduates, presumably interested in retaining an involvement with paid work, although not at a full-time level. Supportive of the findings that older worker economic status could use an additional boost are comparisons of absolute and relative income levels between the aged and non-aged, indicating that although the proportion of aged in poverty is less than existed a few years ago, income both declines with age and is considerably reduced following retirement. For most workers, the replacement ratio of retirement income to pre-retirement earnings could be significantly improved by an expansion of New Concept part-time work opportunities in a broad range of occupations. Given this supportive evidence, it is highly likely that an expansion of New Concept part-time work would be much welcomed by older workers and would both benefit individuals and lessen the burden of social programs.

Opinion polls do not provide a laundry list of criteria for identifying the circumstances under which part-time work is desirable, nor precisely forecast which households will benefit from expanded part-time opportunities. Expressed older worker preference, however, reflects the same signals given by other experience that part-time work with pay rates equivalent to that of full-time work, and with career and fringe benefit qualities, would add in important ways to the array of flexible work arrangements being developed for the workplace environment.

Health Status

Health status joins economic status as a reason why the availability of New Concept part-time work can be important for older workers. In its absence, these two factors often interact in the decision of whether to continue in full-time work or to retire completely in the presence of a health impairment.[27]

Health status and labor force participation. Studies show that a large majority of persons under age 70 live without disabling limitations.[28] And in terms of increasing longevity of men and women, it can be said that a gradual improvement in health is taking place. But some difference of opinion exists as to what this means for the extension of the ability to work longer in later years. Some researchers predict that the period of diminished vigor that accompanies chronic disease will, in the future, occupy a smaller proportion of the life span.[29] But others question this prediction, noting an increase between 1970 and 1980 in the proportion of men aged 50–69 unable to work because of illness.[30]

On a more positive note, although persons aged 65 and over suffer twice as many days of restricted activity as do the general population (40 days versus 19 in 1981), lost *work* days (an average of 4 to 5 a year) are not much different for younger or older workers.[31] In general, age affects productivity insignificantly prior to age 60 (see Chapter 9). In all occupations, there is a wide variation within an age group in individual performance and an overlap in productivity performance among age groups. For many jobs, individual skills and talents exceed the requirements of the job so that even with some diminution in capacity, performance is not affected.[32]

In sum, Americans are longer lived than they used to be. Although health status varies by age, by income, and by race as well,[33] chronological age itself is not the critical determinant of employability or productivity. It is health status in relation to performance of a particular job that is important. The potential of many working persons is greater than the requirements of their jobs, and individual differences within age groups may be greater than productivity differences between younger and older workers. In assessing productivity that influences production schedules and personnel policies, age is not the automatically efficient screening device that some have perceived it to be.

Health status and early retirement. Early retirement, a major transition of life which, once embarked on, is rarely reversed,[34] is influenced not only by the general availability of jobs, but by other factors as well. The age of eligibility for retirement benefits is one, since it colors attitudes about what is a "normal" age for reducing commitments and involvements and tensions of paid work. Early retirement before age 65 began to grow rapidly in the private sector in the 1950s,[35] and was incorporated into social security legislation for women in 1956 and for men in 1961. Research indicates that a second factor is the level of retirement income,[36] affected both by benefit rates and by the cost of living adjustment factor. The availability of supplemental security income has also made possible early retirement for low income elderly by helping them adjust to the actuarial lowering of benefits that takes place when retirement occurs before the normal retirement age of 65.

But within this framework set by age of eligibility and retirement income, health factors are viewed by many researchers as being critically important in making the decision to retire before the normal retirement age of 65.[37] Research studies conducted between the 1960s and 1980s confirm this fact, particularly for workers who retired prior to age 62.[38]

A study of a national sample of men aged 45–59 found that those with health impairments in 1966 were twice as likely to have retired between 1966 and 1971 (or to have died) as those who were free of health limitations.[39] In another analysis of 1966–1976 data based on a national survey that examined the health and retirement decisions of white and black male retirees aged 55–69, it was found that poor health was the cause for early retirement before age 62 for 60 percent of the whites and 67 percent of the blacks.[40] These findings bear out the results of studies of the late 1960s that not only found that poor health was the primary reason for retiring early, but that health as a reason for retirement declined with age.[41] Based on the conclusions of these and similar studies, the House Select Committee on Aging reported that more than 70 percent of men who retired before age 62 did so involuntarily, largely because of poor health.[42]

Those who retire before age 62 tend to be composed of two groups — high income individuals who can afford to retire because of sufficient income and assets and those with low income who have to retire, even though retirement results in economic hardship. There are few in the middle income ranges.[43]

Men who retire because of ill health are more likely to be in low status jobs, to be covered only by social security, and to have lower retirement income than other retirees.[44]

Although health continues to be an important factor in early retirement between ages 62 and 65, economic factors increase in importance as age progresses, and health impairment factors become less important as a retirement cause.[45] One study reported poor health as a reason for retirement in more than 50 percent of retirees aged 62–64; the proportion was less than 25 percent for those retiring at age 65. The percentage also varies depending on whether the health limitation is defined as one of "work limitation" or as "an inability to perform work."[46]

A British study corroborates the American research experience that poor health, more than a voluntary desire for increased leisure, is a cause of early retirement decisions.[47] Studies in both countries support the conclusion that, although the size of the effect may vary depending on the definition of "health" and the adequacy of retirement benefits, health status is clearly and strongly associated with early retirement decisions prior to the normal retirement age.

Health and an expanded concept of part-time work. Health, then, can be a major factor in the decision to retire early, and is an especially important retirement cause for those who retire before age 62. It is a more important reason for early retirement than pursuit of leisure time activities, and it occurs even though the benefits of early retirement recipients, often low income workers, are actuarially reduced as a result. Although it is difficult to measure the precise size of the effect that health has on early retirement without first defining the degree of health limitation, in general the predisposition of employees with some health impairment to retire early stems, not only from an inability to do the job, but also from a decreasing energy level or increasing disaffection with the work of the job. The employee preference is, in many instances, supported by employment policies, which reflect the fact that health status can affect productivity through its effect on absenteeism or efficiency on the job.

But what if New Concept part-time work, more comparable in occupational range and earnings and career potential to that of full-time work, became available? Would there then be an earlier switch to part-time work in response to health needs? Would there be a greater interest in postponing retirement and extending part-time labor market attachment? Or would both effects prevail with greater labor supply? One can only speculate on the answer. It would depend partly on the degree to which health impairment interferes with performance of particular jobs.[48] But it would also depend on interest in part-time work. And here, results of opinion polls indicate that such a preference exists. There is some support, too, for this view in a survey of more than 1,000 male early retirees with long-term service in a number of companies, largely in managerial capacities. Most of the sample earned between $20,000 and $50,000 annually in 1978 dollars prior to retirement. Of the group, 58 percent stated that health factors and the stresses and physical demands of their jobs were important reasons for retirement. In spite of this, about one-fourth re-entered the workforce after retirement as consultants or in self-employed capacities.[49]

One study does not establish a principle, but it does suggest a hypothesis warranting further investigation. Diminished health status does not always make full retirement necessary. Once an interest in part-time work is established, other evidence suggests that its expansion is both possible and desirable (see Chapters 6, 7, and 9). Improved health as a result of a less stressful work program,[50] as well as social benefits to society in the form of reduced retirement, disability pension, or supplemental security income costs, are arguments in support of further experimentation with New Concept part-time work. Encouraging later full retirement by providing later part-time jobs could affect employees, employers, and society as a whole all of whom might benefit from such a policy.

Notes

1. Some phased early retirement programs now developing in academia illustrate this interest in clarifying what the financial commitments are as organizations plan for the future. One college program, for example, permits early retirement with favorable annuity benefits during a five-year period, beginning between ages 62 and 65, or for four years, beginning at age 66, and so on. Faculty can choose an option of total early retirement or partial retirement with half-time teaching. Regular retirement can begin at age 65, but no later than at age 70. Early retirement, once elected, cannot be reversed.

2. Excellent overview discussions of the economics of aging and of policy issues relating to work *or* retirement, are found in Clark, Kreps, and Spengler, 1978; Clark and Spengler, 1980; Clark, 1980, and Schulz, 1985.

3. For a discussion of 26 opinion polls conducted since 1978 and of some of the problems of survey analysis, see Robinson and Sanford, 1983.

4. National Council on the Aging, 1981, pp. xiv, 96–97.

5. Louis Harris survey in Sheppard and Mantovani, 1982, pp. 1–19.

6. National Council on the Aging, 1981, pp. 94–95, 100.

7. American Management Associations, 1982, in Jondrow, Brechling, and Marcus, 1983, p. 2.

8. Work in America Institute, 1981, p. 99.

9. According to Quinn, 1975.

10. Andrisani and Daymont, 1982, p. 43.

11. "Economic status" is defined in several different ways in this section, depending on the definition used in the study cited. Both absolute and relative measures of economic status vary depending on the economic unit used — households, families, or individuals — and the categories of income included — cash, value of owner-occupied housing, and non-cash benefits. For a thorough review and evaluation of research literature on incomes of aged and non-aged, see Grad, 1984.

12. U.S. Department of Commerce, 1983c, pp. 12, 19. A household is defined as all persons occupying a housing unit, both family members and unrelated persons. Unrelated individuals and non-family householders live alone or with non-relatives. In the Census definition, money income includes wages and salaries, income from self-employment, and other earnings; no adjustment is made for non-cash benefits received.

13. National Council on the Aging, 1981, pp. 73–74.

14. Hurd and Shoven, 1982.

15. Danziger, van der Gaag, Smolensky, and Taussig, 1982, 1983, pp. 1–3; Danziger, et al., 1984, pp. 175–96. The study did not attempt to adjust for recent budgetary cuts in social welfare expenditures which began to have strong impact beginning in 1983. The Institute for Research on Poverty estimates that budget cuts accounted for 3 million of the 8 million persons added to the poverty rolls between 1979 and 1982.

16. Hurd and Shoven, 1982. The relative importance of income sources for the aged have changed between 1962 and 1982. The proportion of aged units (married couples and non-married persons aged 65 or older) receiving social security, increased from 73 percent to 90 percent. The percent receiving government pensions rose from 5 percent to 12 percent and aged units receiving private pensions grew from 9 percent to 23 percent. At the same time, the percent of aged units with earnings fell from 36 percent to 22 percent between 1962 and 1982 (Grad, 1984, p. 10).

17. Hurd and Shoven, 1982, p. 18.

18. Sherman, 1976a, pp. 79-80.

19. Schulz, 1985, p. 31.

20. University of Wisconsin, 1983, p. 2.

21. Schulz, 1985, pp. 35-37.

22. Munnell, 1982, p. 24. See also Schulz (1985, p. 74), where the replacement proportion for a middle income worker to maintain a pre-retirement standard of living is estimated to be 65-70 percent of gross income.

23. Schulz, 1983, pp. 247-49.

24. Parnes and Less, 1983, p. 63.

25. Ibid., p. 72.

26. Ginzberg, 1983.

27. Quinn, 1980.

28. Branch, in National Commission on Social Security, 1981, p. 126.

29. Fries, in ibid., p. 126.

30. Schulz, 1983, pp. 244-45.

31. U.S. Department of Health and Human Services, 1982a.

32. Birren in Donahue, 1955; Clark, Kreps, and Spengler, 1978, pp. 927-29, 946; Chapter 7.

33. In a public health survey, 40 percent of persons with incomes over $25,000 described their health as excellent in relation to others of similar age, compared with fewer than 25 percent of those with incomes of less than $7,000. A survey of Massachusetts elderly persons found that poor older Americans can expect fewer remaining years of physical independence than comparable more affluent peers. The health status of elderly blacks is poorer than elderly whites (Taeuber, 1983, pp. 15, 16).

34. Bowen and Finegan, 1969, p. 270.

35. Gordus, 1980, p. 20.

36. Barfield and Morgan, 1969; Tolley and Burkhauser, 1977.

37. Clark, Kreps, and Spengler, 1978, pp. 935-36; Diamond and Hausman, 1984.

38. Some recent studies question the relative importance of health in the decision to retire. See, for example, Fields and Mitchell, forthcoming; Bazzoli, 1983.

39. Parnes, et al., 1975.

40. Parnes and Nestel, 1981, pp. 155-97.

41. Bixby, 1976; Schwab, 1976; Sherman, 1976b, pp. 57-68.

42. U.S. House of Representatives, 1981.

43. Kingson, 1979.

44. Parnes and Nestel, 1981; Sproat, 1983, pp. 40-41.

45. Rones, 1980, p. 15; Bixby, 1976; Schwab, 1976; Sherman, 1976b.

46. Reno, 1971, p. 43.

47. Altmann, 1982, pp. 355-64.

48. Andrisani, 1977.

49. Ginzberg, 1982, pp. 77-91.

50. Eisdorfer and Cohen, 1983.

6

General Economic Conditions and Part-Time Work for Older Workers: Inflation and Unemployment

The previous chapter looked at factors of economic status and health that influence individual preference for part-time and reduced hours of work. Discussion of influencing factors continues in this chapter by looking at the impact of general economic conditions on the potential interest in part-time work. The chapter examines the effects of inflation and unemployment on older workers and how each might have a bearing on their interest in part-time work.

Inflation

INFLATION AND UNCERTAINTY

Inflation—that is, "a substantial, sustained increase in the general level of prices,"[1] has an unsettling effect on members of society by introducing uncertainty about future economic security. According to a national 1981 survey, older persons, as did all Americans, saw "inflation, high cost of living, high prices" as one of the greatest problems facing the elderly today.[2] The evidence of high inflation was especially strong in the late 1970s and early 1980s, when prices overall were rising between 10 and 20 percent a year. At that time, older persons approaching retirement, even when they had planned for the transition, had assumed an inflation rate of no more than 5 percent.[3] The rate of price rise lessened considerably during 1983 (3.8 percent) and 1984 (3.7 percent), but may, of course, increase again. How does inflation affect the well-being of older workers and their attitudes about part-time work?

INFLATION AND ECONOMIC STATUS OF OLDER WORKERS

No one disputes the financial uncertainty that accompanies inflation, but there is less agreement among researchers about the actual effect of inflation on older worker economic status, a status that is influenced by the impact of price increases on both expenditures and real income. For some years, the general assumption was that inflation seriously reduced the standard of living of older persons because they tended to live on fixed retirement incomes. More recently, a reverse position has been expressed — that since social security and Medicare benefits are adjusted to take account of current price changes, older persons are not seriously hurt by inflation.

The Consumer Price Index (CPI), a composite index of prices developed by the government, provides an important measure of the rate of inflation. It is calculated from data on prices of food, housing (including, since January 1983, shelter services consumed by home owners), clothing, transportation, medical care, and other goods and services, weighted according to expenditures for a fixed market basket of goods reflecting actual consumption patterns of urban consumers in 1972-1973. The index is widely used to adjust payments, including wages and social welfare benefits, so as to retain their value in relation to that of a stated past period.[4]

Items affected by inflation differ in different inflationary times, and relative prices change at different rates within a given inflationary period. For this reason, and because expenditure patterns of older persons are known to differ from those of the younger population, there has been some question as to whether the CPI adequately reflects the rates of price changes in goods and services appropriate to the expenditure patterns and standard of living of older persons.[5] Researchers who have compared the CPI with an index using expenditure weights of the elderly have virtually all found that, if the time span is reasonably long, the two price indices have risen the same amount.[6] Hurd and Shoven show, for example, that between 1967 and 1980, despite significant changes in relative prices and differences in expenditure patterns by age groups, the overall price rise for persons under age 60 and for persons aged 60-64, 65-69, 70-74, 75 and over has been about the same. They conclude that use of the CPI is an appropriate gauge of the inflation rate as it affects older Americans. Construction by the Bureau of Labor Statistics of an experimental consumer price index affecting persons under and over age 65 between 1979 and 1981 showed almost identical changes.[7]

Evaluating the effect of inflation on incomes of the elderly is somewhat more complicated, since the elderly are not a homogeneous group and their incomes come from several sources, each of which may be affected differently by price changes.[8] Overall, in 1977, earnings comprised 28 percent of the income of aged families, with a household head age 65 and over.[9] Earnings income adjusts to inflation in different degrees, depending on such factors as the particular occupation or industry from which the earnings come, the existence of a collective bargaining contract, and the firm size. About 37 percent of elderly family income came from social security benefits and another 17 percent from other transfer income. Some transfer income adjusts for price changes (social security, supplemental security income, and food stamps, for example), and some typically does not (veterans pensions, private pensions, and state payments under supplemental security income). Last, 18 percent of aged family income was derived from property. Again, some property income adjusts for inflation; income from intangible financial assets, largely associated with higher income elderly, tends to fall as prices rise.

Under social security, there is a two-step adjustment to inflation. Since 1979, lifetime earnings, on which computation of benefits are based, are adjusted upward by a wage index (after dropping the five years of lowest earnings) to reflect national changes in wage levels up to the time the worker reaches age 60. In retirement, benefits are further increased each year to take account of CPI rises occurring the previous year.[10] The lifetime earnings adjustment incorporates the effect of productivity gains, but there is no adjustment for that effect after retirement. All social security recipients gain from removal of the effects of inflationary price changes in computing benefits; particularly helped are the one-half of aged married couples and over 70 percent of aged unmarried individuals who receive more than 50 percent of their income from social security.

Protection against inflation in private pension plans is less complete and, because of constraints affecting their financing, more difficult to guarantee.[11] Defined benefit plans, a common form of private pensions, pay a specific benefit related to years of service and earnings history. Within this structure, increasingly popular are final-pay plans, which base pensions on an employee's compensation in the few years prior to retirement (commonly five). In this way the benefit reflects much of the price rise and productivity growth that has occurred during the person's career, particularly if there has been stability of employment with an employer and the inflation rate has not been high. Post-retirement adjustments of private pensions are neither widespread nor large in amount. Private pension benefits, a more significant source of income for men than for women, and for middle and upper income than for low income groups, have been severely disadvantaged by inflation. Between 1978–1981, when consumer prices rose 51 percent, retirees with fixed private pensions experienced a one-third decline in the buying power of these annuities.[12]

In view of the differing effect of inflation on the sources of elderly income, it is interesting that 65.8 percent of workers aged 45–64 and 84.8 percent of retired workers responded to a 1979 survey inquiry about the effect of inflation on their retirement by reporting "no effect." Of those not yet retired, only 13.6 percent expected to postpone retirement because of inflation.[13] Despite the expressed fears and the possible realities of an adverse inflationary effect for many older workers, the reported impact of inflation on attitudes and behavior has been small.

INFLATION AND PART-TIME WORK

Because of this seeming lack of responsiveness of behavior to experience, as well as because of the complexity of predicting the inflation impact for individuals whose income is derived in varying proportions from different sources, it is particularly difficult to predict the likely effect of inflation on preference for part-time work. Part-time work could become less sought after in the future if the fear of real income erosion leads workers to postpone retirement and continue to work full time. On the other hand, a continuing inflationary price rise could lead to an increased interest in part-time work among those who would otherwise retire fully, as they seek to buttress their eroding retirement income with current earnings. What is clear, however, is that inflation does have an important bearing on income adequacy through its effect on both the cost of living and the real value of income, and because of this it could influence significantly choices about engaging in part-time work. If workers respond to the realities of the situation, it would appear that the stronger the inflation rate, the greater the tendency to continue in full-time work and to postpone even partial retirement. That this did not seem to happen in the recent strong inflation suggests either that the adjusted social security benefits were adequate to compensate for the inflationary price rise, or that the level of dissatisfaction with the job or the work environment out-weighed the inflationary pull to continue in paid work. Were more New Concept part-time opportunities available within the customary place of employment, the reported response to inflation might have been quite different.

Unemployment

UNEMPLOYMENT EXPERIENCE OF OLDER WORKERS

A number of employment issues affect an older workforce and could lead to policy initiatives. The characteristics claimed to be associated with an aging workforce — job obsolescence, lack of training, restricted mobility, or a decrease in productivity on the job — could raise questions about labor policies. Similarly, changes in consumer demand, competition, enterprise organizational decisions, or government spending cutbacks could result in policies of production retrenchment or plant shutdown that have implications for older worker employment, unrelated to workers' effectiveness on the job. The dynamics of change or of the economy could thus trigger a job change or job redesign within the plant or a temporary layoff or permanent severance from the customary place of employment. It is on these latter outcomes, which are experienced as unemployment, rather than on their causes that this section focuses. It begins with a description of some characteristics of unemployed older workers, then reviews some of the possible costs or consequences of unemployment for them, and finally considers the contribution that an enriched concept of part-time employment might make to lessening adverse consequences of their unemployment or labor market disengagement.

Incidence of Unemployment

Involuntary separations (layoffs, plant closings) are the most important cause of unemployment for older and elderly men. Until the late 1960s, their unemployment rate (that is, the number of unemployed as a percent of the civilian labor force) was slightly higher than that for men in prime working ages, 25–54. It then began to change, and by 1980 and 1981 unemployment rates for the older age groups were lower than those of other adult workers. In 1981, unemployment was 5.5 percent for men aged 25–54, 3.6 percent for men aged 55–64, and 2.9 percent for men aged 65 and over. Part of the reason for these recent lower unemployment rates at later ages has been the location of the employment of older workers in less cyclically sensitive industries and the fact that seniority provisions in collective bargaining contracts provide some protection against being laid off. But the figures also mask a "discouraged worker" effect, particularly prominent for workers aged 55 and over, who retire before the normal retirement age of 65 because they believe that no jobs are available for which they could qualify.[14] Social security retirement income is often what makes leaving the labor force possible for these discouraged workers.[15] Although unemployment statistics relate to those who are available for and seek paid work, the fact is that the "real" unemployment rate, including discouraged workers, is higher than that expressed for both older men and women workers (see Table 6.1).

For older and elderly women, the unemployment rate has been consistently below that of working women in prime adult years, in the 1960s as well as more recently. Full-time working older women are less likely than older men to work in cyclically sensitive industries. For many of them, working full or part time where a career orientation is not strong, the threat of unemployment leads to a "discouraged worker" effect or reinforces an already present tendency to retire before age 65, at the time of retirement of their somewhat older husband. Unemployment rates in 1981 were 6.3 percent for women aged 25–54, 3.8 percent for women aged 55–64, and 3.6 percent for those aged 65 and over.

Unemployment rates for older working women are not only lower than for prime age working women, but also slightly lower than for working men of comparable ages. In 1982, for example, the unemployment rate for women aged 55–64 was 5.2 percent, compared with 5.5 percent for men. For elderly women, the unemployment rate was 3.2 percent, compared with 3.7 percent for men. A major reason is that, more frequently than for older men, labor force withdrawal as a discouraged worker is the way older women respond to a layoff. In 1982, more than three-fifths of all discouraged workers were women.[16]

Duration of Unemployment

Once unemployed, the duration of unemployment is greater for older than younger workers. It rises with age until age 65 and then falls slightly. Older workers aged 55–64 were unemployed for an average of 19.7 weeks in 1982, compared with 15.5 weeks for all workers.[17]

These findings on incidence and duration of unemployment find support in an analysis of unemployment experience during the mid-1960s to mid-1970s of four groups of men and women in a national survey,[18] including a group of older men aged 55–69 and of mid-life women aged 40–54 at the end

Table 6.1. Official Unemployment Rate and Unemployment Rate Including Discouraged Workers, by Sex, Selected Ages, 1968 to 1981, Annual Averages (percent)

Year	Men						Women					
	Age 25 to 54		Age 55 to 64		Age 65 and over		Age 25 to 54		Age 55 to 54		Age 65 and over	
	U^a	$U+D^b$	U	U+D	U	U+D	U	U+D	U	U+D	U	U+D
Total^c	3.7	3.9	3.0	3.5	3.6	6.7	5.5	6.6	3.4	4.9	3.6	8.2
1968	1.7	1.8	1.9	2.3	2.8	6.6	3.4	4.5	2.2	4.2	2.7	8.6
1969	1.6	1.7	1.8	2.1	2.2	5.1	3.5	4.4	2.2	3.5	2.3	7.4
1970	2.8	2.9	2.8	3.1	3.3	5.5	4.5	5.5	2.7	4.1	3.1	7.3
1971	3.5	3.7	3.3	3.7	3.4	5.8	5.3	6.7	3.3	4.7	3.6	7.9
1972	3.1	3.2	3.2	3.6	3.6	6.2	4.9	6.2	3.3	4.8	3.5	7.8
1973	2.5	2.7	2.4	2.8	3.0	6.0	4.4	5.5	2.8	4.0	2.9	5.6
1974	3.1	3.2	2.6	2.9	3.3	6.0	4.9	5.9	3.2	4.6	3.6	7.6
1975	5.7	5.9	4.3	4.9	5.4	9.0	7.5	9.1	5.1	6.9	5.0	9.4
1976	4.9	5.2	4.2	4.7	5.1	8.9	6.8	8.1	4.9	6.4	5.0	9.9
1977	4.3	4.5	3.6	4.1	5.2	9.1	6.4	7.8	4.4	6.1	4.7	10.8
1978	3.5	3.7	2.8	3.3	4.2	7.2	5.5	6.5	3.2	4.6	3.8	9.3
1979	3.4	3.6	2.7	3.3	3.4	6.1	5.2	6.1	3.2	4.3	3.3	7.4
1980	5.1	5.4	3.4	3.9	3.1	6.5	6.0	7.0	3.3	4.6	3.1	7.4
1981	5.5	5.8	3.6	4.2	2.9	6.3	6.3	7.5	3.8	5.6	3.6	8.0

^{a}U = official unemployment rate: total unemployment divided by civilian labor force.

^{b}U+D = unemployment rate that counts all discouraged as unemployed: unemployed plus discouraged workers divided by civilian labor force plus discouraged workers.

^{c}Totals are weighted averages of the 14 years 1968 through 1981: sum of numerators for all years divided by sum of the denominators.

Source: Rones, Philip, "The Labor Market Problems of Older Workers," *Monthly Labor Review* 106, no. 5 (May 1983): 4.

of the period. The incidence of unemployment varied, being highest for the group of young women and lowest for the group of older men. But the average cumulative duration was highest among older men (31 weeks versus 20–24 weeks for the other three groups). In addition, the data showed that unemployment, unequally distributed within each age group, was most unequally distributed among the older men, where the 5 percent of individuals with the most unemployment accounted for more than one-half of all unemployment compared with 29–45 percent for each of the other three groups.

CONSEQUENCES AND COSTS OF UNEMPLOYMENT

Many of the consequences of unemployment are similar for all unemployed. But labor force withdrawal through early retirement, significantly influenced by unemployment,[19] is a way of dealing with unemployment that is unique to older workers. Rather than experience the tensions, subtle age bias, and prolonged unemployment duration so often associated with unemployment in later years, workers who become unemployed near to retirement age frequently elect to retire early on reduced social security benefits. These benefits, which are available to them after age 62, are sometimes supplemented by other retirement income for which they become eligible before the normal retirement age of 65. The recent growth of early retirement schemes in Europe, as well as in the United States, is partially a response to this circumstance and to additional inducements to early retirement, offered by employers, to create more openings for younger workers.[20] Whatever the reason for early retirement (voluntary choice, health, or unemployment), it tends to be a permanent decision. Few older workers who become unemployed and leave the labor force because of unemployment return at some later time.[21]

Monetary Costs of Unemployment

Production and income loss. Economists feel most comfortable when dealing with measurable monetary values, but even among them there is agreement that the costs of unemployment have both a monetary and a nonmonetary component.

Society collectively suffers because of unemployment. There is both a waste of unemployed human resources and a loss in the value of unproduced goods and services that could have contributed to the nation's standard of living. Added to this are the financial costs of public assistance, food stamps, and other transfer payments designed to maintain the unemployed worker and dependents.

Individuals also suffer. Those who enter retirement because of discouragement about employment opportunities forego income and perhaps have a lower retirement income as well, because of benefit adjustment to the earlier retirement date. Older workers who remain in the labor market experience a wage loss throughout the duration of unemployment. Moreover, permanently displaced older workers who remain in the labor market experience a less stable future employment pattern than do workers with similar demographic characteristics whose unemployment is temporary. For the older, displaced worker group, re-employment is frequently at a lower occupational status and earnings level.

A study of men aged 45 and over, covering the period 1966–1973, gives research support to these observations.[22] Parnes and King analyzed the work experience of a 5 percent subsample of a national sample of older men, a group who had worked for the same employer for at least five years and then experienced involuntary separation during the survey period. Twenty percent of this group remained unemployed for at least 6 months before finding another job, and even in 1973, two years after the separation, 6 percent were still unemployed. This compared with a 1 percent unemployment rate for a control group who had similar demographic characteristics but who did not have a permanent job loss. Almost three-fifths of the re-employed, displaced workers had a decline in occupational status, and presumably in earnings, compared with only one-fifth of the control group. The adverse experience, applied to all occupational and educational levels.

A June 1983 study by Shapiro and Sandell of a national sample of men aged 45–59 at the beginning of the study, who were permanently displaced from their jobs, covered the period 1966–1978. The researchers found a decrease of 3.0 percent in real average hourly earnings in the new jobs for men aged 45–49 and a nearly 6 percent decline for displaced men over age 60, which they attributed to difficulty in transferring the skills and knowledge that these workers had accumulated with seniority in the past and that they could not apply to the new job. Although nearly one-third of older displaced workers had held their pre-displacement jobs for more than 10 years, almost twice as many of this displaced older worker group, compared with the entire national sample of mature men, had had a short job tenure of 5 years or less. In their re-employment, displaced workers exhibited both upward and downward occupational mobility, although downward movement appeared to predominate. In terms of wages, about 50 percent of displaced men remained in the same wage category, 28 percent entered a lower wage category, and for 21 percent the wage status rose. Wage losses were more severe in the serious recession of the 1970s than in the slight downturn of the late 1960s. On balance, there appeared to be some suggestive evidence of wage discrimination for workers aged 65 and over.

Replacement income. Workers experiencing loss of a job are not without access to some replacement income. Unemployment insurance, state programs administered jointly by the federal government and the states, provides cash benefits based on previous earnings, customarily payable for a maximum of 26 weeks to temporarily or permanently laid off insured workers and to certain unemployed workers who quit their jobs for just cause.[23] In addition, supplemental and extended benefits may be paid for another three to four months for those who exhaust their regular benefits.[24]

This is not the place to evaluate unemployment insurance as a program of income protection and countercyclical stimulus, but two points are germane to the purposes of this discussion. First, unemployment benefits are currently paid to a much smaller proportion of the unemployed than has been true in earlier years. Only 45 percent of the unemployed received regular, extended, or supplementary unemployment benefits in 1982, compared with 78 percent in 1975. Relative to the number of newly unemployed workers, in recent years (1980–1982), there have been 16–18 percent fewer initial unemployment insurance claimants than previously.[25] The reasons for the low proportion of unemployed who receive benefits are not entirely clear. One economist suggests that they may be related to recent Congressional retrenchment in the federal supplemental benefits program, enacted in 1981,[26] as well as to the combined effect of several measures enacted since 1978. These have resulted in a downward adjustment of unemployment benefits for received pension payments, taxation of unemployment compensation for higher income families, and a decrease in the number of employment offices servicing benefits (making it more difficult to file applications for unemployment insurance).[27] Another economist "guesses" that the *perception* of tightened eligibility rules is a causal factor in the decline in the number of unemployment insurance claimants.[28]

Second, unemployment benefits, although technically allowable for partial unemployment, often contain large potential disincentives. In many states, benefits payable for part weeks of unemployment are computed by subtracting wages earned from the weekly benefit amount. With a benefit amount of one-third of the weekly wage, earnings of partial unemployment quickly exceed potential benefits.[29]

An alternative approach to compensating partial involuntary unemployment represented by the short-time compensation laws now in existence in seven states (Chapter 7), provide unemployment benefits that are proportional to the percent of unemployment during the week. Thus, although income replacement for earnings loss due to unemployment is provided for by federal and state legislation, and indeed is paid to many workers, it not only leaves many others unprotected, but the proportion of unemployed who receive no benefits is growing. Older workers who become unemployed share in this experience.

Non-monetary Consequences of Unemployment

The effects of being unemployed go beyond the economic loss of human resource skills, goods and services, financial costs experienced by society generally, and the income loss of the individual or family. They reach into areas of the quality of life and mental health of the individual on the one hand, and personal relationships and tranquillity of family existence on the other. These are, of course, not issues that affect only one age group.

Brenner, in an analysis of data of a national population sample in the early 1970s, looked at the social stress created by unemployment in relation to several indicators of social pathology.[30] The relationships were not always simply and directly related, nor operating with equal strength for different groups, but Brenner found that in general a sustained 1 percent increase in unemployment resulted with some time lag in a 2 percent increase in the nation's mortality rate, a 4 percent increase in suicide, a 2 percent increase in cardiovascular deaths, a 5 to 6 percent increase in homicides, a 4 percent increase in state imprisonment, and a 3 to 4 percent increase in first admissions to mental hospitals. There has been criticism of methodological aspects of the research and some question about whether the relationships can be so precisely quantified, but there is general agreement with the conclusion that there is a connection between unemployment and these social pathologies.[31] In more recent studies, the findings have been reconfirmed and extended.[32] Declines in labor force participation rates and a rise in business failures, as well as rising unemployment rates, have been found to be associated with an increase in mortality rates. An increase in unemployment affects not only self-esteem and resistance to disease for the unemployed, but impinges as well on their families and on those still employed in the disrupted workplace.

Liem and Rayman have taken a more qualitative approach in their study of the effect of the stress of unemployment on individuals and on family life in several New England areas.[33] They found that unemployment brought both to unemployed men and to their wives more depression, anxiety, and hostility. The considerable stress of unemployment resulted in increased disorganization of family life, with greater prevalence of marriage break-ups and more parent-child conflict and child abuse. They concluded that unemployment has serious long-term human and social welfare as well as economic consequences for individual and family well-being.

Jahoda (1933/1971), who with Lazersfeld and Zeisel was responsible for the classic study of the social-psychological impact of unemployment on members of an Austrian village in 1930, has recently considered the psychological response to unemployment in the 1980s. Although she finds that empirical research does not yet document systematically all of the effects of an absence of a job connection, she suggests that if one looks at employment as an institution, it is possible to see several kinds of benefits provided by paid work:

> the imposition of a time structure, the enlargement of the scope of social experience into areas less emotionally charged than family life, participation in a collective purpose or effort, the assignment by virtue of employment of status and identity, and required regular activity.[34]

These categories, she notes, following from employment as a structure and not from its conditions, are the same in the 1980s as they were in the 1930s. To the extent that they have become a part of the fabric of modern existence, the unemployed will experience their absence. One can also surmise that the void created by their absence relates to the individual and family troubles reported in Liem and Rayman's more qualitative research. In fact, in Jahoda's broad specification of the attributes accompanying employment and the vacuum that is created when persons become unemployed, there appears to be a connection to retirement status. A person experiencing abrupt and total retirement, imposed on an otherwise healthy, active life which may continue for another 20 to 25 years beyond age 65, may suffer from similar problems. There is an important social policy message carried by Jahoda's work.[35]

UNEMPLOYMENT AND PART-TIME WORK

Unemployment has serious ramifications for both society and its members. It not only results in a diminished production of goods and services and social costs of transfer payments and non-cash benefits, but an income and consumption loss for the unemployed worker and his or her family. Equally important and devastating are the potential personal costs of unemployment that affect health and social and family relationships. These are not costs that differentiate among age groups. Nor can they be ignored. Both preventative and ameliorative policies dedicated to full employment goals, as well as toward coping with the consequences of unemployment, are needed. Within that context, part-time work can also play a role.

Obviously, part-time work is not a solution for everyone. For single-parent households or for workers of low skills, the issue is not one of hours reduction, even to preserve jobs, so much as it is one of increasing competence through training, employment opportunities, and support services, so that individuals are equipped and available to fill full-time job openings that provide income adequate for their needs and those of their families. Although not a permanent solution, part-time work in these situations can play a temporary, supportive role during the period of education and training acquisition in preparation for full-time jobs.

There are other unemployment situations in which the availability of an enhanced concept of part-time work could improve the possibilities for coping in a difficult labor market. Although for the individual, the consequences of having no income because of unemployment are the same whatever the unemployment cause, the rationale supportive of part-time work and its institutionalized form may be different, depending on whether unemployment is due to a temporary employment retrenchment or to a permanent displacement of workers from changing or disappearing jobs. This distinction is made in the following paragraphs.

Temporary retrenchment. First, how can part-time work help in coping with temporary cutbacks due to production retrenchment? At present, except for workers in a few states, such unemployment is likely to result either in total unemployment, with unemployment compensation being paid for a period, or in partial involuntary unemployment customarily occurring with no governmental replacement income. Under such circumstances, short-time compensation programs, which prorate state unemployment insurance benefits according to the proportion of reduced worktime, offer an improved alternative. In California, for example, participating employers have customarily instituted a worktime reduction of about one day a week (20 percent) for an average duration of about 13 weeks. Compensation plus earnings for the average worker amounts to about 92 percent of prior full-time income. The program has been favorably received by employees, including the more senior workers, who, in the absence of the program, might not have been required to "share" in the work hours reduction. It has also been supported by employers, who found little difference in their direct labor costs as a result of short-time compensation benefit payments, as compared with unemployment insurance, but experienced a significant reduction in severance and recall and hiring costs (see Chapter 7). For both older and younger workers, short-time compensation saves jobs while retaining some income. At the same time, it minimizes the disruption of enterprise production and permits skill retention of an experienced labor force.

Permanently displaced workers. Permanently displaced or dislocated workers represent a special group of the unemployed, a group that is not only difficult to measure statistically, but even to define. In general terms, a displaced or dislocated worker is one whose job has disappeared because of a plant shutdown (sometimes due to adoption of labor saving technology and sometimes to the effects of international trade competition, for example) and a new job is not likely to develop soon.[36] A more precise definition distinguishes cyclically unemployed from structurally unemployed workers. According to this definition, a displaced, structurally unemployed worker is one in a declining industry, or with long job tenure, who suffers a permanent job loss in a previous employment and for whom a job change will be difficult.[37] Wachter and Wascher estimate that in January 1983 the number of unemployed, dislocated workers in industries with declining employment levels from 1978–1980, was 1.3 million. About one half of these displaced workers worked in the automotive, fabricated metals, primary metals, or wearing apparel industries. Over half were located in the northeast or midwest. If the criteria of displacement combine a declining industry and 10 years of job tenure, then the number of workers affected in January 1983 was about 280,000. Many of this latter group of displaced workers were aged 45 or more. Most affected by such displacement were semiskilled blue collar workers in the automotive, primary metals, textile and wearing apparel industries.

Dislocated or permanently displaced workers are not the same as marginal workers. They may be men or women and they often have skills and strong job attachment. A high proportion have high school diplomas, and their earnings levels are relatively high (one-fourth with a family income of $15,000 or more in a late 1970s study).[38] But in their unemployment dislocated workers share two important distinguishing qualities: their projected wages for future employment are lower than the wages of their last job, and their displacement is likely to result in a long period of unemployment prior to relocation.[39] Older displaced workers are likely to experience these qualities more acutely than others. Skill or location mismatch or age bias in hiring policies are some of the causes of the longer unemployment duration they experience. The findings of the 1977 Parnes study, which documents this longer unemployment duration for older displaced workers than for other older unemployed, is reinforced by research of Gordus, Jarley, and Ferman (1981) and Lipsky (1970), which suggests that a 50-year-old worker will be unemployed twice as long as a 25-year-old.[40]

The phenomenon of structurally displaced workers relates to the latest phase of the technological revolution and the microelectronic innovations that are at its core. The re-ordering and reorganization of the on-going industrial process affect the number and nature of work opportunities and, consequently, future unemployment levels. The impact of changes for older workers can be particularly severe. They could affect the viability of their skills, raise the threat of extended unemployment, and increase the potential for early retirement, with consequences for both retirement income and the quality of life.

Rapid technological change raises a number of important issues. The potential for the creation of new occupations, for example, needs to be considered. How will the occupational structure be affected, and how will the demand for labor for these new jobs synchronize with the size and training of the expected labor supply?[41]

Another question concerns the implications of these new occupations for part-time jobs and for an assessment of their quality. Here, the predictions are mixed. In clerical occupations, for example, there is expected to be a reduction in the demand for full-time workers, correlating with greater sophistication of office technologies. With the re-ordering of jobs into easily monitored components, conversion to part-time job segments is facilitated and there is likely to be an increase in such job openings, partly in response to interests of traditional part-time workers. For some jobs, increased specialization and division of tasks will result in a down-grading of the skill level, while in others, an amalgamation or reorganization of duties will be accompanied by requirements for more technical or administrative skills.[42]

Stepping back from the immediate changes, however, provides a look at the longer-run implications — both social and economic — of the new technological revolution sparked by the microelectronic chip. Nobel Laureate Wassily Leontief notes a disturbing dynamic in the rhythm of current industrial progress that differs from what was found in the past. Industrial change of the late nineteenth and early twentieth centuries was marked by a substitution of machines for the "muscle" of labor, and the strong growth in productivity (output per person-hour) that resulted from this labor saving effect was partially distributed — after a time — in the form of reduced work hours and greater leisure (See Chapter 1). Since the end of World War II, however, the decline in the hours of the standard workweek has ceased, and an important mechanism used earlier for adapting to the decreased need for labor accompanying technological change has thus been eliminated. Moreover, the changes generated by the new technological wave of computers and automation intensify the substitution of machines for labor not only for mechanical tasks, but also for the performance of increasingly complex "mental" functions in production and service industries.[43] Leontief sees the radical and pervasively applied techniques of the new technology as contributing to a slowly but steadily rising long-run trend in unemployment. It is, in fact, already in evidence: the former customary 2 to 3 percent unemployment norm for a full employment economy is giving way to a 6 to 8 percent norm.[44]

How is society to cope with this phenomenon that brings increasing productivity but at the expense of a reduced need for labor? Full consideration of the range of possible policy measures to respond to this situation, suggested by Leontief and by others, is beyond the scope of this discussion.[45] Leontief's view, however, that the solution to the problem of technological unemployment lies in some combination of labor sharing and income policies is quite germane to this discussion.[46] Labor sharing could take several different forms, including a shortening of the standard hours of the workweek or of the number of workdays in the workweek, or of work hours in the workday.[47] These or similar work sharing arrangements, by reducing the labor time of individuals, could help to prevent the creation of two labor groups in the population, one of which is fully employed and the other, technologically unemployed. Leontief does not propose the same pay for less work time, which, among other effects, would increase the rate of substitution of capital for labor. Rather, wages would continue to reflect market factors, and expanded incomes policies would protect the population against the risks of life. To the extent that such work scheduling arrangements are possible and of interest to workers, they can have a value that extends beyond the individual and redound to the benefit of the society as a whole.[48]

Thus, what begins as an institutional change to benefit the quality and economic security of individual lives could have a far broader benefit in meeting the increasing threat of structural unemployment. Indeed, Leontief's prescription has been echoed by at least two other thoughtful and respected commenters of the social scene, who arrive at a similar recommendation from somewhat different perspectives.

Marie Jahoda, Professor Emerita of Social Psychology at the University of Sussex, in her recent study of the social psychological implications of unemployment for individual well-being, states:

> in the long run the shortening of the working hours per day, per year, or per lifetime is the most constructive measure if new technologies actually reduce the amount of work required to give the population a respectable standard of living. The psychological benefits are not tied to an eight hour day or a forty hour week. They would accrue even in the improbable case for this century that working hours could be halved without lowering the standard of living.[49]

Similarly, Alan Pifer, President Emeritus of the Carnegie Corporation, writing about the 50 million healthy, active Americans aged 50–75 (one-fifth of the population), ponders how their productive resources can best be used: "Does this mean they should continue in full time, paid employment for the entire third quarter (of life)? Not at all. . . . The notion of productivity must be broadened to include part-time as well as full-time paid work and full- and part-time volunteer jobs" (*New York Times,* February 7, 1984).

This alternative to unemployment or non-labor market attachment could improve the situation for older as well as younger workers. It is a simple idea, but not a simple concept, for it requires not only a broadened vision for the rationale supporting part-time work, but also a talent and innovative spirit to implement that vision effectively within the industrial structure without diminishing opportunities for those who wish to work full time. There are some pioneers today who are working in the direction of such institutional change. They are experimenting with reduced hours of work and demonstrating when and how an expanded concept of part-time work can both respond to employee interests and serve employer needs. They are inquiring into beliefs and costs of these arrangements in a variety of structures and occupations. These developments will be discussed in Chapter 9. First, however, Chapter 7 will consider some ways in which legislation affects part-time work structures that do or could exist.

Notes

1. For a general analysis of inflation and its relationship to unemployment, see Solow, 1975, pp. 30–66; Thurow, 1983, pp. 50–103; Baily and Okun, 1982, Parts I and II. Clark and Spengler, 1980, pp. 61–63, and Schulz, 1985, pp. 40–44, discuss the impact of inflation on the older population.

2. National Council on the Aging, 1981, pp. 63–64.

3. Ginzberg, 1982, p. 86.

4. For further discussion and references, see U.S. Department of Labor, BLS, 1983b, pp. 317–18; U.S. Congressional Budget Office, 1981.

5. The elderly tend to spend a higher proportion of income than the rest of the population on food consumed at home, home heating and household operation, and medical care. They spend relatively less on restaurant meals, transportation, clothing, home furnishings, and recreation. They are more likely to own their own homes. See National Commission on Social Security, 1981, p. 314.

6. Hurd and Shoven, 1982.

7. Norwood, 1984.

8. Schulz, 1985, p. 44.

9. Grad, 1984, p. 11.

10. Two aspects of the 1983 amendments affect these provisions. The new law delayed from July 1983 to January 1984 the cost of living adjustment for that year. Thereafter, automatic annual adjustments are made in January of each year. Also, although corrections for inflation are generally based on price changes, if trust funds are severely depleted, adjustments will be related to the lesser of price or wage changes (Kingson, 1983, p. 34).

11. For an excellent analysis of the economics of private pensions, see Munnell, 1982.

12. Ibid.; U.S. Department of Labor, 1980; Schulz, 1978; Schmitt, 1984. Between 1970 and 1980, median annual wages and salaries rose 103 percent, average social security primary insurance amounts for retired workers ages 62 and over rose about 184 percent, and median annual private pensions for units aged 65 and over, increased about 75 percent. The CPI increased 112 percent during the period (Grad, 1984, p. 11).

13. Morgan, 1981. Unless otherwise indicated, data in this section come from Rones, 1983.

14. The number of discouraged workers has grown from 971.5 thousand in 1980 to 1.6 million in 1982. In the second quarter of 1983, workers aged 55 and over were 23 percent of discouraged workers, although they represented only 14 percent of the total working population (U.S. House of Representatives, 1982b, pp. 62, 72).

15. Renes, 1978, p. 4.

16. U.S. Department of Labor, BLS, 1983b, pp. 69, 34.

17. U.S. House of Representatives, 1982b, pp. 62, 71.

18. Parnes, 1982, pp. 1–2, 53–54.

19. Bould, 1980, pp. 123–26; Kingson, 1982.

20. Rones, 1983, p. 4; Sheppard and Rix, 1977, p. 6; International Labour Office, 1984.

21. Bowen and Finegan, 1969, p. 270; Clark and Spengler, 1980, p. 112.

22. Parnes and King, 1977; Parnes, 1981.

23. In 1981, the average benefit amount was $106.69, 35.9 percent of average weekly wages. Average benefit duration was 14.5 weeks (U.S. Department of Health and Human Services, 1982b, p. 227).

24. Hamermesh, 1977; Runner, 1983, p. 38; *Employment and Training Report of the President,* 1982, pp. 52 ff.

25. University of Wisconsin, 1984, p. 5.

26. In the 1974–76 recession, about 40 weeks of extra compensation were made available by the federal government to extend state unemployment benefits. The Federal Supplemental Compensation program, enacted in September 1982, provided only 6 to 10 additional weeks for individuals who had exhausted their rights to other benefits. In April 1983, this was changed to 8 to 14 weeks (*New York Times,* Sept. 9, 1983; Holen, 1984).

27. Burtless, 1983, pp. 246–49.

28. Summers, 1983, p. 251.

29. Hamermesh, 1978; Work in America Institute, 1981, pp. 92–93.

30. U.S. Joint Economic Committee, 1976; Brenner, 1982.

31. Brenner, 1982, p. 45; Jahoda, 1982, pp. 45–48; *New York Times,* April 6, 1982, pp. 1–2.

32. Brenner, 1984; Gordus and McAlinden, 1984.

33. Liem, 1981; Liem and Rayman, 1982, pp. 1116–23.

34. Jahoda, 1982, p. 59.

35. Jahoda does not ignore the effect that dehumanizing work conditions can have on an interest in an extended job attachment. She urges a continued striving to improve the work envi-

ronment (Jahoda, 1982, pp. 86–90).

36. U.S. Congressional Budget Office, 1982a, p. 4; Wachter and Wascher, 1983, p. 181.

37. A "declining industry" is one where employment has decreased because of a smaller output or reduced manpower needs. "Long job tenure" is considered to be 10 years or more.

38. Bendick and Devine, 1981, p. 209.

39. Ibid., p. 178.

40. Ibid., pp. 193–94; U.S. Congressional Budget Office, 1982a, p. ix.

41. Projections show a large increase in the computer and health fields and strong growth among scientific, technical, and computer jobs that design and develop high tech products. These occupations are expected to grow faster than employment in general (Silvestri, Lukasiewicz, and Einstein, 1983). Many of the new jobs will not be in the high tech industries themselves, but in the banks, insurance, and other business offices that high tech products service and influence (*New York Times,* September 18, 1983).

Despite these new fields, new occupations are expected to account for only 7 to 8 percent of job growth in the 1980s. Traditional occupations will continue to be in strong demand. Changing demand within occupational categories and some job displacement and job mis-match between skills and job requirements is projected. But this will be less than previously expected because of the sharp decline in the rate of increase of the labor force. Between 1978 and 1980, the labor force grew at about 2.2 percent a year. Between 1983 and 1990 its rise is expected to be only 1.5 percent a year, representing a drop of 6.9 million workers over earlier expectations. (Wachter and Wascher, 1983, pp. 178–180; *Wall Street Journal,* August 17, 1983).

42. George, 1984. Although the claim has been made that the demand for labor in high tech industries will respond to the more highly educated supply of labor now available, increasing evidence indicates that for large areas of work, this may not be so (Silvestri et al., 1983) and that job rationalization leading to "de-skilling" of the job may predominate over a more skilled job reorganization (George, 1984; Levin and Rumberger in *New York Times,* September 4, 1983). Shaiken (*New York Times,* September 4, 1983) finds a growing tendency for a "two-tier work force" – that is, a small group of creative people at the top and many low paid wage earners at the bottom. With office automation, some traditional female jobs may disappear and others will become much more routine. Part-time work in these occupations may come to have many of the worst features formerly associated with piece work – low pay, no fringe benefits, and monitering of production rhythms (*Wall Street Journal,* May 6, 1983). These negative aspects temper the enthusiasm about increased hours flexibility that computer-based improvements can bring.

43. Leontief, September 1983b, p. 405; 1982, p. 188.

44. In December 1973, for example, recovering from an early 1970s recession, the unemployment rate for civilian workers was 4.9 percent. In January 1980, a peak period of recovery from the 1974–1975 recession, the unemployment rate was 6.3 percent. In May 1984, making a third recovery from the recession of 1981–1983, it was 7.5 percent (U.S. Department of Labor, BLS, communication; U.S. Department of Commerce, *Business Conditions Digest,* April 1973, p. 115; May 1977, p. 11; January 1983, p. 10).

45. U.S. Congressional Budget Office, 1982a; Wachter and Wascher, 1983.

46. Leontief, 1982, 1983a.

47. In the past, downward adjustment of standard workweek hours was made possible by increasing productivity, which permitted the fruits of a higher standard of living to be shared. In recent years, the rate of productivity growth has slowed considerably. Private non-farm output per hour grew by about 2 percent a year between 1968 and 1973 and only 0.9 percent each year between 1979 and 1982, after which it dropped to 0.4 percent. For the near future, experts project this downward trend to be reversed, nurtured by new capital investment, strong growth in demand for goods and services, and a rising skill level of the labor force. Productivity is projected to reflect a 1.6 percent annual growth rate in 1982–1990 and a 1.3 percent rate in 1990–1995 (Personick, 1983, p. 25). With rising productivity, reflected in higher real wages, there could be a greater willingness on the part of some workers to trade a number of work hours for more leisure and a greater flexibility in scheduling work time.

48. Leontief is not alone in this view. There is also considerable concern in Europe about the effects of automation on the numbers and quality of jobs, with impact particularly on women and unskilled workers. Advocated social policies in Europe include shortening of work hours to prevent further spread of unemployment (Wieczorek-Zeul, 1983).

49. Jahoda, 1982, p. 99.

7

Social Policy and Legislation: Influence on Part-Time Work for Older Workers

Legislation—and the lack of it—affect the way institutional structures develop. Part-time work has been around for a long time, but until recently little consideration has been given to the issue from a legislative perspective. Until the past few years, statutory policy has affected part-time work only indirectly, as a byproduct of the pursuit of other social goals.

Federal legislation has, nonetheless, exerted an important influence on part-time work for older workers. At first it did so through provisions that influenced the choice to work or to retire. Much of this legislation was enacted in periods of limited job opportunities and sought to encourage retirement of older workers. More recently the influence has become both more direct and more positive, with legislation that facilitates the development of reduced-hour work schedules or provides a part-time role model of its own in public employment.

This chapter looks first at provisions of three legislative acts that affect the preference of individuals for part-time work (although their primary purpose has to do with other issues). A second section describes recent legislation that provides positive support for part-time work schedules. The final section comments on desirable directions for social policy with respect to part-time work for older workers.

Indirect Social Policy Influence on Part-Time Work for Older Workers

OLD AGE, SURVIVORS, AND DISABILITY INSURANCE
(OASDI), 1935, 1939, 1956

OASDI, or social security, is a compulsory, federal, social insurance program that protects most Americans against the risk of lost earnings due to retirement, disability, or death of a breadwinner.[1] More than 94 percent of persons aged 65 and over receive social security benefits and for about two-thirds of them, social security accounts for more than one-half of total income. In this social insurance program, individual equity considerations of a fair rate of return on contributions made are tempered by a social policy to provide an adequate income base for all retirees.[2] A number of provisions in addition to the level and replacement ratio of retirement benefits to pre-retirement earnings influence attitudes toward work participation (affecting interest in part-time as well as in full-time work) — eligibility provisions, mandatory retirement age, earnings restrictions, early and postponed retirement provisions. Three of these, and their implications for part-time work, are examined below.

Early Retirement

Early retirement provisions, applicable to women since 1956 and to men since 1961, evolved as part of a policy supportive of retirement. Early retirement was seen as a way of rewarding older workers for their long years of employment, of compensating workers forced to leave the labor market due to unemployment or poor health, and of opening up jobs for younger workers.[3] An additional argument in support of women's early retirement was to permit retirement to occur at the same time as that of their husbands, who were often somewhat older. The provisions permit retirement at age 62 with actuarially calculated benefits to ensure, on average, benefit equivalence whether workers retire early or at the customary retirement age. The maximum reduction, applicable to those who retire at age 62, leaves the recipient with 80 percent of the normal retirement benefit.

Early retirement proved to be popular both for those who had other income or private pensions and could afford to retire and for others for whom continued attachment to the labor market for health or employment reasons was difficult.[4] In the late 1960s and 1970s, the generally improved levels of social security benefits increased the adequacy of early retirement income for many workers, and provided further encouragement for early labor force withdrawal.[5]

Recently, however, two conflicting trends appear to be emerging that raise a question about a continuing preference for early retirement. On the one hand, private sector early retirements, encouraged in the mid-1960s by unions as a way to open up employment opportunities for younger members, have shown a resurgence of growth.[6] Known as "open windows" or "golden handshakes," most plans have not been discriminatory. They have offered substantial bonuses or benefits as early as age 55, sometimes after as few as 10 years of service and often at less than full actuarial reduction of benefits, in an effort to encourage labor market withdrawal.[7] In 1983, for example, two-thirds of all pension plan participants in medium and large firms could retire before age 65 with unreduced benefits.[8] The measures have sometimes been introduced to enhance the competitive position of the firm in the face of a recession by severance of older, higher paid workers. Sometimes their purpose has been to facilitate adaptation to technological change, or to deal with corporate restructuring by reducing labor costs.[9] Employees who accept these early private pension inducements also become eligible at age 62 for early social security retirement benefits.

But, at the same time that these early retirement trends are receiving more publicity, economists are injecting some cautionary comments into discussions about them, noting the possible shortage of skilled and experienced workers that accompany such retirements,[10] and the mismatch of workers with available jobs that may occur.[11] Both add to employer costs. In addition, questions are being raised about the psychological and economic effects of retirement over the long term. Moreover, the pool of younger workers is shrinking and the low birth rates of today are expected to produce fewer new workers by the year 2000.[12] Thus, from a societal perspective, the labor market consequences of early retirement are not necessarily all positive. In addition, early retirement adds to immediate (although not longer-run) pressures on social security finances and runs counter to the planning goals of the 1983 Amendments to the Social Security Act, which include a gradual raising of normal retirement age beginning in the year 2000.

It is interesting to note that there are some indications of a second, conflicting current resulting in a slowing down of the rate of early retirement.[13] In 1978, for example, 66 percent of male and female retirements occurred prior to age 65; in 1980, the proportion of people retiring early declined slightly, to 64 percent.[14] Bankers Life and Casualty Company of Chicago found that in the five years prior to 1980, 70 percent of workers reaching retirement age elected to remain at work.[15]

This recently emerging new wrinkle in retirement rhythms has yet to be explained fully. At the least, it appears that there is some uncertainty as to the continuation of early retirement trends, as illustrated by the slowing down in the decline in labor force participation rates of older men, on the one hand, and the lessening of the increase in the participation rates of older women on the other (see Table 2.3).[16] Good social policy should be neutral in affecting the work/retirement decision of workers who have earned the right of choice through long attachment to the labor market. Yet, for those who prefer to continue in some paid work, the work choices are limited and often undesirable. Opening up a greater range of options beyond that of full-time work or full retirement could permit a more accurate expression of work preferences at the same time that it would respond to on-going demographic changes, labor force needs, and pressures on social security financing.

Postponed Retirement

Part-time work is also an alternative to postponed retirement. Prior to 1982, social security benefits increased 1 percent for each year that retirement was delayed up to the age of 72. This was raised to 3 percent in 1982, and the age beyond which earnings did not lower benefits was reduced from age 72 to 70. Under the 1983 Social Security amendments, the delayed retirement credit is to be further increased gradually, beginning in 1990, until it reaches 8 percent per year for workers who become 65 in 2010. At that time, on average, the benefits, like those for early retirement, will be close to the level that equalizes the present value of future benefits and are actuarially neutral to the age of retirement.[17] What this means is that by continuing to work, individuals will be assured that the higher benefit they receive at a later age will have the same value over their remaining expected lifetime as that due them at age 65. Given this fact, those for whom part-time paid work has appeal would seem more likely to choose it if it is available in a desirable job, which for many may be their job in the customary place of employment,[18] with prorated earnings and fringe benefits. Such workers will still, however, under the present provisions have to contend with the "earnings test."

Earnings Test

The "retirement test" or "earnings test" is a provision of the Social Security Act adopted to ensure that social security benefits are paid for the purpose for which they were intended — partially to replace lost *earnings* with a retirement benefit. The provisions currently in effect represent a compromise that permits a minimum level of earnings wth no benefit reduction (in 1985 $7,320 for nondisabled beneficiaries aged 65–69 and $5,400 for those aged 62–64). For income that exceeds this amount, one dollar of benefits is withheld for every two dollars of annual earnings. Benefits are thus reduced gradually as earnings increase. A man aged 65 in 1985, with a wife eligible for benefits based on his record, who always earned the national average wage, could earn as much as $27,062 before the entire benefit would be withheld. No more than 5 percent of beneficiaries have any benefits withheld under the earnings test. In December 1983, only 337,000 of those affected by its provisions received no benefits, compared with 21.4 million who did receive them.

Opponents of the "earnings test" are very vocal. In a recent Harris Poll, 43 percent of Americans, particularly the more affluent, favor repeal of the provision.[19] Persons who urge its repeal point out that not only are benefits reduced when earnings exceed the exempt amount, but earnings income is taxed, both as income and for social security purposes, leading to a marginal tax rate for working that may be as high as 70 percent.[20] Among the group of workers whose earnings in retirement would exceed the maximum allowable without benefit reduction, employers report some inclination to work only up to, but not beyond, the exempt income limit.[21] A problem of high employee turnover is thus created.[22] In an Andrus Gerontology Center survey inquiring about company plans for expanding part-time work, one out of four organizations indicated that the earned income limitation discouraged them from developing reduced-hour options for older and retired workers.[23]

And yet, repeal of the "earnings test" would raise several equally serious problems. It would represent a major departure from the social insurance principle of protection against earnings loss through replacement of a proportion of lost earnings. Moreover, it would run counter to the social adequacy tenet of the law, in that nearly two-thirds of the benefits arising from the repeal would go to higher-income beneficiaries, such as autonomous professionals who continue to maintain active consultancies and practices in their later years.[24] A simulation study in the late 1970s found that in the event of repeal, one-half of the new benefits created would have gone to the top one-third of the aged income recipients with incomes over $10,000, and 20 percent would have gone to those with incomes greater than $20,000.[25] A strong argument could be made for an alternative of raising the general level of benefits to provide a more socially desirable use of available funds for benefit enhancement.

This is a knotty problem involving conflicts of valued social goals — reconciling social adequacy with individual equity considerations in social security benefits, and removing obstacles to part-time work. The 1983 amendments to the Social Security Act address the problem by providing for a decrease in the benefits withheld when earnings exceed the exempt limit. Beginning in 1990, the benefit withholding rate will decrease from one-half to one-third (that is, $1 of benefits will be withheld for every $3 of earnings in excess of the exempt amount for fully retired beneficiaries aged 65 in 1990).[26] Schulz suggests an alternative approach whereby the exempt amount would be set at the average level of wages covered by social security ($13,000 in 1981).[27] In this way, the major beneficiaries of the amendment would be lower income groups, and the social security cost would be less than with outright repeal. In preserving the fundamental principle of earnings replacement on which the American social security program has been built, and giving continuing emphasis to the principle of social adequacy in the use of its limited funds, the Schulz proposal has much to recommend it. Doubling the current earnings exemption would provide some relief from the penalty for paid work (including part-time) and encourage the use of part-time schedules for and by older workers for longer periods of the year.

EMPLOYEE RETIREMENT INCOME SECURITY ACT (ERISA), 1974

Although less universal than social security, private pension benefits probably have more of an impact on the decision of many older workers to work or to retire than does the receipt of social security.[28]

About one-half of men and one-third of women aged 14 and over, working full time in wage and salary jobs (in 1979), are covered by a private retirement plan, compared with only 9 percent of persons working part-time.[29] Coverage is uneven among industries and occupations, being highest in manufacturing and in transportation, communication, and utilities industries, and among professional and technical, managerial, and skilled and semiskilled jobs. Large unionized firms are more apt to be covered than are small, non-unionized ones.[30]

ERISA, enacted in 1974, had as its principal objective the protection of pension rights of workers covered by private plans.[31] Its provisions affect those working groups for whom private pension coverage is available. The impact of the law is thus not uniform across industries or for all men and women, nor is it the same as that of social security.

Several provisions, by creating disincentives for work, also adversely affect the potential for part-time work. First, only limited work is permitted when a pension is being paid. A Department of Labor regulation, effective in 1982, limits such work hours to no more than 40 hours a month if the retiree is working for the employer who maintains the retirement plan, or, in multi-employer plans, in the trade, craft, or industry covered by the plan. If hours exceed this number, there can be a loss of private pension benefits.[31] Similar to the social security earnings test but with less impact, the provision limits the amount of part-time work that can be engaged in without benefit loss.

Second, the fact that pension vesting must occur after employees work 1,000 or more hours in a year (about one-half time) has led enterprises to limit the annual hours of work for part-time employees to less than this number, or to hire one full-time employee rather than two part-time employees, each with pension coverage. It raises, in a different context, the issue of fringe benefit costs that is discussed in Chapter 9.

Third, little discussed in the literature is the effect that phased retirement or other part-time work near retirement could have on benefits in those plans that are based on earnings in the period before retirement. Should benefits be computed on the basis of equivalent full-time earnings, as is done in the federal government? Should pension contributions be continued at a full-time rate, although work is only part-time, as is possible for California teachers? Should benefits be frozen at the earnings rate of some prior full-time period? Should they be prorated? The problem is not insurmountable, but as reduced-hour work expands for older workers, it poses a further issue that must be addressed.

In addition to these provisions that may constrain the offer of part-time work generally, two additional provisions have implications for part-time work for older workers. To prevent higher labor costs for employers who hire older workers, and to encourage their hiring, ERISA permits the exclusion from an existing company pension plan of workers who are hired within five years of normal retirement age (customarily age 60). In addition, pension credits can cease to accrue for employees beyond the normal retirement age. Nearly one-half of all employers freeze pension benefits at age 65, and almost 30 percent of all workers are covered by private pension plans that do not accrue benefits after eligibility for regular retirement benefits have been established,[33] although studies indicate that such a policy has no cost justification.[34] The lower compensation rates that result for older workers because of these provisions could serve as a disincentive to their working, whether full or part time.

AGE DISCRIMINATION IN EMPLOYMENT ACT (ADEA), 1967

The ADEA, effective in June 1968, provides protection from discrimination for persons between ages 40 and 65 on the basis of age in hiring, promotions, training, layoffs, compensation, and other terms of employment. Amendments in 1978, almost all of which were effective by January 1, 1980, raise the upper age limit for most workers — including that at which mandatory retirement could be required — from age 65 to age 70, and virtually eliminate mandatory retirement for most civilian employees in the federal government. Prohibition of mandatory retirement before age 70 was gradually phased in between 1979 and 1982, in an effort to respect existing collective bargaining agreements and to respond to needs of academic institutions in adjusting untenured and tenured faculty employment terms and financial arrangements. Some high level executives and policy makers continue to be exempt from the law's provisions.

Even though the law emphasizes protection of older workers from age discrimination, it has until recently supported the ERISA provision and specifically permitted continuation of the practice of pension exclusion for recently hired older workers as long as the provisions were not established to evade the purposes of the act. In June 1984, the Equal Employment Opportunity Commission (EEOC) voted to rescind the regulation that denied additional pension credits to employees who worked past age 65, but a staff proposal to implement this has yet to be developed.[35] The provisions that in effect limit fringe benefits for older workers, continue.

On the other hand, the 1978 amendment that raised the age of mandatory retirement make an important statement in support of the employment of older workers, even though its effect on retirement is expected to be small. Prior to the 1978 ADEA amendments, it was estimated that only 5 to 10 percent of retired workers were forced to retire.[36] Although about one-half of the private non-agricultural workforce is subject to mandatory retirement provisions,[37] the Department of Labor projects that raising the retirement age from age 65 to 70 will result in only a 5 percent increase in male workers aged 65 to 70 remaining in the labor force by the year 2000.[38] What the actual effect will ultimately be will depend partly on future trends in early retirement decisions. Professional and managerial occupations in which work-related health limitations are relatively fewer, income loss from retirement is relatively greater, and jobs are often more challenging, could be the most likely ones to be affected by raising the mandatory retirement age.[39]

Even though this employment effect is likely to be more symbolic than real, the statement about older worker employment is an important one to make. Demographically, we are moving into an era where not only are the numbers of older persons in the society growing, but their skill and experience may be increasingly needed as the pool of younger workers becomes smaller. Removing older workers from the labor market in an arbitrary manner would serve societal interests no more than those of individuals. Moreover, as will be discussed in Chapter 9, numerous studies document the fact that work performance does not necessarily worsen with advancing chronological age. Mandatory retirement does not provide the simple, efficient, impersonal device for removing inefficient workers or facilitating company reorganization needs. A much more accurate screening mechanism would be a test for functional competence applied in relation to needs of the job. Functional job analysis, combined with an expanded range of part-time jobs as an alternative to mandatory retirement, would better meet enterprise needs, as well as be more in tune with societal and individual interests.

Legislation That Directly Supports Part-Time Work

Legislative provisions in social policy relating to older workers have affected the preferences for and availability of part-time work, but their primary focus has been on other issues — retirement benefits, private pension standards and payments, and prevention of older worker discrimination. The effect on work schedules has come not directly, but through an influence on individual decisions with respect to work *or* retirement, most often emphasizing incentives for the latter. Beginning in the mid-1970s, however, there also began to percolate a more direct interest in federal policy to foster alternative work structure options, of which part-time work was one. It was not a work schedule whose adoption was sought to solve a labor shortage; indeed, these were years of labor surplus. It was a form that had strong support from women's groups, among others, and one of its effects was to expand employment opportunities not only for women, but for older persons, students, the handicapped, and others interested in a more flexible lifestyle. With some exceptions, neither organized labor nor management was particularly supportive of the idea.[40]

FEDERAL EMPLOYEES PART-TIME CAREER ACT, 1978

In 1978, Congress enacted two laws to foster the development of alternative work structures in the federal sector. The Federal Employees Flexible and Compressed Work Schedules Act of 1978 provided for a three-year experiment with flexible work hours and compressed workweeks within the federal sector. By the end of the three-year period, when almost 350,000 federal employees were on a compressed workweek schedule and more than one million were working flexible full-time work hours, the experiment was seen as a success.[41]

More germane to this discussion was the second act, the Federal Employees Part-Time Career Act, signed into law in October 1978. Its purpose was to facilitate the establishment of permanent, part-time positions (between 16 and 32/hours weekly) in federal government jobs from GS-1 to GS-15, to set goals and time tables, and to evaluate the experience. Part-time workers were to be paid at a wage equivalent to that of full-time employees, with prorated fringe benefits. In an effort to minimize agency resistance to the new schedule, a part-time job no longer counted as one position when setting agency personnel ceilings, but as an appropriate fraction of a full-time equivalent position. The part-time program was to be administered by the Office of Personnel Management.

An evaluation of the law covering the period January 1979 to May 1982 offered a number of interesting observations.[42] Most important, the report estimated that the number of permanent, career part-time employees in the federal government, excluding the Postal Service, increased by almost 14,000 from January 1979 to January 1981, when part-time employment peaked at 60.6 thousand persons. It then fell to 54.5 thousand by mid-1982, declining somewhat faster than the shrinkage of federal employment generally that took place during the period. The earlier increase in part-time jobs, often arising from a conversion from full-time positions, was somewhat counteracted in the later period by a conversion in the opposite direction, as employees sought greater employment security in full-time positions.

Women constituted about 69 percent of the government's part-time workforce as of July 1981, compared with 39 percent of the full-time workforce. Contrary to expectations, a smaller proportion of part-time (10 percent) than full-time (15 percent) employees were over age 55, due perhaps to the relatively sedentary nature of government work, which poses no physical problem for older workers, and to the fact that higher pensions result when retirement follows a period of full-time work. A slightly higher percentage of part-time than full-time workers, most likely students, were under age 23 (7.5 percent versus 6.7 percent).

Unfortunately, evaluation of the program coincided with a period of employment uncertainty and cutbacks, and this affected both opportunities and expressed preferences for part-time work. Between January 1979 and January 1981, for example, agency personnel ceilings were raised for part-time positions at the same time that ceilings for full-time permanent positions were reduced. The freezes frequently led to increased hiring of part-time employees. On the other hand, budgetary constraints and uncertainties about reductions of the federal workforce led to postponements and failures to fill existing part-time vacancies. Federal managers feared that conversion of a job to part time would mean a permanent loss of a full-time slot, lowering the stature of their office. Workers were worried that part-time jobs would be less secure than full-time jobs; in fact, in a number of departments part-time workers were disproportionately at risk in employment reductions in force (see the *Washington Post,* July 2, 1984).

In addition to the effects of the government employment climate and of departmental procedures with respect to part-time jobs, evaluation of the experience was also hampered by the fact that government agencies often failed to implement provisions designed to foster interest and participation in part-time work. At the time of the 1982 evaluation, only two (out of seven) evaluated agencies had examined vacant agency positions to determine the feasibility of conversion of full-time to part-time jobs. Only three agencies had established annual part-time goals and time tables. Five agencies had no procedures for evaluation.

Because of these staffing uncertainties and administrative problems, it is difficult to assess what the potential of part-time work scheduling would be under a more vigorous implementation of the law. It remains to be seen whether there will be more support for the law's goals during the period of extension of the legislation to September 1985.[43]

HOURS REDUCTION DUE TO EMPLOYMENT RETRENCHMENT

Short-time compensation (STC), a form of compensated work sharing undertaken as an alternative to full-time layoffs, has had a happier experience despite its more complicated history.[44] Its growing acceptance and support in the states where it has been enacted indicates both its viability as a work scheduling form in jobs traditionally thought to be alien territory for reduced work hours and its usefulness in periods of necessary temporary employment cutbacks. STC is currently seen as a useful supplement to more basic macroeconomic fiscal and monetary policies that buttress and promote a full employment goal. It offers another rationale in support of reduced-hour schedules, additional to those of attracting skilled labor resources or responding to employee work scheduling needs.

The concept of work sharing has long been used in a number of European countries.[45] The German program, dating from 1927, is the oldest and most heavily studied here because of the similarity of its administrative structure to the unemployment insurance framework of American programs.[46] European employers support work sharing programs because they are concerned about the loss of their human capital investment in trained workers and are aware of the often large expense involved in first laying off workers and then, when times improve, rehiring and retraining a new workforce.[47] European workers have found the concept of work sharing compatible with their egalitarian and collectivist approach to work.[48] They favor the programs because they permit retention of an employment connection and fringe benefits, while only slightly reducing money earnings during the temporary period of partial work combined with short-time compensation.[49]

Partial Unemployment Benefits

In the United States, although there has been provision for payment of benefits for partial unemployment in almost all state unemployment insurance laws (Montana being an exception), until recently the provisions have been extremely restrictive. Their purpose has been less to preserve jobs than to ease the administrative burden of paying benefits based on a small amount of earnings.

No distinction is made between eligibility requirements that apply to partial or full unemployment insurance benefits. Partial unemployment benefits are roughly equal to the value of full weekly unemployment benefits less the income earned during the week of partial work. Thus, if an employee earns $300 for a 40 hour week and is eligible to receive a benefit of $120 for each week of unemployment, he or she could work no more than two days before becoming ineligible for benefits, because after two days of work earnings would exceed the unemployment benefit.[50]

Partial unemployment insurance benefits account for no more than 5 to 6 percent of the total weeks compensated under regular unemployment insurance. The proportion declines as unemployment becomes greater.[51] Because of the stringency of the provisions, partial unemployment compensation plays almost no role in preventing layoffs and spreading employment in periods of temporary recession. Rather than providing a means of fostering reduced-hour work in such circumstances, because of benefit loss with minimal earnings, they reduce the incentive to work at all during a week in which full benefits can be paid.[52]

State Short-Time Compensation (STC) Programs

Since the enactment of the California Shared Work Program in July 1978, six other states have passed similar programs: Arizona (1982), Oregon (1982), Florida (1982), Washington (1983), Illinois (1984), and Maryland (1984). The programs, using unemployment insurance to compensate for reduced worktime, have an orientation similar to that of work sharing programs in Europe.[53] Like these programs, they were developed to cope with periods of temporary employment retrenchment. Once legislation was developed, the critical factors in support of their rapid enactment were their ability to preserve jobs,[54] retain skilled employees, provide income through prorating of unemployment insurance benefits, retain fringe benfits, and permit rapid, easy transition back to full-time employment when economic recovery occurred. The programs were not viewed as a way to achieve full employment. They responded to the reality of a temporary period of less than full employment and sought an equitable formula for distributing work and supplementing income in an environment where employment opportunities were limited. Although not in name, they in fact converted full-time to part-time jobs by reducing hours of work below those of a normal full-time workweek. These programs furnish useful information about what is structurally possible for reduced-hour work and where lie some of the problems in designing part-time work schedules. Not all the experience is transferable, however, since income reimbursement is not usually an accompaniment of part-time work taking place outside these programs, although it could be for some forms, such as phased retirement.

The California program provides a good illustration of how the STC programs work. It has the longest tenure, has undergone one thorough evaluative scrutiny, and has been used as a model on which to pattern, with some adaptive changes, the other state programs.[55]

The California Shared Work Program was instituted as a temporary emergency measure in response to enactment of Proposition 13, which embodied drastic property tax reforms and raised the possibility of widespread layoffs in the public sector. Although the public sector unemployment never materialized, thanks to other pockets of financial support for state services and skillful management of the state's human resources, the program has been widely applied in the private sector and has now been extended until 1986.

The California work sharing program is integrated with the California regular unemployment insurance law. Participation is voluntary, taking place at the initiation of an employer who certifies that a decrease in work hours is economically necessary and submits information about the planned wage and hours reduction. If the firm is unionized, the union representative must also approve the program in writing. To ensure that the program has some minimal impact and to justify the administrative expense involved, worktime reduction must apply to at least 10 percent of the regular permanent workforce in the work unit; hours and wages must be decreased at least 10 percent.[56]

Employees who meet the regular unemployment insurance eligibility requirements (in 1980, minimum earnings of $900 during the 12-month base period) are entitled to pro-rated regular weekly benefits related to base period earnings and to the proportion of reduced time. Weekly benefits range between $30 and $136.[57] A worker eligible to receive $120 in weekly benefits could be paid 20 percent of that ($24) for each full day of non-work time. Benefit duration has recently been increased from 20 to 26 weeks, following a one-week waiting period, and can be extended to a 52-week period if the effective unemployment rate exceeds 7.5 percent.[58] If workers are laid off following the exhaustion of reduced-hour benefits, regular unemployment insurance benefits are paid for the remainder of the worker's unemployment insurance entitlement (less the amounts already paid out for STC benefits).

Administrative features of the program are simple. For example, since the reduced worktime is presumed to be temporary, employees are not required to register with the job service agency as looking for work, and this results in some administrative cost saving. The issue of fringe benefits was not addressed in the legislation; in practice, firms maintain some fringe benefits (medical benefits), while other benefits (accrued vacation leave) are reduced in proportion to the amount of time worked. Employees on STC who "moonlight" or perform paid work in excess of their reduced-hours schedule assigned by the employers have such earnings deducted from their shared work benefits. There is no interference with decisions about personnel, including discharges, transfers, and new hires.

The short-time compensation program is financed by an annual payroll tax of between 0 percent and 3.9 percent on the first $6,000 of wages, with variations depending on the solvency of the fund and the employer's tax/benefit experience. To increase the financial strength of the trust fund, a 1983 amendment provides that if an employer has a negative reserve balance (that is, benefit charges exceed contributions) on June 30 for the two previous years, contributions must equal the amount of the benefits paid during the previous year. A refund or credit will be provided if collections are greater than benefits paid.[59]

What, then, can be said about the operation of the program? Has it served well the purpose for which it was designed? What have been the views of participating workers, particularly older workers who, because of their seniority, might not have had to reduce work hours in the absence of short-time compensation?

The program is popular. Usage has increased since 1978, fostered by high levels of unemployment, increased use by large employers, and the positive view of STC held by both employers and employees. By the end of 1982, STC enrollees amounted to almost 15 percent of all initial unemployment insurance claims.[60] The average duration of worktime reduction for workers was 13.3 weeks.[61] The average worker maintained 92 percent of full-time take-home pay and fringe benefits while working a little more than four days a week.

One of the most important lessons of the California program derives from the characteristics of the employers who elect to participate. For the fiscal year ending June 30, 1980, manufacturing represented a higher proportion of

STC employers (45.0 percent) than of regular unemployment insurance employers (11.4 percent) or of their representation among all employers in the state (7.9 percent). Employers in trade and services and in construction, on the other hand, were less heavily represented. The discrepancy in experience was even greater in terms of the industrial distribution of claimants. Of all work sharing claimants, 80.3 percent were in manufacturing, compared with 31.7 percent of all regular unemployment insurance claimants. Construction, trade, and services, on the other hand, were more heavily represented among regular unemployment insurance claimants (14.9 percent and 33.1 percent respectively) than among work sharing claimants (2.3 percent and 11.4 percent respectively). Consistent with this industrial pattern, work sharing claimants were more likely to be in blue collar occupations and less likely to be in white collar and service occupations than were regular unemployment insurance claimants. Public service employees were also not commonly covered by short-term compensation. The importance of these figures lies less in their absolute magnitude, which is influenced by the industrial composition of the state and by specific economic conditions, than in the fact that they demonstrate the feasibility of reduced-hour/part-time work for blue collar workers in the manufacturing sector. It is clear that when there is an economic necessity, work can be scheduled on a less than full-time basis among a wide variety of industries and occupations.

The evaluation showed that employees, both union and non-union, were highly satisfied with the program, especially after an experience with it. There is no decisive evidence that short-time compensation helps affirmative action. But there is also no evidence of junior/senior worker conflict or a dissatisfaction of senior workers with the program, at least over the short run. This is so, even though simulations indicate that older workers probably experience a greater proportion of worktime reduction under work sharing than they would have had layoff by seniority been the policy; there is also some income redistribution to younger workers.[62] Union representatives reported that senior workers were more likely to favor the program after they had participated in it. Apparently the large proportion of all workers who gave high value to additional free time through work sharing (71.7 percent saw it of moderate or high value) also applies to older workers. Perhaps older workers, like the 75 percent of all married participants, have a high proportion of employed spouses. If so, a moderate, temporary income loss would not put family expenditures in jeopardy. A lessening of work pressure might be a welcome experience as retirement nears, particularly when few, if any, changes in job assignments are associated with work sharing. It is important to learn more about this, since experience suggests that an expansion of phased retirement, which also incorporates part-time work, might receive a similar positive reception.

FEDERAL SHORT-TIME COMPENSATION LAW, SEPTEMBER 1982

The 1982 Federal Short-Time Compensation Law, a section of the Tax Equity and Fiscal Responsibility Act of 1982, represents the culmination of long interest, study, and discussion among a number of employee, employer, and public interest groups who were interested in developing a design for work sharing that could be applied by states as an alternative to layoffs in periods of temporary employment retrenchment.[63] A number of proposals were discussed, and in 1980, federal legislation was proposed, its provisions based on the California Work Sharing Unemployment Insurance law.

Representative Patricia Schroeder led congressional efforts to develop a formula acceptable to interested groups, providing for government assistance to and federal evaluation of enacted state programs of STC benefits. The need for such benefits increased with rising unemployment rates in the early 1980s. In August 1981, the AFL–CIO Executive Council reversed its earlier opposition to work sharing by endorsing a resolution in support of the concept of worktime reductions supplemented by unemployment insurance benefits, if adequate safeguards for employees were also adopted.

The federally enacted law neither imposes a policy of STC nor interferes with the tradition of state autonomy in developing programs under the federal-state unemployment insurance system. What it does provide is technical assistance and model legislative language to assist states interested in developing such laws. An evaluation report to Congress by the Department of Labor, scheduled for October 1, 1985, will look at the operation, costs, and effects of state STC programs.[64]

Data are still insufficient for a full evaluation of STC, both as a concept and as an operating program. Apart from the findings that emerge, however, there is a separate issue of political philosophy to be resolved. In 1982, the Department of Labor objected to the proposed legislation, fearing excessive costs of evaluation and administration and claiming that there was no need for the legislation, nor was it an appropriate role for the federal government to play. Supporters of the bill, pointing to the experience of earlier, comparable studies, questioned these cost estimates. They foresaw societal benefits emanating from a reduction of welfare expenditures for otherwise laid-off workers and an increase in tax receipts from workers who remained on the job. Representative Schroeder suggested that work sharing would be much less expensive than a public works program, which might cost $10,000 for each job created (see the *Wall Street Journal,* May 2, 1980). Program experience and evaluation will resolve some of these arguments. In the meantime, existing state programs are reported to be working well and receiving support from all groups who are affected by their provisions.

Social Policy Influence on Part-Time Work for Older Workers: Desirable Directions

American social policy has been consistently supportive of its older citizens. The focus of that caring has responded to the paramount needs of particular historical periods. As a result of earlier legislation, elderly workers at retirement are assured a basic foundation of income related to their pre-retirement earnings and benefit from government supervision and protection of their accrued private pensions. More recently, there has been a federal policy commitment to older workers to prevent and correct age discrimination in the labor market.

But in focusing on these important priorities, other policies affecting work of older workers have sometimes not been addressed or have been treated negatively to reinforce a higher priority goal. As a result, a patchwork of conflicting provisions influence the decision to engage in paid work or the preference for patterns of work scheduling alternative to that of full-time employment.

The United States is now well into a new era in which demographic and educational changes influencing the sex, age, and skill composition of the labor force are coming to grips with changing industrial and occupational needs, sparked by new technologies and a growth of service-oriented demands. Greater longevity accompanying medical advances can mean for many an ability to perform occupational tasks for an extended period of time beyond the normal retirement age.

Unfortunately, employment policy, except for the area of work sharing in times of temporary employment retrenchment, largely continues to support either work *or* retirement. As yet there is no recognition that additional options with respect to work scheduling are both possible and have much to recommend them.

Except for work sharing with STC, the effect of federal legislation on part-time work is still largely indirect and restrictive. Social policy has not yet addressed in a coordinated way the issue of part-time and reduced-hours work scheduling. Social policy and federal legislation could play a role in sponsoring model programs, bringing together the evidence about benefits and problems of part-time work, and offering technical assistance in the design of programs, as well as evaluative analysis of their performance. It is an issue of vital importance to older workers, but not to them alone. It is an issue that requires not only that policies of the past become more rational and respond to the growing interest in worktime flexibility, but that they also conform to the already enacted policy extending the retirement age of the future. By removing obstacles and penalties to reduced-hour work, as well as facilitating the development of a range of alternatives for combining work with other activities, life satisfaction can be enhanced for individuals, and improved productivity,[65] skill utilization, and financing of social services will become possible for society as a whole.

Notes

1. The Social Security Act was passed in 1935. Survivor benefits were added in 1939. The disability insurance program became part of the law in 1956. This section looks at the way specific provisions of the Social Security Act affect the preference for part-time work. It does not consider an equally important issue, on which evidence is inconclusive — namely, how the receipt of social security income affects the labor supply through its effect on the decision to work or to retire. There is a general consensus that retirement income is only one of a number of factors that affect labor supply, but there is as yet no complete explanation of the retirement decision (Schulz, 1983, p. 246 and references; Thompson, 1983, pp. 1446–48 and references; Clark, Kreps, and Spengler, 1978, pp. 930–39 and references). Nor is it possible to quantify the effect

precisely, although it has been estimated that social security benefits may account for one-half the reduction in the labor force participation of elderly men since 1950 (Danziger, Haveman, and Plotnick, 1981, pp. 996-97; U.S. Congressional Budget Office, 1982b, p. 19 and references; Gustman and Steinmeier, 1983b). Aaron points to the complexities of defining "retirement," the inadequacy of presently available data for answering the question, and the inherent analytic difficulties in demonstrating interaction among relevant variables. He finds that most studies conclude that social security has decreased the labor supply of elderly workers, but that the size of the effect is unclear (Aaron, 1982, and references). Even if a precise measure of the effect were possible, it would only say something about the choice of retirement in relation to other options, including traditional part-time work as presently conceived. It would not indicate how preference would be expressed if New Concept part-time work were widely available.

2. Social security benefits, paid to eligible retired workers and their dependents and survivors, are based on earnings in covered employment, adjusted for changes in the average wage level, and then averaged after deducting five years of lowest earnings. The worker's primary benefit amount is based on a fixed formula (adjusted to reflect growth in covered wages) that provides a higher replacement rate (proportion of benefits to pre-retirement earnings) for persons with lower average pre-retirement earnings, in order to assist lower income families cover basic living needs. The amount of the primary benefit is always more for workers with a higher lifetime earnings covered by social security, however, than for those with a lower covered lifetime earnings. Dependent and survivor benefits are a proportion of the primary benefit amount. For a low-wage earner who always earned the federal minimum wage and retired at age 65, the program is designed to replace about 56 percent of earnings; for workers who always earned the maximum taxable amount under social security, benefits would replace 27 percent of pre-retirement earnings (Social Security Administration communication, December 1984). Old age, survivors, and disability insurance benefits in 1985 are financed by a 5.7 percent tax on employee earnings up to a maximum of $39,600, matched by an equal employer tax.

For a more complete discussion of the background and operation of social security, see Ball, 1978; Schulz, 1985, chapters 4, 5, and 6. Research on the economic impact of the social security program is discussed in Aaron, 1982, and Thompson, 1983. An excellent discussion of the short-run and long-run financing issues is found in Munnell, 1983a and 1983b. See also National Commission on Social Security Reform, 1983.

3. National Commission on Social Security, 1981, p. 127.

4. Sproat, 1983.

5. Clark and Spengler, 1980, pp. 94-95. Between 1968 and 1976, even after adjusting for inflation, both normal and early retirement benefit levels increased over 50 percent. Adjustment of benefits for changes in the cost of living has taken place since 1975 (U.S. Congressional Budget Office, 1982b, p. 20). Although early retirement provisions attempt to be neutral in their actuarial adjustment, because of the usually higher earnings in later work years, and because these earnings would raise the benefit level above that based on earnings computed at age 62, the expectation is that rational behavior would result in continuation of work rather than in early retirement. The fact that for many workers it does not, has led one social security expert (Aaron, 1982, pp. 60-64) to characterize the effect as "puzzling."

6. McConnell, 1983a, p. 176; Chapter 5.

7. McConnell, 1983a, p. 177; Schulz, 1983, pp. 255-58. A number of companies have provided early retirement incentives as a way of cutting costs and adapting to change—Bethlehem Steel Corporation, Deere and Company, Firestone Tire and Rubber Company, American Telephone and Telegraph, Bank America Corporation, Eastman Kodak, and Sun Company (*Wall Street Journal,* April 24, 1984).

8. U.S. Department of Labor, BLS, 1984c.

9. Leavitt, 1983, pp. 3-4.

10. Schulz, *Wall Street Journal,* April 24, 1984.

11. Rosenthal, *Washington Post,* May 7, 1984.

12. National Commission on Social Security, 1981, p. 128.

13. Several reasons may explain a change in attitude about early retirement. There is some evidence that inflationary uncertainties have slowed slightly the pace of early retirement (Schulz, 1983, p. 254; Morgan, 1981). Employees may also be more aware of the implications of increasing longevity. In 1900, for example, when average life expectancy for men was 48.2 years,

about 6.5 percent of life expectancy was spent in retirement. In 1980, with a life expectancy of 68.3 years, that percent rose to almost 17 (Best, 1981, p. 8). How retirement time is used becomes a matter of more concern when 11 years are involved than when retirement years number about 3.

Employer concerns about early retirement relate both to monetary and lost skill costs, which can be substantial, especially with the "sweeteners" offered in recent years to induce retirement. A negative effect on employee morale and productivity has also been noted.

14. Eisdorfer and Cohen, 1983, p. 58.
15. National Commission on Social Security, 1981, p. 131.
16. Ibid.; U.S. Department of Labor, BLS, 1983b, p. 16.
17. Kingson, 1983; Svahn and Ross, 1983, p. 26; Thompson, 1983, p. 1428.
18. McConnell in U.S. Senate, 1981, p. 41.
19. National Council on the Aging, 1981, p. 125.
20. Tolley and Burkhauser, 1980, p. 97.
21. Root and Zarrugh, 1983, p. 21.
22. Paul, 1983b, p. 27; Paul, 1983a, p. 16.
23. Paul, 1983b, p. 54.
24. Kingson, 1983, p. 53.
25. Schulz, 1983, p. 260.
26. Svahn and Ross, 1983, p. 26.
27. Schulz, 1983, p. 260.
28. U.S. Congressional Budget Office, 1982a, p. 21.
29. Women's lower proportion of coverage is related to their differing employment characteristics. They tend to work in industries and occupations with low coverage and in smaller and nonunion firms, which are less likely to have pension plans. Greater work discontinuities and shorter tenure on the job, together with earlier termination from paid work, mean that vesting is also less likely for them than for men. When covered, because of these factors and lower earnings, pension benefits are lower than for men (Rogers, 1980; Schulz, 1978; Kahne, June 1981).
30. Rogers, 1980. A discussion of pension benefits in medium and large establishments of at least 100 or 250 employees (depending on the industry) is found in U.S. Department of Labor, 1983a, and 1984c. In the 1983 survey, 82 percent of employees were covered by private retirement pension plans.
31. For an excellent general discussion of ERISA and its relation to employment and retirement policies for older workers, see Munnell, 1984.
32. U.S. Congressional Budget Office, 1982b, p. 30.
33. McConnell, 1983a, p. 181; U.S. Congressional Budget Office, 1982b, pp. 30–31.
34. U.S. House of Representatives, 1982a.
35. A 1978 regulation stated that employers "are not bound to credit years of service worked beyond age 65 to final pension benefits" (Batten, 1981). In July 1984, the Equal Employment Opportunity Commission ruled that workers were entitled to accrue private pension credits after age 65 (*Wall Street Journal*, July 2, 1984).
36. Rones, 1980, p. 15.
37. Stone, 1980, p. 32.
38. U.S. Congressional Budget Office, 1982b, p. 31.
39. Rones, 1978, p. 10.
40. Whittaker, 1980, p. 7.
41. Shroeder, 1982, p. ix.
42. Gould correspondence, 1982.
43. Reduced-hour schedules, sometimes in formal programs and sometimes arranged informally, are becoming increasingly visible in state employment. In 1981, more than 35 states had permanent part-time work arrangements; job sharing was present in 19 states. Only two states had phased retirement programs in 1981; two more states adopted such programs in 1984 (Chapter 9). The purposes of reduced-hour scheduling has been to attract and retain skilled labor, to increase employment opportunities for women, older workers, and the handicapped, and to seek productivity improvement. Increased job satisfaction, morale, and productivity, as well as reduced absenteeism, tardiness, and overtime, have been cited as program accomplishments, as has been an expansion of employment opportunities for groups of workers. For a description of arrangements in individual states, see Long and Post, 1981.

44. For two excellent discussions of historical background on federal policy on reduced hours, see Ittner, 1984, and Nemirow, 1984 (and references).
45. Crowley and Huth, 1983; Nemirow, 1984; Mesa, 1984.
46. Best, 1981, p. 84–87; Meisel, 1984, pp. 53–60.
47. Grais, 1983, p. 7.
48. Nemirow, 1984, pp. 179–80.
49. Grais, 1983, p. 7.
50. In fact, computation is more technical than this. The unemployment insurance programs in all but four states have an "earnings disregard," which permits some earnings, usually no more than the earnings of one day of full-time employment, before unemployment benefits are reduced. If earnings exceed the amount of the "disregard," benefits are generally reduced one dollar for each dollar earned. No partial benefits are payable when earnings exceed the weekly benefit plus the "disregard." Under the present provisions, it is unlikely that partial unemployment benefits would be paid if employees worked more than two days in a week.

In four states (Connecticut, Kentucky, Nevada, and Washington), the earnings "disregard" is based on a fraction of wages ($\frac{1}{3}$, $\frac{1}{5}$, $\frac{1}{4}$, $\frac{1}{4}$, respectively). After adjusting for this, unemployment insurance benefits are reduced by a fraction equal to one minus the fraction of wages in the "disregard." Benefits cease when earnings exceed the weekly benefit amount in one state (Nevada) or a little more than this, in the others. The "disregard" amount is larger than in the first model and the marginal tax rate on earnings (that is, benefit reduction for each dollar of earnings) is less than 100 percent. In these states, there is thus somewhat more incentive for a worker to work reduced hours and receive partial unemployment benefits. But partial benefits here, too, are ineffective if work hours are cut back for less than two days of the workweek (Hamermesh, 1978, pp. 233–38; Grais, 1983, pp. 135–40).
51. Hamermesh, 1978, p. 236.
52. This raises another issue of whether permanent part-time workers are eligible to receive unemployment insurance. The same criteria for coverage under the unemployment insurance system apply to part-time as to full-time workers. Employers pay the same federal and state unemployment insurance taxes for both kinds of workers. In general, voluntary part-time workers work long enough in the year to meet the monetary qualifying criteria. But they face a problem of establishing eligibility for benefits, which depends on their "availability for work." A few laws specify a requirement of full-time availability; most, however, permit administrative interpretation of the clause. Only about a quarter of the states interpret "availability" to allow payment to otherwise eligible part-time workers, if there is a market for their services at the time and wages they seek (Dahm and Fineshriber, 1979, p. 13). Clarifying the circumstances under which unemployment compensation is payable to permanent part-time workers (and other reduced-hour workers) will become increasingly important as part-time work becomes more prevalent.
53. Work sharing can take many forms, depending on the organization of the productive process and administrative preference — rotating layoffs, periodic plant shutdown, reduced daily or weekly hours. Most commonly used in states with work sharing programs is a reduction of weekly days of work from five to four (MaCoy and Morand, 1984, p. 4).
54. Nemirow, 1984b, p. 37.
55. Information in this section comes from California, 1982, unless otherwise stated. For further discussion of union views about short-time compensation, see Chapter 8.
56. Best and Mattesich, 1980, p. 3.3.
57. Lammers and Lockwood, 1984, p. 64.
58. Ibid., pp. 78–79.
59. Ibid., pp. 64, 79; Best and Mattesich, 1980, pp. 13–23.
60. Lammers and Lockwood, 1984, pp. 65–68.
61. Ibid, pp. 64, 74–76.
62. Ibid., p. 76.
63. Ittner, 1984, pp. 123–29.
64. In order to assure minimum uniformity of legislation, states are encouraged to consider a number of provisions: (1) definition of a "short-time compensation program" (for example, where workweeks have been reduced by at least 10 percent by a qualified plan, and where there is a prorating of unemployment benefits); (2) definition of a "qualified employer plan" (for example, where an employer or employer association certifies to the state agency that reduced hours are an alternative to layoff for at least 10 percent of employees, where health and retirement ben-

efits continue to be provided, where the union representative has consented to the plan). The Secretary of Labor's report is to cover financial questions relating to the impact of programs on the unemployment trust fund, administrative costs, and employer tax rates, and to assess issues relating to job preservation — especially for women and minorities, health and retirement benefits, layoffs, and effect on entitlement to unemployment compensation (MaCoy and Morand, 1984, Appendix).

   65. Nemirow, 1984, pp. 37–38.

8

Trade Unions, Part Time, and Reduced Hours of Work

Of all the forces molding and constraining the development of part-time work, none are more powerful than the views of unions and employers about its viability as a work form and its potential benefits and costs. Chapter 8 looks at part time and reduced hours of work in relation to the American trade union movement and its guiding principles. The chapter begins with a discussion of the size and strength of trade unions and the context and philosophy affecting expression of union views. It then moves to consider union attitudes about representation of part-time workers in collective bargaining agreements, and the current position of the AFL–CIO with respect to part-time and reduced hours of work, both as a collective bargaining goal and as a measure of social policy. It concludes with comment about union policies in the future with respect to part-time work for older and women workers.

Importance of Trade Union Views

There has been a decline in trade union membership or union density since the AFL–CIO merger. In 1980 unions represented only 20.9 percent of the total labor force, compared with 25.2 percent in 1956.[1] Is the decline due to an irreversible trend of structural changes in the economy that makes union views increasingly irrelevant to any discussion of a new concept of part-time work? Evidence suggests not.

It is true that there has been a lagging union membership in goods-producing areas that have been the traditional base of American trade unions (for example, in construction, mining, and electrical manufacturing), and also a general shift in the structure of the economy from goods-producing to service-producing industries. Although union membership is growing faster in the service-producing than in the goods-producing areas, it has not, with the notable exception of the public sector, where the proportion of employees in unions has risen from 12 percent in 1956 to about 50 percent in the early 1980s, kept pace with the rate of expansion of the industries themselves.[2]

Recent research acknowledges that a decline in the proportion of the workforce in areas that are traditionally unionized influences the ease with which new trade union organization takes place,[3] but questions the primacy of this factor in determining the degree of unionization. Rather than changing economic structures, this research suggests that it is the increasingly vocal managerial opposition to unions beginning in the 1960s, expressed through illegal as well as legal "positive labor relations," that has played a major role in explaining the trend, accounting for perhaps 40 percent of the decline in union density.[4] Also contributing to the decrease in union membership has been a drop in organizational real expenditures per non-union member.[5] Managerial and labor union behavioral activities, rather than inevitable economic trends, appear to account in large part for the decline in the proportion of the labor force that is organized.

But despite this declining trend of union strength, trade unions, representing 13.7 million workers in 1983 (see *New York Times,* May 31, 1983), exert a strong voice in both the industrial and political arenas. They work through a nationally effective political organization. On issues of industrial policy, the influence of their views extends far beyond the numbers on their membership roster. Perspectives of individual union members are readily transmitted and sympathetically reflected in the views of other family members, whether or not they themselves belong to trade unions. Moreover, the provisions of collective bargaining agreements affect non-unionized as well as unionized groups. Once a union shop is negotiated, the agreement applies to all workers in the plant, union and non-union alike. Collectively bargained policies are often the pace setters for non-unionized as well as unionized firms in an industry or region where the management aim is sometimes to maintain high employment standards and sometimes is directed to forestalling trade union organization. Trade union positions on social legislation and in collective bargaining wield a strong influence on the evolution and conditions of the industrial environment, including policies of part-time and reduced-hour scheduling of work. Unions are major contributors to the architecture of the working environment and, as such, play an important role in facilitating or hindering the acceptance of part-time work.

Context of Trade Union Views on Part-Time Work

Union views on part time and reduced hours and their priority ranking among collective bargaining goals must be viewed against the backdrop of the general philosophy that underlies industrial relations. It has been suggested by one labor relations expert that because of the influence of rapidly changing economic conditions and other environmental factors, industrial relations may be at a crossroads.[6] He notes three possible collective bargaining scenarios that could mold its long-run future directions: (1) a partnership approach, represented by developments in labor-management cooperation, quality-of-worklife programs, and concession bargaining; (2) an adversarial relationship, a consequence of organized labor's declining membership, which would set the course toward implementing a union-free sys-

tem; and (3) a "rerun theory" that foresees a continuation of past union prag-
matism responding to the conditions of the given economic environment,
typified by Samuel Gompers's philosophy that labor must focus on obtaining
"more, more, here and now."[7] Which theory will emerge as the most referant
to future industrial relations will depend on the course of economic and some
political events.

The dynamic and often volatile short-run currents at work are probably
poor predictors of what is to come. Rather, future union philosophy and industrial relations will be influenced, Derber suggests, by underlying factors
such as demographic and labor force changes, trade union membership
trends, the evolving role of government, and the impact of technological
developments.

Demographic trends (see Chapter 2), including the rate of growth of the labor force and its age and sex characteristics, will affect both the demand for
and supply of labor and attitudes toward specific collective bargaining issues.
Trade union membership is related to, but not controlled by, these demographic changes. In their recent study of unions, Freeman and Medoff note
that trade union membership has fallen in the past and rebounded with new
forms such as the CIO and National Education Association, new areas of
membership as in public sector unions, and new government supportive legislation, exemplified by the National Labor Relations Act.[8] There is no reason
why there should not be another resurgence as groups act to realize the economic expectations they feel are their due.[9] The complexion of future trade
union membership will undoubtedly reflect both on-going demographic
changes of working groups and industrial and occupational economic trends.
As an example, the number of women trade unionists is expected to double
over the next 10 years (AFL–CIO *News,* April 28, 1984) with some effect on
the trade union power of women and prominence of issues of interest to
them. But it will be even more influenced by managerial and union goals and
behavior.

The role and effect of government in matters of industrial relations provide a second important and imponderable factor. The degree of government
intrusion, the form it takes, and the consequences of its policies for unions
and for collective bargaining — illustrated in recent years by the declining rate
of success of unions in National Labor Relations Board elections[10] — all have
implications for the future of industrial relations.

Debate continues with respect to the impact of technology on employment
levels, needed occupational skills, and trade unions. Leontief's view (see
Chapter 6) that the current wave of technological change will result in a slow
but steady rise in the long-run unemployment rate is countered by the assess-
ments of Hunt and Hunt and Vedder, who predict that, despite job displacement by 1990, as a result of automation and the introduction of robots —
affecting welders and painters in the automobile industry, for example
— massive general technological unemployment will not occur, at least for
the near future.[11] According to this view, a number of semiskilled and unskilled jobs will be eliminated, but a number of new skilled technical and
white collar jobs will also be created. Skillful management of human re-

sources, including retraining programs, and a careful monitoring of robotics developments can prevent major employment dislocation. Whichever effect predominates, there will be a more intense focus on measures of change to adapt to and to counter the effects of technological advance, with consequences for employment, union membership, and union policies.

How these economic and political forces are played out will affect whether the approach of industrial relations will be cooperative or adversarial, and what will be the issues of paramount concern in collective bargaining. Although part-time work could conceivably be an issue under any of the three scenarios, the potential for its development is probably greater under the partnership or "rerun" philosophies. Here, negotiation could minimize the threat of competition between part-time and full-time workers. Maximized would be the potential of part-time work for enhancing life's quality and/or pragmatically lowering labor costs to save jobs in the face of short-run cyclical or long-run structural unemployment. Overall, the stronger the demand for workers relative to supply, the more advantageous the bargain that can be struck on behalf of unions.

Union Attitudes: Part-Time Workers and Part-Time Work

Attitudes of unions about part-time work are influenced by the structure of the industry or occupation, prevailing economic conditions that affect the available alternatives of full-time or part-time work, and the values of union leaders and members about full-time and part-time work itself. With a number of exceptions, trade unions have viewed part-time work with some skepticism. One reason for this has been the low status and pay of many traditional part-time jobs. This has resulted in a fear, sometimes substantiated by experience, that the introduction of part-time work will lower the economic status of an occupation and increase competition between full-time and part-time workers for the work that is available.[12]

A competitive tension can exist between full-time and part-time workers even when earnings and fringe benefits are prorated. Longevity of service, for example, can increase employer liability for vacations, pension payments, and earnings over time. Thus, given an opportunity, some employers will prefer part-time workers to fill certain jobs since such workers, thought to have a higher labor turnover, will be less costly to employ. Reacting to this, unions have sometimes supported a policy of limiting the availability of part-time work. They perceive the competitive nature of part-time work as intensified during periods of economic downturn, and as a means of masking the critical issue of pushing for full employment policies to counteract the general deficiency of demand for labor.[13] Part-time work can help in periods of labor scarcity, the unions claim, but it does not play a beneficial employment-creating role when the economy is suffering from labor surplus.[14]

Moreover, some unions view part-time workers as being difficult to organize and to involve in union activities,[15] because it is assumed that they have a divided commitment in their loyalties, reflecting their several spheres of activity. Because of the uncertainty among both employers and unions about how part-time workers will vote in an organizing election, they have often been excluded from the initially conceived bargaining unit, although they have sometimes been brought into the unit following a successful organizing campaign and election.[16]. In fact, a lower proportion of part-time workers than full-time workers are represented by unions.[17]

Part-time workers are not always excluded from the bargaining unit; estimates of the proportion who are unionized range from 5 to 17 percent of all part-time workers.[18] For many years, part-time employees in newspaper work, acting, writing, music, and teaching have been represented by unions. In education, for example, collective bargaining for teachers exists in about one-half the states, mostly in K–12 grade levels. A survey last conducted in the mid-1970s showed that although provisions vary by state, in general part-time positions are not excluded from the bargaining unit on the basis of work load, funding source, or voluntary status of employment. When part-time teachers (for example, substitutes or specialty teachers) are in the contract, they receive prorated earnings and benefits.[19] The National Education Association passed a resolution in 1981 in support of part-time work and in 1984 considered, but rejected, a proposal to prorate union dues (now totaling about $225 annually) as a spur to organization.

Airplane pilots and flight attendants also include a form of part-time work—job sharing—as part of their collective bargaining agreements. Part-time workers in traditional jobs in service industries and in occupations in hotels, restaurants, hospitals, and retail stores are routinely represented in union negotiations. The United Food and Commercial Workers, for example, has a long history and tradition of incorporating part-time workers into the union. A sizable percent of the Service Employees International Union (SEIU) work part time, and the union has established a District 925 for clerical workers, many of whom are part-time workers. The American Federation of State, County, and Municipal Employees (AFSCME) and the Newspaper Guild provide model contract provisions to assist in negotiation of contract clauses that relate to interests of their part-time members. A number of workers affiliated with unions that represent the public sector—SEIU, AFSCME, and operating engineers—are part-time job sharers.

Although the pay in many part-time non-professional fields continues to be low, it is higher for unionized than for comparable non-unionized workers. In some cases, the collective bargaining contract provides seniority rights giving part-time workers access to other benefits such as promotion, choice of shift, or vacation preference, to which they would otherwise not be entitled.[20]

Because of the strong linkage between part-time work and women's employment, it is important to understand women's status in trade unions as a prelude for thinking about reduced hours in relation to collective bargaining. The proportion of women in labor organizations is less than their proportion in the labor force overall, and their increase in union membership has been much less than has their increase in the working population.[21] Part-time women workers are even less well organized than full-time women workers. Why is trade union organization of women so low?

It has been shown that over 80 percent of the male-female difference in union membership can be explained by the fact that women work in less unionized occupations and industries than do men, have lower job tenure, and are less interested in benefit offers, such as health insurance, that are often less valuable to them than to male workers, because of coverage under a husband's policy.[22] The reason for the lower degree of organization in these areas lies partly in the historical origins and traditional strongholds of American unions, which have been the skilled blue collar trades rather than low status white collar jobs where women are more apt to work. Partly it may be related to the slower pace in organizing voluntary, part-time workers, heavily populated by women, because of some question about the strength of their trade union commitment. Thus, the difference between the degree of unionization of women and men is not caused by apathy or antagonism to unions on women's part nor to some gender-based reason why they are less active in union affairs, but rather to the characteristics of their jobs and the energy with which organization of part-time workers is pursued.[23]

A study of trade union working women in Sweden, which looked at the question of trade union activity in relation to full-time and part-time status, has some relevance here. The findings indicated no significant difference in trade union activity between full-time and part-time workers if homogeneous groups were compared.[24] The study concluded that the apparent lower trade union membership proportion and activities of part-time unionized women workers were explainable by their work in less well organized sectors of the economy and by differences in their demographic (women with preschool children) and socioeconomic (relatively more blue collar than white collar) characteristics. Blue collar workers, although more likely to belong to unions, were less likely to be active in union affairs. The research findings suggest that as organization of part-time working women proceeds in these less well organized occupations, there will be a net gain in union strength and effectiveness.

Organizing women workers, including part-time working women, will be more successful if unions support those benefits that respond to the interests of working women, whose work, although described as "voluntary," is frequently necessitated by family responsibilities. It is important that the Coalition of Labor Union Women (CLUW), which focuses on promoting issues of importance to women's well-being, gives part-time work a high priority as a trade union goal.[25]

Part time and reduced hours of work, although part of a long tradition, do not have an easy life within labor organizations. In good times, part-time weekly hours as a collective bargaining issue must compete with issues supporting higher wages or fringe benefits or an increase in leisure time through more days off (for example, vacations and holidays), or less worktime related to a shorter standard workweek. In the face of a recession, part-time work is sometimes viewed as intensifying the competition for jobs by increasing the supply of labor. To reduce the supply of labor, some negotiated pre-retirement, voluntary part-time work arrangements were abandoned in recent years — for example, in steel — and replaced by retirement benefit increases to encourage full and early retirement.[26]

At the same time, part-time work has appeal for specific working groups, occupations, and industries and offers, under certain circumstances, a preferable alternative to no work. In recent years, work sharing arrangements, accompanied by short-time compensation, have been viewed enthusiastically both by union leaders and worker participants. Unions emphasize their supportive role to other employment-generating measures that are to be simultaneously undertaken by government.

Traditional attitudes, however, especially those which have evolved from past negative experience, do not change easily. This is particularly true for the majority of workers for whom a full-time wage is necessary to support a family. Thus, a discussion of union views about reduced hours must consider not only the interests and needs of workers for work schedule flexibility, and the contribution of part-time work as a union goal for increasing the appeal of union membership, but also the potential effect of part-time work on standards of work and on the availability of jobs.

This last issue will be explored in the next two sections by looking first at reduced hours as a collective bargaining issue designed to save jobs and then at trade union views with respect to state or federal legislation that affects the number of working hours.

Part Time and Reduced Hours of Work in Collective Bargaining

LAYOFFS VERSUS REDUCED HOUR SCHEDULES

Work sharing was initiated on a broad scale during the 1930s depression when mandatory work-time reductions accompanied by major wage cuts were introduced under the Hoover administration. Its most common type by far is a reduction of weekly work hours below normal to spread the work, and in this respect it is a form of part-time work. Work sharing sometimes also occurs as specific rotating periods of employment and unemployment, with payment of unemployment insurance during unemployed periods, or takes the form of division of work, normally found when piece work is used.[27] Historically, unions opposed work sharing measures in their collective bargaining agreements and elsewhere as a device for "asking labor to bear the major costs of unemployment relief."[28] In recent years, although present in a number of collective bargaining agreements, work sharing clauses have continued to be viewed by many not as a source of work schedule flexibility, but as a method of transferring to workers the burden arising from unemployment.

COLLECTIVE BARGAINING AGREEMENTS AND REDUCED HOUR SCHEDULES

A 1970–1971 analysis of provisions in 1,845 major collective bargaining agreements indicates that about one-quarter of them, covering 36 percent of workers affected by the agreements, provided for the possibility of work sharing in the event of a temporary cutback in employment.[29] Some clauses were introduced as a way of avoiding favoritism in application of hiring hall procedures when employment retrenchment occurred. About one-half of the agreements and over three-quarters of the work sharing provisions were in manufacturing.[30]

Even when work sharing clauses exist in collective bargaining agreements, however, they are rarely invoked (except in the very unstable garment industry), because there is no provision for income replacement. In general, when a cutback becomes necessary, unionized workers and firms have been more apt to use a specified layoff procedure based on seniority, rather than reductions in hours of work.[31] This reliance on layoffs, provided in about 80 percent of the agreements in the 1970–1971 survey, is more prevalent in unionized than in non-unionized firms and appears, at least until the mid-1970s, to be a tendency of growing rather than diminishing importance.[32]

A comparison of layoff and work sharing provisions in collective bargaining contracts in the mid-1950s and early 1970s — unfortunately last updated in 1972 — reflects this tendency to use layoffs as an employment adjustment device. In 1954–1955, 5 percent of major contracts with hours reduction provisions provided for layoffs to begin when reduced hours had been in effect for a specified period of time of four weeks or less. By 1970–1971, the proportion had risen to 23 percent.[33]

Speaking of the mid-1970s, Oaklander notes,

> Examination of the many collective bargaining agreements negotiated year after year in the unemployment-prone 1970s, fails to turn up innovative job security provisions. There is little sign of more intensive application of older provisions intended to bring increased job security such as dividing work and *reducing hours* [emphasis supplied], attrition arrangements, or advanced notice of layoff. Reports analyzing the contents of major collective bargaining agreements through 1976 indicated little intensification of benefits. . . . [34]

Bednarzik suggests that by the mid-1970s, fewer than one in five major agreements contained work sharing clauses.[35]

Why is there this preference for layoffs over work sharing when temporary cutbacks become necessary? Freeman and Medoff suggest that one important explanation is that the perspective of senior workers dominates union decisions, and this has been their preference since layoffs customarily reflect seniority.[36] Reinforcing this preference is the fact that the cost of the unemployment resulting from layoffs, in the form of unemployment insurance, is only partly borne by the firm where it occurs and is partly shared with other firms. With the exception of a few states, the general availability of unemployment insurance for full weeks of unemployment, not for partially unemployed weeks, is a third factor. Collective bargaining agreements do not provide for income reimbursement for the partial involuntary unemployment that accompanies this form of work sharing cutbacks in hours.

REDUCED HOURS AND WORKER/UNION PREFERENCE

Publication of government data on work sharing ceased just about the time that work sharing reappeared in some collective bargaining negotiations as an adaptation to economic downturns, and, for totally different reasons relating to gender role and lifestyle changes, a new interest in more flexible work schedules arose. What we know about the effect of these two recently converging forces on attitudes about part-time and reduced-hour arrangements in collective bargaining agreements comes largely from case studies and interviews with trade union officials, rather than from national surveys of collective bargaining agreements or work schedule arrangements.[37] More can be said, however, concerning the current attitude of workers and unions with respect to part-time reduced work hours.

First, there is undoubtedly an increased interest in flexibility of work scheduling, brought about not only by changing workforce characteristics but by the increased diversity in the way lives are being lived. Women need more flexibility in order to integrate family demands on time with their increased paid work commitments. Men, too, either because of changing or expanding home and social roles, or because of a growing importance of non-work–related activities in their lives, more often than formerly seek flexibility in carrying on their income-earning responsibilities. Not all workers favor part-time work, nor do they necessarily want part time as a permanent work arrangement. A 1980 Gallup Poll, for example, showed that 59 percent of the 1,600 men and women surveyed were in favor of more flexible work hours, but only 19 percent wanted more part-time work.

At the same time, women continue to plead — or demand — release from the rigidity of full-time work hours when children are young and when elderly parents in later years require care, even though their commitment to continuous paid work throughout their lives is growing.[38] It is not at all clear that individual workers are aware of the variety of reduced-hour work schedules that exist or of the ways in which full-time and part-time scheduling could be integrated over the course of a work life. That is not surprising, since the broad experience resulting from reduced work hours, including prorated earnings and benefits, has taken place largely in relation to temporary employment retrenchment, rather than in response to a fostering of flexibility in worktime arrangements.

Two simultaneous currents seem to be operating at present within the union movement. One current is represented by those unions that readily include part-time workers and see them both as a group in need of union support and as a potential source of membership strength. These unions, aware that Old Concept part-time work is undergoing a metamorphosis, see a need for a better understanding of the alternative ways of structuring part-time schedules, the guidelines to follow in negotiating provisions for part-time work, and the education of union members about what is possible as a prelude to deciding what is desirable. They are interested in analysis and evaluation of the potential impact that an expansion of part-time work might have on union interests in career paths, training and educational leave, seniority, earnings, fringe benefits, child care, and job opportunities. They see part-time work becoming a more important issue as women continue to enter the labor force and join unions, and as older workers become more articulate about their interest in continuing a labor market attachment that is less intensive than previously.

A second current focuses in its policy direction on the general deficiency of demand in the economy and the need for creating full-time job openings to lessen the impact of cyclical unemployment and structural displacement. Within this framework, part-time work as a collective bargaining issue is for the present put on the back burner.

This union view acknowledges the need for adaptive response to changing circumstances. But the current policy emphasis with respect to working hours seeks change through the social arena rather than through collective bargaining and focuses less on the need for work flexibility than on hours adaptation to alleviate unemployment. The next section considers two approaches, each a form of reduced hours, though not of permanent part-time work, that are presently receiving official union support and attention.

Trade Unions, Part Time, and Reduced Hours of Work in Social Legislation

Social policy in relation to work displacement has developed slowly in the United States. There is little national data on the characteristics of layoffs, and historically the government has rarely intruded into industrial decision making. Except for work sharing arrangements directed to the problem of temporary layoffs, trade unions have largely focused their energies not on collective bargaining approaches to adjustment, but on support of public policy that minimizes the financial consequences of industrial change for workers. Decisions about initiation of that change have resulted largely from the operation of the market mechanism.[39]

In recent years the threat of foreign competition, the impact of the recession, and the potential for major dislocation posed by technological change have brought some revision in this market-mechanism–directed approach to job displacement. Trade regulation, government loans to preserve a faltering corporation, and discussions about a need for a national industrial policy are a few examples of an increased government concern about the impact of industrial change, both temporary and permanent, on society as a whole. This is the area in which social policies relating to hours reduction of work play a role.

REDUCED STANDARD HOURS OF WORK

The current union drive to reduce the standard hours of the workweek — unchanged since World War II — is a social policy, distinct from, but very germane to, a discussion of reduced hours of work as a form of work sharing.

In contrast to the ambivalence with which trade unions viewed work sharing historically,[40] they gave strong support to the Fair Labor Standards Act (FLSA) of 1938, which sought a similar goal of reduced worktime in a more acceptable way. Under the law, the workweek standard was set first at 44 hours, and in 1940 at 40 hours, the then-customary workweek length. Pay at time and one-half was required for hours worked in excess of this standard. The penalty pay provision, by encouraging new hiring rather than extending work hours of already employed workers, provided public policy support for sharing of work through lessened use of overtime. Average hours of workers on manufacturing payrolls fell from 44.2 in 1929 to 40.5 in 1932 and 38.1 in 1942.[41] Since then, weekly working hours in manufacturing have continued to hover around 40; in 1982 they were 38.9 hours.[42]

Although the standard workweek length has not been significantly modified since 1938, union support for its reduction has continued. In 1962, the Executive Council of the AFL–CIO called for amendment of the FLSA to provide for a 35-hour workweek, and in several subsequent Congressional sessions bills were introduced to bring this about. An All Unions Committee to Shorten the Workweek was organized in 1977, and in 1978 Congressman Conyers of Michigan introduced a bill that would gradually shorten the standard workweek to 35 hours, increase premium pay to double time,[43] and abolish mandatory overtime, a provision already existing in many collective bargaining contracts.[44] The bill provided for a reduction of earnings to accompany the fewer work hours, a position at variance with the traditional union position, and thus for the first time raised the issue of an "income-leisure trade-off," a stance that has been puzzling to many full-time male and also some female workers already concerned with making ends meet on a full-time wage.[45]

The proposed amendment to the FLSA, re-introduced into Congress in March 1983, provided for a stepwise reduction in work hours over an eight-year period, to 32 weekly hours (four days of eight hours). In early 1984 increased prominence was given to this issue of a reduction of the standard workweek, and there were reverberating echoes of similar demands among European unions.[46] The legislative form of the current American union proposal is still not firm. One suggestion would allow workers to accumulate credit hours, increasing each year, to be applied to a six-week vacation period taken when production schedules permitted. Both the United Automobile Workers (*AFL–CIO News,* March 17, 1984) and the Steelworkers Union (*New York Times,* April 14, 1984) have announced support for a shortened workweek as a way of spreading the work and offsetting employment losses caused by technological change.[47] Several unions already have a 35-hour standard workweek.[48] In 1982, 19 percent of full-time professional and administrative employees, compared with 6 percent of full-time production employees, had a standard workweek of less than 40 hours.[49]

Why this resurgence of support for a shortened standard workweek? What is the relationship between a reduced standard workweek and part-time work? Both options relate to fewer work hours and, in this sense, represent alternative approaches to designing a shortened work period. Each provides a mechanism for sharing of worktime to prevent creating two groups of workers, one employed and one unemployed. The goal of employment sharing among all job seekers is of growing interest to unions as they perceive the increasing job displacement effects of the current technological changes.[50] An AFL-CIO Committee, reporting in 1983 on "The Future of Work," saw "no simple and easy solutions to the difficult problem of job creation in a labor surplus economy."[51] The Committee recommended a variety of labor programs to combat this complicated situation, including an approach to a shorter workweek, reduced work hours per year, and higher overtime penalties to open up more job opportunities.[52] One of the goals of reducing the length of the standard workweek, achieved either through federal legislation or collective bargaining, is to prevent (or minimize) long-term technological unemployment. So, too, could the availability of more part-time jobs.

But part-time work and a shortened full-time workweek are not the same in their production or cost/benefit impact.[53] Although the two "hours" policies could be complimentary, they have yet to be recognized as such by the unions. Reducing the length of the standard workweek to mitigate the effects of long-term technological unemployment is currently the only hours policy receiving strong AFL–CIO support.

SHORT-TIME COMPENSATION

When the concept of short-time compensation (see Chapter 7) first came under discussion, it was resisted by unions because it emphasized a sharing of work rather than a job-creating full-employment philosophy, and because it posed some potential threat for cherished seniority provisions. But the increasing necessity for some response to high unemployment rates, the positive experience of the operating programs — and especially the existence of an income replacement mechanism that minimized income loss — became strong counterarguments that increased support for the state programs, from both union leaders and members.

In August 1981, after considerable discussion and with some continuing reservations, the national AFL–CIO Executive Council endorsed the principle of short-time compensation. Concluding that "On balance, short-time compensation with appropriate safeguards is a worthwhile approach," the Council's statement urged the adoption of several provisions when states saw fit to incorporate short-time compensation into their unemployment insurance legislation:

> (a) adequate funding for the unemployment insurance trust fund to protect the rights of all who are unemployed; (b) where workers are represented by a union, agreement with the union on short-time compensation; (c) wage replacement level of at least two-thirds of each worker's lost pay for up to 40 percent of the workweek; (d) full retention of pension, insurance, or other fringe benefits; and (e) protection against manipulation of short-time compensation that would discriminate against recently hired workers, especially minorities and women.[54]

With the exception of the recommendation on the wage replacement level, which continues to follow the standards set by the regular state unemployment insurance laws, provisions of short-time compensation programs are generally in conformity with these Executive Council recommendations.

The positive union response to the functioning California program is illustrative of the way state short-time compensation programs have been accepted by union participants. In California, about the same proportion of union members participate in the program (22.2 percent) as the proportion

of union members in the workforce (25 percent).[55] Their employing enterprises tend to be small and medium-sized manufacturing firms.[56] There has
been both strong union leader and worker satisfaction with the program and
an increase in support following an experience with it. Union business agents
have frequently taken credit for participation of the firm in the program and
have worked closely with company representatives in implementing its provisions. In the evaluation of the California program, more than 90 percent of
union representatives in participating firms felt that union members favored
the program, whether member views were categorized by age, sex, or minority status. A much lower proportion of union representatives of non-
participating firms reported that their members favored the program —
between 22.6 percent and 65.5 percent for comparable categories. Only for
the category of senior workers did there seem to be a lower level of enthusiasm for the program. But even this proportion rose considerably — from two-
thirds to 85 percent — once there was an experience with the program. In contrast, only 11 percent of union representatives of non-participating firms
reported a positive response on the part of senior workers.[57]

Union representatives saw as major advantages more leisure time, maintenance of union strength, increased group solidarity, maintenance of job
skills and job attachment of a skilled labor force, and a fairer method of adjustment than layoffs. They also reported that a number of fears were never
realized. Ninety-six percent of union representatives reported no evidence of
work speed-ups, 89 percent reported that fringe benefits had not been altered, except for prorating of vacation time, and 90 percent said there was no
negative effect on senior work pensions. There was no indication that the
senior/junior conflict was a major problem, and there was a sense that, although senior workers undoubtedly absorbed more of the costs of reduced
hours than they would have if a policy of layoffs had been followed, their historical gains were not threatened by the program. The increased proportion
of senior workers favoring the program after experience with it supports this
view and suggests that the program held some benefits for them as well, perhaps due to the temporary increase in leisure time. Overall, 85.4 pecent of
participating union representatives were sufficiently impressed with the program's advantages to be willing to recommend it to others.[58]

Union support for extension of the short-time compensation concept has
been strong. In the 1982 hearings on the federal Short-Time Compensation
bill (see Chapter 7), both the United Automobile Workers and the American
Federation of State, County, and Municipal Employees testified in favor of
the measure.[59] There is no evidence that the basic union tenet of seniority has
been weakened by short-time compensation programs. Rather, the serious-
ness of the recessionary employment climate, the presence of income reimbursement, and the good experience with operating programs, together with
the redeeming administrative features that include low administrative costs
and a guarantee of union participation in decision making, provide a combination of convincing reasons why unions and short-time compensation programs can co-exist without difficulty in conditions of less than full
employment.

Future Union Policies and Part-Time Work for Older
and Women Workers

Despite the obvious need and expressed interest of some worker groups for part-time work and the experience of some unions with it, both within specific unions and in union experience with short-time compensation programs, the general union view remains ambivalent about reduced-hour work as a trade union goal. Historically, the experience of unions with work sharing has not been a happy one, since wage reductions have commonly accompanied the reduction in hours, leading to a view that workers were bearing the cost of unemployment. In prosperous times, unions have chosen to press for other benefits for their members (a majority of whom are full-time male workers) over part-time work, which traditionally has had most appeal for the minority membership group of women. In periods of economic retrenchment, they have given highest priority to more general policies that create jobs and maintain full employment. In the event of employment cutbacks, with the exception of support for short-time compensation, they have traditionally favored use of collectively bargained layoff provisions according to seniority, which permit income reimbursement for total unemployment through unemployment insurance. Work sharing provisions in union agreements, which generally have no source of compensating income, are rarely involved.

The increasing threat of long-term unemployment — a predicted accompaniment of automation and technological change — has brought new vigor to a long-standing union interest in reducing the length of the standard workweek as a means of saving jobs. Union energies currently flow into this goal without at the same time seeking to increase a potential for extending voluntary part-time work, which might similarly increase employment opportunities.

The one area of reduced hours that has received strong union support is that of state short-time compensation programs. Although in their work sharing quality the laws challenge the concept of union seniority, in practice the benefits have outweighed the disadvantages, and support has grown with experience, among senior as well as less senior workers. The fact that the programs support a temporary employment retrenchment; that if a union exists, short-time compensation is introduced only with union approval; and that with compensation, income loss is not large, and is compensated for in part by the temporarily increased leisure, combine to give a high level of worker satisfaction with the program. This is so even though there has been some redistribution of income from senior to junior work sharers.

The short-time compensation experience has some important implications for thinking about union policies with respect to part-time work. It shows that the responsibility of such scheduling is possible in a broad variety of occupations, including assembly line work of skilled and semiskilled workers, groups that hitherto have had little experience with part-time work. And it exemplifies how, with a cooperative union-management approach, it is possible to implement a well-received program of part-time work that functions without competition among several categories of workers.

In an era where unions face a labor market with a changing occupational and industrial composition and emerging new emphases in the sex and age characteristics of the working population, innovative thinking not only about techniques of organization but about issues that will attract unorganized workers to trade union membership is essential. New Concept reduced-hour work is one such issue. As a work schedule form it is compatible with occupational and industrial trends and has appeal for both older and women workers, two groups of growing importance in the labor market. It has a proven track record as a useful program of adjustment in the face of temporary employment retrenchment. Even without compensating income, it could supplement other measures fostering full employment that would help to adjust to the longer-run employment problems related to technological change. Union-management cooperatively developed scheduling arrangements, which would serve production needs as well as employee interests, could bring benefits to both union and nonunion workers as well as to enterprises affected by the new plans. More Old Concept part-time jobs at low pay and with few fringe benefits developed in response to employee needs could prove to be more competitive and less palatable to full-time trade union members than an alternative extension of collectively bargained New Concept part-time work.

Notes

1. U.S. Department of Labor, BLS, 1980, p. 412; U.S. Department of Labor News Release, September 18, 1981.
2. Wachtel, 1984, p. 384; Reynolds, 1984, p. 337. If bargaining associations that function much like unions (for example, National Education Association, American Nurses Association) are included, one half of all federal employees, 40 percent of state employees, and 55 percent of local government employees are organized (Reynolds, 1984, p. 337).
3. Freeman and Medoff, 1984, chapter 15; Freeman, forthcoming.
4. Freeman, forthcoming.
5. Ibid.; Voos, 1982, in Freeman and Medoff, 1984.
6. Derber, 1983.
7. Livesay, 1978, p. 85.
8. Freeman and Medoff, 1984.
9. Ibid., 1984, pp. 243–45.
10. Freeman, forthcoming.
11. Hunt and Hunt, 1983; Vedder, 1982.
12. Hourly rates of pay for equivalent work are lower for traditional Old Concept part-time than for full-time workers (see Chapter 3). Fringe benefits in traditional part-time jobs are also frequently lacking. For example, although elementary and secondary part-time teacher job sharers have acquired job security and parity with full-time teachers, faculty on college campuses, in these days of tight budgets, are aware of an increase in "off-ladder" part-time instructors who are paid at a much lower than full-time salary rate for their teaching and have few, if any, fringe benefits (Moorman, 1982a).
   It is interesting that Swedish trade unions, despite a difference in political philosophy and in trade union organizational structure, view part-time work with similar skepticism and for the same reasons as in the United States. In the author's discussions with Swedish trade union members and leaders concern was expressed about the substitution of part-time for full-time workers. Chemists' assistants, for example, have reported greater difficulty over time in finding full-time work because the openings had increasingly been filled by part-time workers. Despite

research evidence to the contrary (p. 116), many Swedish trade unions believe that part-time workers have a limited commitment to their jobs and to the union and thus represent a threat to union standards (Quist, Acker, and Lorwin, 1984, pp. 275–76).

13. Work in America Institute, 1981, p. 103.
14. Nollen, 1982, p. 126.
15. Wertheimer, 1984, p. 292.
16. Zalusky, 1983.
17. Nollen, 1982, p. 126.
18. AFL-CIO estimate in *Washington Post,* July 2, 1984; Nollen, 1982, p. 18.
19. Robinson, 1976, pp. 82, 88–89.
20. Zalusky, 1983. For example, communications workers at the Rochester Telephone Company have a contract that provides seniority for part-time workers, as do other groups in the telephone industry. The machinists' union at Lockheed has shift preference through seniority for part-time workers.
21. In 1980, although women were 42 percent of the civilian labor force, they were only about 31 percent of employed wage and salary workers in labor organizations. The percent of employed women who were members of labor organizations has increased only from 15 percent to 16 percent between 1955 and 1980. Reflecting their occupational concentration, over one-half of women trade union members belong to eight labor organizations (Marshall, Briggs, and King, 1984, p. 135; U.S. Department of Labor, BLS, 1983b, pp. 12–13; Estey, 1981, p. 9).
22. Freeman and Medoff, 1984, pp. 28–29.
23. In fact, there are several illustrations of the strong union commitment of part-time workers. Part-time members of the SEIU have sometimes led union organizing drives. One recent survey found that part-time nurses were just as militant and cohesive a group as full-time nurses in their behavior response to two hypothetical problems posed abut their work situation. One union representative attributed the strong pro-union response of these part-time workers to the prorating of dues on the basis of weekly hours of work, and even more, to the high level of professional commitment of part-time nurses (Moorman, 1982b, pp. 10–11).
24. Sundström, 1982. Eighty-one percent of full-time employed women in Sweden and 69 percent of part-time employed women are trade union members. Their "trade union activity" is reflected in attendance at union meetings during the 12 months prior to the study, self-report on their degree of union participation, and election as a union representative.
25. CLUW, independently organized in 1974, is now endorsed by the AFL–CIO (Marshall, Briggs, and King, 1984, p. 138) and functions within union structures. At its 10th anniversary convention held in March 1984, delegates adopted a list of wide-ranging resolutions, including ratification of the ERA, support for affirmative action, equal rights, pay equity, and child care, and opposition to "computer homework" (ch. 6, p. 88), a form of part-time work that includes a number of negative aspects of work associated in the past with piece work. A resolution in support of part-time work was noticeable by its absence.
26. Zalusky, 1983.
27. U.S. Department of Labor, BLS, 1972, p. 3.
28. Best, 1981, p. 3; Nemirow, 1984a, pp. 158–64.
29. U.S. Department of Labor, BLS, 1972.
30. Work sharing has been applied where the hiring hall concept is strong, such as in the longshore industry, and in the garment and performance trades. It has also been provided for a period prior to layoff in large contracts such as in auto, steel, and communications (Work in America Institute, 1981, pp. 91–92). Three-fourths of all agreements providing for work sharing stipulate a reduction in weekly hours during slow periods (Morand and McPherson, 1981. See also Nollen, 1982, ch. 4).
31. Henle, 1981. Application of these layoff provisions assumes a temporary cutback, where there is some retention of seniority and other benefits and the right of recall to the job. Permanent employment reductions trigger a different adaptive procedure that can involve major wage concessions to save jobs (Freeman and Medoff, 1984, pp. 55–57). But there is considerable ambiguity in distinguishing between a temporary and permanent job suspension when the cutback first occurs (Oaklander, 1982, p. 191).
32. Medoff, 1979; Freeman and Medoff, 1984, pp. 114–15; Oaklander, 1982, p. 190.
33. Freeman and Medoff, 1984, p. 116; U.S. Department of Labor, BLS, 1972, p. 24. The

1970-71 survey showed union participation to be much more common in the decision to reduce hours than to initiate layoffs (62 percent versus 23 percent). Unions were interested in retaining the option of modifying the period of hours reduction preceding layoff in response to improving or deteriorating economic conditions (U.S. Department of Labor, BLS, 1972, pp. 15, 30).

34. Oaklander, 1982, p. 190.

35. Bednarzik, 1980, p. 4.

36. Freeman and Medoff, 1984, pp. 115-16.

37. The Work in America Institute reports that since the 1975-1976 recession, *Labor Arbitration Reports* includes the index heading "Work sharing, to avoid layoff," an indication that this provision has become more common (Work in America Institute, 1981, p. 91).

38. Mallan, 1982; Oppenheimer, 1982.

39. Oaklander, 1982, pp. 187-90.

40. Nemirow, 1984a, pp. 164-65.

41. Best, 1981, pp. 3-5; Olmsted, 1983, p. 479.

42. U.S. Department of Labor, BLS, 1983b, p. 186.

43. Fringe benefits, rarely available when the FLSA was first enacted, now account for about 25 to 40 percent of employee compensation. Under the present penalty rate of time and a half, it can cost employers less to pay overtime than to recruit and pay wages and fringe benefits to new employees. The cost of an overtime hour is less than 120 percent of the cost of a straight time hour (Testimony of Oswald, AFL-CIO, reported in Bureau of National Affairs, 1979, p. A-12).

44. Bureau of National Affairs, No. 206, p. A-12.

45. Whittaker, 1979. The "income-leisure trade-off" suggests that at higher incomes some persons will be willing to give up some income in order to achieve more leisure, a leisure that could be taken in the form of a shorter work day, workweek, or work year, as more holiday or vacation time or as early partial retirement (Best, 1978). Unions question the assumption that workers have the luxury of thinking in these terms. An important issue in this debate is whether, given more stability in job tenure and a growing proportion of two-worker families, interest in this "trade-off" possibility will increase. At present, the union position with respect to reduction of hours in the standard workweek is that because of rising productivity and profits, no sacrifice of income should be required when the workweek is reduced.

46. In European countries between 1960 and 1975, unlike the situation in the United States, annual working hours decreased, due partly to a decrease in the standard workweek, partly to an increase in paid holidays, and partly to changes in employment structure that have led to more part-time work. The changes were made possible by a strong rise in productivity during the period. European unions continue to press for further reduction of the standard workweek to 35 hours and for reduction of overtime, as a measure to counter rising unemployment (Van Ginnekan, 1984, p. 35).

The West German I. G. Mettall Engineering Workers Union, the largest union in Germany, has negotiated an agreement with the metal working industry that provides for an average reduction in the workweek from 40 to 38 ½ hours beginning April 1, 1985. Workers received an immediate pay raise of 3.3 percent and another 2.2 percent is scheduled for April 1985. The agreement, which runs to October 1, 1986, is seen as an opening wedge to a 35-hour workweek in Germany (AFL-CIO *News,* July 7, 1984).

47. The UAW demand reiterates the union goal of reduced worktime through more vacation and holidays. It continues a 1979 tradition whereby 26 paid personal holidays were agreed to in collective bargaining to lessen the rigors of the assembly line and to create jobs for younger workers.

48. For example, the Hatworkers' contract with the Millinary Association, and the contracts of the Graphic Arts Union with the Chicago Lithographers Association, Hotel Workers with the New York Hotel Association, and the International Ladies' Garment Workers Union with the Coat and Suit Association (Testimony by Oswald, AFL-CIO, reported in Bureau of National Affairs, no. 206, 1979, p. E-2).

49. U.S. Department of Labor, BLS, 1983a, p. 16.

50. Congressman Conyers, in presenting his bill in 1983, noted, like Professor Leontief (see Chapter 6), that the impact of technology on long-term unemployment is growing. Over time, unemployment rates at peaks of economic recovery have been rising dramatically (U.S. Congress, 1983, p. E-594; Chapter 6, note 44). Conyers sees technological unemployment as un-

responsive to traditional fiscal and monetary measures, thus requiring other policies of adjustment (U.S. Congress, 1983, p. E-594).

51. AFL–CIO, 1983, p. 18.

52. Ibid., p. 19.

53. A reduced standard workweek or shorter daily hours could each have an effect on a number of economic variables — employment, productivity, labor costs, retirement payments, tax revenues, inflation rates (Bureau of National Affairs, 1979). In Congressional testimony, union leaders stressed the employment, income, and expenditure benefits flowing from the reduced standard workweek. Several labor experts questioned the certainty of these effects, however, and emphasized the advantages in flexibility and adaptability to individual enterprise needs that would flow from an emphasis on reduced hours, to be achieved through collective bargaining or publicly supported part-time work sharing.

54. AFL–CIO, 1981.

55. Lammers and Lockwood, 1984, p. 73.

56. California, 1982, p. 8.2.

57. Ibid., pp. 8.4–8.9.

58. Ibid., pp. 8.8–8.15. Arizona and Oregon show similar evidence of union support (St. Louis, 1984, p. 92; Hunter, 1984, p. 105; Paris, 1983, p. 7).

59. Ittner, 1982.

9
Enterprise Experience: Part-Time Work and Older Workers

Part-time work has been around for a long time, and thus it is surprising that little data exists to describe the experience of its several newer forms.[1] Partly this is so because the issues do not easily lend themselves to measurement. The benefit of increased job satisfaction and the cost of a more complex supervisory function cannot be readily converted to dollar terms. Yet enterprises do have a perspective about the usefulness and costliness of part-time work and the kinds of reduced-hours structures that serve particular employment and work scheduling purposes. This chapter will look at some of these issues in relation to the employment of older workers.

Employer Views on Part Time

In writing about employers' views, one authority on part-time work suggests that an employer decision about whether or not to institute part-time work is not a policy decision, nor is it made on the basis of a cost/benefit analysis.[2] Rather, the introduction of a part-time work schedule follows a pragmatic judgment that it will solve a particular problem with respect to the human resource contribution to production, such as a shortage of workers or of specific skills, or serve a desire to retain a valued worker. The adjustment to uneven or peak loads in production or service, for example, is sometimes made by hiring, on a part-time basis, workers or annuitants who have formerly worked for the company. Similarly, Rosenberg and McCarthy conclude from a study of 36 firms which adopted reduced hour programs that neither job characteristics nor firm size determine the decision about part-time work scheduling, but rather "a humanistic philosophy coupled with business needs play dominant roles." They note that reduced-hour schedules have been successfully adopted in a range of production occupations as well as in managerial, technical, and professional positions.[3]

Employers today maintain a cautious interest in, but not an enthusiastic advocacy of, reduced-hour work. Although they are neither convinced of its cost advantages, nor even of the wisdom of making that choice specifically based on costs, they do expect an increased demand for reduced-hour schedules. Managerial leadership, seeing the necessity of responding with equitable and economical policies when that increased demand materializes, need a fuller understanding of the implications of reduced-hour scheduling.

Earlier chapters have documented that the climate of interest in part-time work is becoming stronger, both because of changing labor force and labor market characteristics and changing values and preferences about the use of time. Accompanying these trends have been a number of case study analyses of part-time provisions for particular enterprises and working populations.[4] This chapter will not repeat the excellent interpretive descriptions of individual firm experience contained in these studies. Rather, the chapter looks more generally at some of the issues with which employers are concerned: the kinds of jobs for which part-time work is feasible; the cost savings and cost increases associated with part-time work; the impact on work performance of older workers; and the future prospects of part-time work for older workers.

Kinds of Jobs for Which Part-Time Work Is Feasible

Until the emergence of New Concept part-time work with generally prorated earnings and fringe benefits, the notion of part-time work conjured up a conception of low status, low paid jobs with no fringe benefits and with little opportunity for career advancement. As indicated in Chapter 3, early studies of part-time work indicated that jobs with discrete tasks, with functions that were repetitive or stressful, and those associated with uneven demand for goods or services were the most likely candidates for part-time work. These include such part-time jobs as hospital auxiliary personnel, retail sales clerks, and waitresses. A 1976 analysis of part-time occupational traits questioned this description, noting the existence of a number of part-time jobs with continuous work flow, and with considerable training and communications requirements.[5]

Since the late 1960s and 1970s, the emergence of new forms of part-time work has further expanded the kinds of tasks found to be compatible with reduced-hour schedules. The broader range of occupations offering part-time work sometimes resulted from social legislation that provided for work sharing accompanied by short-time compensation. Sometimes it occurred because of employee initiative in applying job sharing to a variety of similar or complementary blue collar or white collar skills.[6] Reduced-hour work was also extended in a regular New Concept part-time mode, rewarded with prorated earnings and benefits equivalent to that of full-time work. Such structures also responded to the needs of older workers gradually moving into retirement.

WORK SHARING WITH SHORT-TIME COMPENSATION

One of the major lessons of the work sharing/short-time compensation experience of California is that this form of reduced-hour work, averaging one day of a traditional full-time workweek in 1982, is compatible with assembly line production. For the fiscal year ending June 30, 1980, for example, 45.0 percent of short-time compensation employers were in manufacturing, a much higher proportion than was found either for regular unemployment insurance employers (11.4 percent) or for all employers in the state (7.9 percent). Because of the large size of manufacturing firms, the variation in the proportion was even greater when work sharing claimants were compared. For example, 80.3 percent of work sharing claimants worked in manufacturing, compared with 31.7 percent of all regular unemployment insurance claimants. The occupational distribution of claimants reflected this industrial pattern of usage. In 1980, almost 70 percent of all claimants were blue collar workers compared with about 40 percent of regular unemployment insurance claimants.[7] The work sharing experience of California demonstrates that discrete tasks are not a prerequisite for the scheduling of part-time work. In fact, the inter-relatedness of skills in the production process increases the value of retaining workers on the job and sharing the limited available work time, rather than resorting to layoffs where readjustments in dovetailing of worker functions is necessary.

Not all occupations are equally well served under work sharing with short-time compensation. The reasons do not have to do with a technical inability to adapt jobs to a shortened work period, but to particular provisions of a work sharing program and to characteristics of occupations in which the traditional connection of the worker is to the job rather than to the firm. In such circumstances, sharing of work when completion of the job results in work-time reduction is a less appropriate adjustment than are layoffs.[8]

JOB SHARING

Because job sharing has thus far been so largely a response to individual initiative (to permit child or elderly relative care, for example), the range of occupations where it is present still reflects the needs and preferences of individuals in those jobs. A number of job sharers are found in highly professional positions — physicians, lawyers, teachers, social workers, even middle-management administrators. At the same time, job sharing has been successfully applied in blue collar operative work, where reduced costs of absenteeism and over-staffing to cover it, reduced overtime, and improved worker effectiveness have been found to balance an added cost that comes with provision of fringe benefits. In one firm, for example, the absentee rate, which had been 7.6 percent, became 0.4 percent when workers were permitted to find a partner and convert to a job-shared position.[9]

Although there is a general belief among observers that job sharing is more useful for career-linked positions than is regular New Concept part-time work, evidence on this is mixed. Job sharing sometimes, but not always, preserves the authority that accompanied the previous full-time duties. In one company, a professional recruitment position requiring full-time attention, allowed for the effective division of responsibility in the shared position; in another, job sharing of duties of an administrative secretary resulted in an imbalance in authority between the two employees.

Job sharing is not limited to professional work. Indeed, the preponderance of job sharing is still in non-managerial low or mid-level white collar jobs, although at higher levels than standard, Old Concept part-time jobs.[10] In a recent national survey of reduced-hour arrangements among over 400 organizations, two-thirds of the job sharing arrangements were in manufacturing, sales, and health care industries.[11]

Gradually, an understanding is growing of the kinds of job skills that lend themselves best to job sharing. Job sharing seems equally suited to public or private sector positions, although at present it is more common in the public sector. Equally appropriate skills amenable to job sharing are those of a repetitive and stressful nature (for example, data processing), or those that require autonomy in highly professional work (for example, physician-in-training). Work that can be planned in advance, is of a non-crisis nature, provides an ability to delegate, and is without tight deadlines lends itself to job sharing. Managerial and supervisory functions offer no problem, especially if they are of a liaison or advisory rather than a direct overseeing nature.[12] The experience in one firm suggests that job sharing works best when participants work as a team, rather than as competitive individuals vying with one another for records of accomplishment.

REGULAR, NEW CONCEPT PART-TIME WORK

The reduced-hour schedules discussed above are easy to identify because of the distinctive program that gives rise to them (work sharing) or the distinctive way in which the part time is structured (shared job). These reduced-hour forms share a quality of "full-time-ness" attributable to the full-time *position* with which each is identified. Having this attribute means that the part-time quality of the job may represent a less radical departure from a full-time position than regular New Concept part time, easing its acceptance.

Regular New Concept part-time work does not necessarily relate to a full-time position. It is difficult to distinguish it from standard Old Concept part-time work without a knowledge of the specific earnings and fringe benefit attributes of the job. In the absence of general information about these financial rewards, case studies are the major source of information about occupations where regular New Concept part-time work exists.[13] Recent case studies center on a broad variety of work — a manufacturer of electronic test measurement instruments, an academic institution, a firm that manufactures computers and provides software applications services, a bank, a state insurance fund, a city port. The prevalence of regular, New Concept part-time work depends partly on the skill and bargaining strength of individuals who seek it, and partly on the responsiveness of employers to the humanitarian aspects of the concept, the potential benefit of part-time work for the firm, and the ability of the enterprise production or service process to adapt to such an alternative work scheduling mode. Within this frame of reference, employers are more willing to accommodate employees whose value to the firm has been proven; they pay attention in policy development to general precedent-setting implications — that is, how many others must receive similar treatment — as well as to implications for the individual worker.

PHASED RETIREMENT

The United States has very limited experience with phased retirement.[14] These are voluntary programs of gradual retirement offering older workers a reduction in working time in stages — daily, weekly, yearly — usually in the customary job and always in the customary place of employment preceding full retirement. As indicated in Chapter 3, a few companies offer potential annuitants, often those with long service, this kind of work in the months or years prior to retirement. The time period of the phasing can be limited — for example, four months prior to retirement — or it can cover two to four years before reaching retirement age. The non-work time is sometimes offered as additional weeks of vacation, and sometimes as reduced work days (one or two, perhaps) in the workweek, gradually increased over time. There may or may not be compensating income for lost worktime. Social security may be payable if eligibility is established and permitted income levels are not exceeded. Some companies adopt a policy that avoids adverse effects on future pension benefits, which often relate to earnings levels in years just prior to retirement.[15] For example, the pension may be based on the salary that would have been received if full-time work had continued.

Although providing a number of advantages to the firm, including a continued availability of skills and experience for training younger workers and for continuing productive roles, phased retirement plans are not widespread. The absence of role model programs and the focus on an alternative of early full retirement have undoubtedly contributed to enterprise hesitancy to establish phased retirement programs. There is also evidence of employee reluctance to participate in existing plans — this has been attributed to lack of knowledge about program benefits and concern about effects on power and status as an employee and on retirement benefits.

Phased retirement programs are much more common in Europe than in the United States.[16] They are often established unilaterally by employers, but are sometimes negotiated through collective bargaining.[17] Successfully functioning plans, which often continue full-time wages and fringe benefits, and always continue accrual of pension benefits as though wages and salaries were unaffected, exist in the insurance industry in France; cover all firms, including the self-employed and public sector in Sweden; and are available to both blue collar and white collar workers in manufacturing companies across Europe. These plans are not limited by industry or occupation.[18]

What this brief review indicates is that part-time work is much less constrained by occupational and industrial characteristics than is conventionally thought. Reduced hours of work have been successfully incorporated as work sharing and phased retirement in manufacturing industries as well as in service and clerical jobs. Job sharing, reflecting employee or employer interest, has been adopted both for part-time jobs in traditional areas and for a range of both blue collar and high status white collar occupations. Reduced work hours have been introduced in both public and private sectors. Support for an extension of part-time work scheduling is indicated by expressed employee preference, a humanistic personnel approach, need for labor resources to fill production and service needs, and supportive social policy.

Although employers expect reduced-hour schedules to spread, there is as yet no strong pressure for their expansion. Why? What can additional knowledge about costs and cost savings aspects of part-time work contribute to an understanding of their current prevalence and to attitudes about their future development?

Cost Savings and Cost Increases Associated with Part-Time Work

The next two sections discuss some issues in cost savings and cost increases, first, in relation to what is known about the functioning of part-time work, and then in relation to the known effects of age on the effectiveness of workers. The final section of the chapter discusses recent trends in industrial policy with respect to part-time work for older workers.

COST SAVINGS

Table 9.1 presents an interesting overview of economic effects of part-time work for firms, based on survey findings combined with qualitative impressions from case studies of permanent part-time employment and job sharing. Enterprises give a largely positive report on productivity of part-time work and associated costs of absence and tardiness. Overtime payments may be reduced when part-time work increases.[19] On the other hand, employers see the cost of scheduling operations as mixed in their effects and give a largely negative report about supervisory and record keeping problems. Unfortunately, only the direction and not the size of these effects is known.

Productivity and Absenteeism

The positive cost-reducing effects of part-time work on productivity and absenteeism presented in Table 9.1 are confirmed by other studies. Although the view of one authority is that part-time workers are less productive than full-time workers,[20] caused at least partly by the fact that fixed labor costs per employee (for example, recruitment and training) must be prorated over fewer work hours, in general, enterprises report that employees on reduced schedules are either more productive than their full-time equivalents or no less productive.[21] A variety of reasons might account for an improvement in productivity: part-time work attracts new skilled labor force members who are not available for full-time work; part-time work reduces fatigue and stress of the job and the use of worktime to attend to personal chores; part-time work can be accompanied by an increase in commitment and motivation and may even bring about some job redesign that results in a better match between employee talents and needed job skills; part-time work can improve energy application and work flow.

Related to the higher productivity, enterprises consistently report, as do 40 to 50 percent of the firms in the Nollen tabulation, that absenteeism is less than with full-time employment.[22] A 1976 study of federal workers reported lower resignation rates and less absenteeism for part-time than full-time

Table 9.1. Economic Effects of Part-Time Employment on User Firms

	Direction of Effect	Frequency and Size of Effect
Labor performance and costs		
Productivity	positive	One-quarter to one-half of all users; size of effect is not documented.
Absence and lateness	positive	40 to 50 percent of all users; size of effect is unknown.
Turnover	mixed	20 to 40 percent of all users have reduced turnover, but one-third may have worse turnover; economic impact is small.
Wages	positive	Wage rates paid to part-timers (compared to full-timers) are lower in 15 to 30 percent of user firms; gap is 8 to 30 percent, due to lower job levels.
Overtime pay	positive	70 percent of all users report less overtime; size of effect is unknown.
Fringe benefits	mixed	20 percent of all users have proportionally higher costs; 60 percent have lower costs because not all benefits are offered; size of effect is hypothetically $150 to $1500 per employee per year.
Capital and production operations		
Scheduling, coverage, communication	mixed	One-half or more of all users solve scheduling problems of part-timers with large, but undocumented, cost savings; one-third of all users have more difficult production operations.
Management and personnel administration		
Supervision	negative	35-50 percent of all supervisors have more difficult jobs due to part-time employment; cost impact is unknown.
Record keeping	negative	One-third of all users; size of cost increase is not documented but is probably small.
Recruiting	mixed	One-third of all users report each outcome; size of effect is unknown.
Training	negative	20-30 percent of all users have marginally higher training costs.

Source: Stanley D. Nollen, New Work Schedules in Practice: Managing Time in a Changing Society, New York: Van Nostrand Reinhold, 1982, p. 17.

workers.[23] Use of overtime is also often reduced because of the improved balance between demand for labor hours and labor hours offered.

What this experience suggests is that although the optimal workweek length in relation to productivity may not be known, and in fact may differ for different tasks and jobs, there is also no reason to assume that the present standard of 40 hours is an ideal workweek length for maximizing productivity. In fact, experience of reduced working hours indicates that, in a number of cases, it may not be. Indeed, the improved labor-management relationship that results from the process of developing a part-time work option can itself give a boost to productivity of a workforce and be a reason for offering part-time work.[24]

Labor Turnover Costs

Labor turnover that gives "mixed results" and with "economic impact [that is] small" (Table 9.1) for firms with permanent part-time or job sharing positions becomes a major cost saving factor under conditions of compensated work sharing. It is the minimizing of layoff-related turnover cost that plays a major role in the employer election of work sharing with short-time compensation.[25]

The California evaluation study provides some interesting comment on labor turnover costs. It describes turnover costs of a firm as having two components. The first, intangible costs, are related to the disruption and disorientation associated with changes taking place in a working team and can affect morale and eventually such factors as productivity and accident rates. These are difficult to measure. The second, tangible costs, include lump sum costs of severance pay and recall and the even larger costs of new hiring, including recruitment, selection, and training costs.[26] Although turnover costs are known to be high and with considerable variation by occupation, enterprises do not often calculate them. In a 1979 study by the Bureau of National Affairs, only 18 percent of the 137 personnel executives surveyed were found to calculate the cost of employee separations.[27] Turnover costs of those that did ranged from $500 to $7,000 per separation. A 1981 survey of 105 companies in southern California found that average turnover costs varied by type of work. They averaged $1,291 for office and clerical and technical employees, $3,611 for production, service, and maintenance workers, and $10,356 for salaried employees.[28] The same kind of variation in turnover costs that applies to full-time work applies to part-time work, with the amount of cost related to the occupational and industrial characteristics.

Work sharing in a short-time compensation program is a special case of part-time work, where the appropriate comparison of costs is between work sharing and layoffs, and not between part-time and full-time work. Maintaining the employment relationship for workers through work sharing means not only less separation and recall expense than under layoffs, but — more important — lower new-hire costs. It is this relative saving that makes turnover cost with work sharing a "benefit" of part time. The saving is more for some occupations than for others. It is greater in manufacturing occupations than in construction or mining, for example, because skills are more firm-specific in the former case, making new-hire training costs larger. The value attached to preservation of the work team, with its positive effect on morale, is also more evident in manufacturing than in industries where hiring hall employment is used and skills are more industry- than firm-specific. Turnover cost saving of work sharing in contrast with layoffs is particularly evident in tight labor markets, because with strong labor demand, laid-off employees are more apt to have found jobs elsewhere, thus triggering a need for a new recruitment, selection, and training cycle when rehiring begins. In the California program, not only are turnover costs relatively less with work sharing than with layoffs, but exist despite additional costs of fringe benefits that accrue with work sharing.[29]

COST INCREASES

Administrative and Supervisory Costs

Unlike productivity and absenteeism and labor turnover costs with work sharing, there is a general consensus that supervisory and administrative costs are often higher with reduced-hour programs. Job sharing is an exception, where administrative aspects are carried by the job sharers (see Table 9.1).[30] This is, of course, not surprising since reorganization of work must take place when alternative work schedules are introduced, and coordination and monitoring functions are greater when there are more workers and a variey of work hours to be meshed with production needs. What is noteworthy is that the costs are not perceived to be greater than they are; it is not unusual for employers to conclude that the savings in labor performance aspects — for example, absenteeism — more than compensate for the additional administrative costs involved.[31]

Fringe Benefits

Whereas the greatest cost saving aspect of short-time compensation programs is a lessened turnover cost, the expense of fringe benefits, if maintained at the same level as for full-time workers, constitutes the major cost stumbling block to expansion of new forms of part-time work.

Fringe or non-wage benefits constitute between 30 and 40 percent of direct labor costs.[32] In the Nollen tabulation (Table 9.1), 20 percent of surveyed firms had proportionately higher fringe benefit costs for part-time than for full-time workers.

There are several kinds of fringe benefits. Mandatory or statutory benefits, which comprise almost 30 percent of the employee benefit package and equal 9.6 percent of wages and salaries,[33] include social security, unemployment insurance, worker compensation insurance, and sometimes railroad retirement and sickness insurance benefits. Employer contributions for these, set by law, usually take the form of a payroll tax. Because of an income ceiling for social security and unemployment insurance federal taxes, above which the tax does not apply ($37,800 for social security in 1984, $7,000 for unemployment insurance effective in 1983), employer tax liability can be greater if two or more part-time employees with below ceiling earnings replace one full-time employee, some of whose income is above the ceiling.[34] This is not a major issue with respect to social security, since 94 percent of employees earn less than the maximum social security taxable income. The unemployment insurance tax ceiling is lower, however, and although the federal tax rate is also less (6.2 percent as of January 1985), the additional tax costs could affect more persons. The added fringe benefit cost for worker compensation is negligible. In general, in relation to individual employees, additional statutory benefit cost is not significant.

Discretionary, taxable fringe benefits, not required by law, and fully taxable as compensation, constitute about 43.4 percent of the benefit package and 14.1 percent of wages and salaries.[35] They include holiday, vacation, and sick leave paid to the employee at worktime pay rates. The benefits are easily prorated and are frequently offered to part-time workers on this basis.[36]

Discretionary, tax-favored fringe benefits, which constitute about 27 percent of employee benefits and 8.8 percent of wages and salaries,[37] may include health insurance, life insurance, dental insurance, pensions, or profit sharing. They are tax-favored in the sense that they are either not taxed or are tax-deferred. For example, in accord with provisions of the Employees Retirement Income Security Act of 1974 (ERISA), employers must include employees in qualified retirement plans if they work 1,000 hours (about half time) or more a year. In 1979 (the last year for which data are available for part time), 9 percent of part-time workers, compared with 51 percent of full-time workers, were covered by a pension or other retirement plan on their current job.[38] The benefits, often based on a proportion of the workers' earnings, are not a fixed cost, but they often have another disadvantage that can result in added administrative costs. Two-thirds of workers belong to a "defined benefit" plan; these include one-third of all pension plans.[39] Once vested (permanently insured under the plan), the employee's benefit rights are assured even after leaving that employment. The administrative burden for employers who have had a large number of part-time employees, charged with the responsibility of maintaining records and tracking them through the years, can be large.

Health insurance has another aspect that makes the cost particularly high for part-time workers. Health insurance premiums are a per capita charge to employers and therefore are a more costly proportion of wages as the number of working hours decreases. Moreover, these costs are rising rapidly, reflecting the continuing increases in the cost of medical care, and often range between $600 and $1,200 for each part-time worker. For these reasons, although most employers provide health insurance for full-time employees, only about one-half do so for part-time workers.[40] Prorating health insurance charges is frowned upon by the insurance industry because it can result in adverse selection and thus a higher cost of the plan if the employee elects not to participate and pay the remaining cost not covered by the prorated employer contribution. The problem has become more acute because these benefits are highly valued by workers, making benefit programs a competitive bargaining issue for attracting and retaining desired skilled part-time employees. The cost problem is particularly acute for small employers.

A number of alternative options are gradually being developed to meet problems of high fringe benefit costs. In addition to prorating benefits, where possible, or offering fewer benefits than to full-time workers, firms sometimes decide to "cash-out" discretionary benefits, paying higher wages and no benefits. Alternatively, it is becoming more common for employees to be responsible for paying part of the health insurance costs, thus lowering the employer liability. A third approach, growing in prominence, although still with some lack of regulatory clarity, is exemplified by flexible or "cafeteria" benefit plans. Here the employee receives a percent of wage or salary income as benefit "credits" and with this sum chooses among a variety of benefits offered. Again, there can be a problem of adverse selection, since health coverage tends to be selected as a benefit by those employees most likely to need it. Even though employers sometimes require at least minimum enrollment by all employees in the "low option" health plan to ensure some spreading of risk, this has not been enough to solve the problem of rising health costs due to adverse selection in coverage.

Development of defined contribution plans (two-thirds of all pension plans, although covering only one-third of all workers) provides another way of easing the financial burden of pension plans for employers. In this case, the part-time or full-time employee who leaves a firm is given a lump sum payment equivalent to the defined employer contribution (plus interest) made on the employee's behalf during the employment with the firm. The employee then purchases an insured pension with this sum and retains responsibility for its administration. Pensions become a form of retirement savings rather than accruing as a form of group insurance.

These evolving provisions reduce the employer administrative responsibility and financial burden of fringe benefits. They do so partly by constraining options available to employees and partly by removing them and their benefits from a group insurance mode. As a result, there is a greater willingness to provide benefits for part-time workers, but the benefit levels are lower (or premiums higher) for equivalent costs (benefits) than for full-time workers. The problem of offering fringe benefits to part-time workers is complex, as are the regulatory provisions affecting the insurance industry. There is need for close study and evaluation and dissemination of information, concerning both the present situation and developing trends, to assure that all parties both understand and are treated fairly as changes occur.

Work Performance of Older Workers

Assessing the potential of part-time work for older workers requires not only a knowledge of issues surrounding part-time work, but also knowledge relating to older worker effectiveness in the workplace. The importance of these issues stems partly from the fact that by 1995 about two-thirds of men and two-fifths of women aged 55–64, and perhaps 13 percent of elderly men and 7 percent of elderly women, will be in the labor force (see Chapter 2). They are also important because the current interest in preserving and creating work opportunities for older workers represents a reversal of a philosophy, dominant since World War II, that stressed the beneficial effects of older worker labor market withdrawal in order to open up job opportunities for younger workers with families to support. Accompanying this earlier social policy thrust was a somewhat understated, but nonetheless present, view that a decrease in workplace effectiveness was part of the aging process.

There is no doubt that aging, accompanied by changes in the nervous system, has an effect on both physical and psychological characteristics of human beings. Physical traits of muscular strength and lung capacity and sensory traits of vision and hearing are affected by age, and there is some reduction in short-term memory.[40] But the decline, particularly in areas of mental functioning, has in the past been much exaggerated for persons who are generally healthy. In fact, a number of newer research studies challenge long-held beliefs by demonstrating that intellectual growth can continue strong well into an individual's ninth decade.[42]

In considering the select population of older working persons, the issue becomes one of how the aging process affects productivity on the job.[43] Here, the range of responses depends on personal attributes of the individuals involved and the relationship of these to job characteristics and the human resource needs of the firm. The way these factors mesh determines how productivity relates to age.

In a review of past research on specific work-related qualities,[44] Julia French reports research findings that older workers are more successful participants in creativity development programs than their younger counterparts,[45] and that as managers they may be more cautious risk takers.[46] They may less easily undertake new training, but once trained, they tend to have greater employment longevity with the firm.[47]

Other studies, examining the effect of physical well-being on work performance, note that most jobs do not tax the physical capacities of workers, despite some decline in motor skills with age. The incidence of work injuries does not increase with age: in 1980, workers aged 55 and over accounted for 12 percent of worker compensation cases, although they comprised 14 percent of the civilian labor force. Once injuries occur, however, their duration is longer for older than younger workers.[48] Absence rates due to illness do not show great variation by age. In 1982, workers aged 65 and over had 5.3 work days lost per year, compared with 4.3 days for workers aged 25–44 and 5.6 days for workers aged 45–64.[49]

Studies of the overall relationship of productivity and age have tended to focus on particular work situations or categories of workers. Although few in number and frequently dated, those that exist show a remarkable consistency in their findings. McConnell refers to several studies of industrial workers, clerical workers, and supervisory personnel that suggest that age is unrelated to "performance appraisal ratings, efficiency, and overall productivity."[50] French describes several studies undertaken by the Department of Labor in the 1960s (including *The Older American Worker*, 1965) that note a broad range of productivity levels within age groups that sometimes overshadow the differences between age groups.[51] This generalization is supported by more recent studies.[52] Daymont concludes from his survey of research literature that as a worker ages there may be some decline in those aspects of productivity affected by knowledge obsolescence or physiological changes, and an increase in those dimensions that rely on maturity and work experience.[53] Such findings have led researchers to conclude that, in general, chronological age has little effect on productivity prior to age 60,[54] and that there is a large overlap in productivity performance among age groups.[55]

This is not to deny that a slowing-down process takes place with aging, but emphasizes that the effect is different for different individuals and is differently expressed, depending on the strength and combination of influencing qualities and how they interrelate with the needed tasks of the workplace. While longer illness duration, obsolescent skills, vision and hearing impairment, or general decline in effectiveness may occur during later ages, some changes may not be important for the job at hand or may be overcome by modifying the work task. Some aging effects can be compensated for by loyalty, motivation, and experience built through long association and identification with the firm, and reflected in lower mobility rates, stronger work commitment, and steady, consistent performance. It is the combination of all the negative and positive influencing qualities that comprises the overall productivity effect.

It is increasingly recognized that longevity is growing and health is improving in the sense that debilitating aspects of chronic diseases are lessening and are expected in the future to occupy a smaller proportion of the life span (see Chapter 5). Moreover, it is becoming more apparent that because of individual variation and workplace needs, a rigid index of chronological age is neither an accurate nor a useful device in delineating the effectiveness of work performance. There is increasing discussion about the use of a concept of functional age, which reflects the intertwining effects of inheritance and environment, and which seeks to assess in measurable ways the ability of a person to perform the job tasks required.[56] Functional job analysis is an old, respected tradition. Even the conept of functional aging is not new, but it has far to go in its evolution and testing as a tool of human resource policy. When that has occurred, it will no doubt turn around some of the outmoded views about chronological age and work performance that have resulted in distorted descriptions of the work capacity of older individuals and have been counterproductive to the labor resource needs of firms. A change in approach could result in private enterprise as well as social benefit.

Part-Time Work for Older Workers: Future Prospects

Despite the fragmentary nature of data about the monetary implications that accompany part-time employment of older workers, attitudes about retaining or hiring older workers are gradually becoming more positive. A 1981 survey of chief executives of major U.S. firms reported a significant change from the 1960s and 1970s, when the general view was that workers "peak" at age 50. Seventy-six percent of the executives in the survey said they would hire workers over age 50, and 80 percent expected that their companies would employ a larger proportion of older workers in the near future. Ninety percent believed that the on-the-job performance of older workers is as good as that of younger workers.[57] This section will briefly discuss the purposes of New Concept part-time work today as it applies to older workers, in order to gain some sense of overall trends and future directions.

Company policies — other than pension and retirement programs — specifically directed to the older workforce are not widespread, but their varieties are growing. Part-time work in its several forms is a relatively recent addition to the list.[58] In a 1983 development of a roster of plans that benefit older workers, half of the 231 identified programs were found to be for part-time or temporary employment, and these excluded work sharing, phased retirement plans (because they were designed to provide a gradual transition to retirement rather than to expand jobs) and job sharing plans (which were allocated to a "job redesign" category).[59] Most strongly represented were part-time plans for white collar workers — they represented more than 70 percent of the programs that were occupationally specific rather than focused on the general labor force. At the other end of the spectrum — and strongly underrepresented — were programs for skilled (7.5 percent) and other blue collar workers (20.3 percent).[60] Lest there be confusion about the technical feasibility of applying part time to these latter occupations, it must be remembered that reduced-hour work sharing programs are heavily located in blue collar manufacturing organizations. The potential occupational/industrial base for part-time work is broader than that exemplified in this study.

There seems to be some identification of different forms of part-time work with different purposes for which part time is used, and sometimes with different occupational (and industrial) areas. Just mentioned, and earlier discussed (in Chapters 7 and 8), has been work sharing, designed to preserve jobs generally, and affecting older workers largely in a sharing of existing work rather than in a capacity of creating new jobs.

A second purpose of part-time work is to provide a mechanism for extending worktime of workers whose technical or interpersonal skills or other qualities are important to the firms, by making scheduling more attractive. This could mean an extension of work life by permitting a phasing into retirement, rather than requiring an earlier sudden transition to full-time retirement. The same result could be achieved by providing regular part-time work or job sharing in an effort to retain or recruit older (or younger) workers who could not or would not work full time. This approach has been used in high-tech firms.[61] The fact that this was the most frequently cited benefit of firms using job sharing or phased retirement in the Andrus Gerontology Center survey[62] indicates its importance as a reason for extending part-time work in the future.

Phased retirement, which can be a mechanism for retaining the talents of older workers, also illustrates a third purpose of part-time work, a humanitarian purpose of easing a difficult life transition for those who must retire because of impaired health or because of enterprise preference. A decline in performance effectiveness, or a wish to lower the labor costs by reducing the proportion of senior workers, or a desire to open up opportunities for younger workers may lie behind the enterprise decision. Phased retirement, still rare in the United States, need not have an industrial or occupational limitation, although Paul notes that it is a popular part-time form in mature industries such as banks and insurance companies.[63]

Some researchers point out that voluntary part-time work is instituted with the purpose of giving stability to an otherwise volatile labor force. Fast food chains, for example, now recruiting older workers for entry level positions, hope to counter in this way the high turnover and absenteeism and tardiness rates of the teen-age segment of their labor force.[64]

Last, mention should be made of a growing category of temporary part-time workers, often rehired retirees, who work on a contract basis or in a consultant capacity. They provide a pool of experienced, temporary labor available to respond to short-term changes in the demand for labor, thereby ensuring a smaller but stable full-time labor force. Private pensions based on past service can be paid to these workers because of their temporary attachment to the company. At least one firm provides fringe benefits for a younger group of "buffer zone" part-time employees to compensate for the lack of job security in their positions. Although short-term part-time work attachment may represent a welcome connection to productive activity for some, the implications of the temporary nature of the work arrangement and the compensation structure for the "buffer zone" part-time workers in relation to that of full-time workers needs careful evaluation.

The new concept of part-time work is not at a crossroads; it is just taking off. It will grow more rapidly if the economic climate is one of expansion, increasing the value of having an expanded pool of experienced, trained workers, and reducing the possibility that choice of a part-time schedule will be viewed as a lack of work commitment and motivation. But some kinds of part-time work will grow also in a more restricted employment environment, since they have the humanitarian function of offering a gradual transition to retirement and providing work sharing during periods of employment retrenchment. Part time will work better if, as Root and Zarrugh attest,[65] there exists a "symbiotic relationship" of mutual worker and employer benefit. It will develop more easily if the potential threat of competition between full-time and part-time workers is minimized — perhaps through development of openings in consultation with worker representatives and careful assignment of jobs, or through a requirement that the option of part-time work be related to prior full-time employee status. It will expand more readily if workers become knowledgable about the available reduced-hour options and how each might be used, both within the work environment and in life planning.[66] Social policy provisions are not neutral with respect to reduced-hour work forms; they play an important role in facilitating or constraining employer and employee decisions.

Although having a cost saving "sense" is itself of value and is frequently used by management in its decision making, having a more precise measure of cost savings and cost increases of alternative work schedule options is even better. Careful evaluation of monetary aspects of part-time work and analysis of costs and benefits associated with different rhythms of production timing would provide a firmer foundation from which to consider worker preferences.[67] In the face of current demographic, labor market, and occupational and industrial trends, part-time work is sure to increase. The issue is whether it will develop "willy nilly" or whether its development will be monitored and guided to maximize its usefulness for employing organizations and workers, as well as to provide social benefits along the way.

Notes

1. Olmsted, 1983, p. 488.
2. Nollen, 1982.
3. Rosenberg and McCarthy, 1982, p. 29; McCarthy and Rosenberg, 1981.
4. Nollen, 1982; McCarthy and Rosenberg, 1981; Meier, 1978; Jacobson, 1980; Olmsted, 1983; Nollen, Eddy, and Martin, 1978; Swank, 1982; Work in America Institute, 1981; Harriman, 1982; Olmsted, Smith, et al., 1981. Case studies of reduced hours relate to both standard and regular part-time work, job sharing, voluntary work sharing, work sharing accompanying employment cutbacks, phased retirement, and some variant forms involving rehiring of annuitants.
5. Nollen, Eddy, and Martin, 1978, pp. 85-91.
6. Some public sector employing agencies have institutionalized this process by identifying the goals and tasks of a job and evaluating prospective candidates (both full time and job sharing) in terms of an ability to fulfill job needs (Nollen, 1982, pp. 197-98).
7. California, 1982, pp. 4.4, 4.8.
8. Work sharing with short-time compensation has not been highly used in the public sector in California, for example, partly because public sector employers do not build up financial reserves through an unemployment insurance tax contribution as do employers in the private sector. Although short-time compensation could be useful to them, the prospect of making additional budgetary allocations to reimburse directly the unemployment insurance fund for benefits paid, has not been a welcome one. Public employee disinterest in the program has been attributed to an absence of a tradition of labor-time reduction to compensate for a decreased work load, as there has been in manufacturing.

The relatively low use of work sharing in agriculture and in the building trades, on the other hand, is related to factors of job structure. In these industries, the employment connection ends when the job is completed. Workers do not have a steady attachment to one employer, and this makes it difficult to construct a work sharing arrangement within a firm. (California, 1982, pp. 1.20, 8.5-8.6; Macoy and Morand, 1984b, pp. 29-30, 72). For further discussion of factors leading to a firm's use of the California shared work program, see Tibbs, 1984.
9. Nollen, 1982, pp. 53-58.
10. Ibid., p. 53; Meier, 1978, pp. 39-40, 60; Paul, 1983b, p. 34.
11. Paul, 1983b, p. 14.
12. Meier, in Nollen, 1982, p. 61.
13. McCarthy and Rosenberg, 1981, pp. 113-28; Nollen, 1982, pp. 106-11.
14. In one inventory taken by the National Council for Alternative Work Patterns, fewer than 20 private sector U.S. firms were found to have phased retirement programs (Swank, 1982, p. 3). The recent national survey of the Andrus Gerontology Center found that one-fourth of the 427 organizations studied had phased retirement programs, over half of which were located in businesses of less than 1,000 employees. About two thirds of the plans were in manufacturing, sales, and health care industrial sectors (Paul, 1983 p. 9, 14). Two state governments, California and Iowa, implemented phased retirement options for their employees in 1984, and New York established a Mature Worker Unit to study and evaluate initiation of such options for state employees (New York, forthcoming).

Partial retirement, increasingly common in the United States, differs from phased retirement. It does not have to do with a gradual transition to retirement in the customary job, but refers to part-time employment in other work and often in another firm following retirement. The part-time job is often at a lower level than that of the customary employment, is often temporary, and makes no provision for fringe benefits (see Chapter 3). In contrast to the 25 percent of organizations using phased retirement in the national survey, more than two-fifths (42.6 percent) of organizations rehired their retirees on a part-time temporary basis (Paul, 1983b, p. 9).

    15. Olmsted, Smith, et al., 1981, pp. 16–18.

    16. Some researchers attribute the difference in European and American experience to limited knowledge of American employees about potential gains (Shkop and Shkop, 1982), or lack of information about employee preferences, or resistance to change on the part of employers (Lyons, 1981; Foreman, 1982). Others point to a difference of philosophy between Americans and Europeans (Morrison, 1979; Nusberg, 1980), whereby American policy lays stress on employment flexibility for older workers through legislation prohibiting age discrimination, while European policy emphasizes flexibility resulting from personnel practices, including work scheduling (Swank, 1982, p. 3).

    17. In their 1981 study of European experience, the National Council for Alternative Work Patterns identified over 84 individual firms, excluding those in countries with national plans, with phased retirement programs (Swank, 1982, p. 4).

    18. Ibid., p. 11.

    19. Olmsted, Smith, et al., 1981, pp. 3–4.

    20. Owen, 1982, p. 117.

    21. Harriman, 1982, p. 152; California, 1982, p. 6.35; McCarthy and Rosenberg, 1981, p. 36.

    22. MaCoy and Morand, 1984b, p. 26; Nollen, Eddy, and Martin, 1978, pp. 52–54; California, 1982, p. 6.35; McCarthy and Rosenberg, 1981, p. 33.

    23. Barrett, 1984, p. 27.

    24. MaCoy and Morand, 1984b, p. 26.

    25. Because work sharing is linked to an employment retrenchment, its evaluation by employers is often compared to an alternative option of layoffs. In the evaluation of the California program, 78 percent of the employers who chose to participate in the work sharing program instead of instituting layoffs, indicated that maintaining valued employees, was a reason that influenced their decision. (See also Motorola experience in Arizona, St. Louis, 1984, p. 93). One half used this adaptive mechanism because it was acceptable to firm managers, and 47.6 percent used it because of its potential for labor cost reductions relative to layoffs (California, 1982, p. 6.27; Mesa, 1984).

    26. California, 1982, pp. 6.7–6.9. Expenses of recruitment include the cost of advertising the opening, employment agency fees, cost of time involved in writing the job description. Selection costs have to do with screening and testing and checking references of applicants. Training costs involve formal and informal on-the-job training and could include lost productivity due to the use of newly trained workers.

    27. Ibid., p. 6.7.

    28. Ibid., p. 6.8.

    29. Ibid., pp. 6.8, 6.18.

    30. Harriman, 1982, p. 152.

    31. Nollen, Eddy, and Martin, 1978, p. 27. When asked about costs of the company phased retirement program, the Personnel Vice President at Volvo in Göteburg, Sweden, replied, "How do you measure human 'hardware' or a person's satisfaction with the job?" Plant officials estimated that additional personnel time needed to administer the partial pension and other leave programs were more than offset by the decline in absenteeism among workers (Swank, 1982, p. 169).

    32. Best, 1981, pp. 21–22; Chollet, 1983. Unless otherwise indicated, this section is based on material provided by Deborah Chollett, Employee Benefit Research Institute, Washington, D.C.

    33. Chollett, 1983.

    34. Ibid.

    35. Salisbury and Chollett, 1983, pp. 3–4.

36. Nollen, 1982, p. 104.
37. Salisbury and Chollett, 1983.
38. Rogers, 1980, pp. 10–11.
39. In a defined benefit plan, workers are guaranteed benefits based on earnings for a specified period or for total years of service. Employers' wariness of this fixed commitment of benefit income for part-time as well as for full-time workers is one reason for turning to defined contribution plans, in which liability is clearly limited to the agreed-upon employer contribution, made on the employees' behalf, plus interest.
40. Nollen, 1982, p. 104; U.S. Department of Labor, BLS, 1983a.
41. Welford, 1958, in Clark, Kreps, and Spengler, 1978, p. 927.
42. *New York Times,* February 21, 1984, pp. C 1ff. For example, John Horn, a psychologist at the University of Denver, reports that "crystallized intelligence," that is, a person's ability to use an accumulated body of general information to make judgments and solve problems, continues to increase throughout life, with smaller increments at later age levels. This can occur despite the simultaneous decline of "fluid intelligence"—an ability that involves perceiving and using abstract relationships. Mental alertness is nurtured by social and mental involvement with one's surroundings.
43. For an excellent discussion of productiyity and older workers, see Daymont, 1983.
44. U.S. Senate, 1982, pp. 50–51.
45. Taylor, 1968.
46. Vroom and Pahl, 1971; Taylor, 1975.
47. Meier and Kerr, 1976.
48. U.S. Department of Labor communication, 1984.
49. U.S. Department of Health and Human Services, 1982a.
50. McConnell, 1983a.
51. U.S. Senate, 1982, p. 50.
52. New York State, 1972.
53. Daymont, 1983, p. 11.
54. Birren, 1955, in Clark, Kreps, and Spengler, 1978, p. 927.
55. Clark, Kreps, and Spengler, 1978, p. 927; Daymont, 1983, p. 12.
56. McFarland, 1973, pp. 1–19; Sheppard and Rix, 1977, ch. 5, pp. 70–80. Functional criteria used to assess job performance are the standards and norms of specific occupations according to which the worker's job performance in a range of physical, mental, and interpersonal abilities is measured and compared.
57. Gollub, 1983, p. 4.
58. Temporary full-time openings filled through special hiring agencies or from a pool of company retirees, availability of training programs, job redesign, and job/worker appraisal programs offer ways alternative to part-time work for expanding work opportunities for older workers.
59. Both phased retirement and job sharing are included in the definition of part-time work used here. The former has a clear focus on older workers; the latter, although with a strong potential application to older workers (for example, in pairing with or teaching skills to younger workers), does not at present apply to older workers in large numbers (Nollen, 1982, pp. 156–57).
60. Root and Zarrugh, 1983, p. 10.
61. McConnell, 1983b, p. 23.
62. Paul, 1983b, p. 23.
63. Ibid., p. 13.
64. McConnell, 1983b, p. 23; Paul, 1983a, p. 5.
65. Root and Zarrugh, 1983, p. 5.
66. The low participation rate of older workers in part-time programs applicable to them (Paul, 1983a, p. 13), suggests that workers may not always be aware of the benefits offered. The increase in positive employee attitude that followed participation in the California work sharing program is an indication that experience with reduced-hour work can increase the degree of support for it.
67. Winston (1982), a recent addition to the economics literature, introduces readers to the complexities of the timing of economic activities by firms and households.

10

A New Concept of Part-Time Work: Prospects for the Future

We are living in an era in which change marks the movement of time — in demographic and labor force trends, in occupational and industrial directions, in technological change, and in values and life styles. But despite knowledge of our aging population, a concern with the potential skill needs in the labor market, and the growing emphasis given by society to quality of work and family life issues, we give surprisingly little attention to whether the institution of the workplace is responding to the new directions and values and needs of society. We continue to adhere to a standard 40-hour workweek, without assessing the relative productive efficiency of alternative work scheduling arrangements, or attempting a better fit between the interests of the working population and the timing of productive activities.

As we have seen, changing economic and social trends have been accompanied by the emergence, since the late 1960s, of several new forms of reduced hour schedules that constitute a new conception of part-time work. Growing demand for and supply of part-time opportunities, combined with emerging new forms that prorate earnings and at least some fringe benefits, create an environment that can only lead to growth in the use of reduced-hour schedules. It is therefore important to understand the benefits and problems associated with part-time work so that we can better guide the development that is sure to come. I hope that this book on part-time work will contribute to an understanding of what this form of worktime flexibility is and what advantages it offers.

Since issues become clearer when viewed in specific context, this study has focused on workers aged 55 and over, and in one central chapter, on the special case of women, for whom part-time work is not only useful in later life, but often essential at various times throughout the life span. The lessons of the experience, however, are more generally applicable. They could apply equally well to young women and men who seek part-time work as an accompaniment to education and training, or to somewhat older workers who, while gradually becoming less locked into full-time work as an unremitting course of life, experiment with breaks in full employment to gain further training, develop new careers, pursue an avocation, increase their role in the family, or simply take a break from the pressures of work.

In this concluding chapter, the major themes and information are summarized in terms of the questions first raised in Chapter 1. The chapter concludes by discussing what are perhaps the most important questions of all — now that we have a clearer understanding of the implications of part-time work scheduling, how does part-time work fit into the scheme of things? Where do we go from here?

What Can Be Said About the Preference for Part-Time Work by Older Workers? What Is the Evidence of Interest and of Apathy and Resistance to This Work Schedule Form?

CONTEXT

Demographic and occupational/industrial trends combine to make part-time work a major issue of interest (see Chapter 2). The population is gradually aging; by 2030 perhaps 30 percent of the population will be aged 55 and over. Changes are also occurring in the growth rates of different age groups in the labor force, influenced by these population trends, but also by decisions about paid work, work in the home, schooling, occupational training, and retirement. At present, it is expected that the proportion of older workers in the labor force at or over the age of 55 will be decreasing somewhat. Women in the future may constitute a slightly increased proportion of older workers. One of the reasons is that the labor force participation rate of older men is declining and, barring changes in conditions surrounding work and retirement, may continue to do so. The participation rate of older women, on the other hand, rose from 1950 to 1969 and has remained roughly constant since then. In 1995 their labor force participation rate is projected to be at about the same level as today. The combination of population and participation rate changes are likely to result in somewhat fewer older male workers and a relatively constant number of older female workers. Expected skill shortages leading to active recruitment of older workers and greater availability of more desirable part-time jobs could, of course, result in a larger number of workers coming from these age groups, thus altering projected figures. One question that might be addressed is whether it would be desirable to have more of these workers aged 55 and over working part time rather than continuing in full-time work or retiring. My own view is that where such part-time schedules can be developed without additional cost or with other compensating advantages for the enterprise, such a choice should become more readily available to older and other workers. In light of expressed preferences and the available data of experience with part-time schedules spelled out in the book and summarized below, it appears that benefits could accrue not only for workers, but also for employers and for society as a whole.

A second question has to do with projected industrial and occupational trends. In the next ten years, 75 percent of the new jobs created will be in service industries; among occupations the greatest growth will be experienced by service workers and those in professional and technical categories. Many of the new jobs will be located in areas where part-time work is already common (Chapter 3). In 1982, of all voluntary part-time workers, two-fifths were in service industries. One-fifth of all workers within service industries worked part time voluntarily. Among occupations, almost 15 percent of voluntary part-time workers were professional, technical, and kindred workers, and more than one-fourth were service workers. Presently, 30 percent of workers within non-domestic service occupations work part time voluntarily, and 12 percent of those within professional, technical, and kindred areas. For a large number of jobs in the expanding fields, structuring part-time work will present no difficulty.

Because of the strong and increasing representation of women in the civilian labor force, and the very high proportion of voluntary part-time workers who are women, the relationship between part-time work and women's employment deserves special attention (Chapter 4). An analysis of research about the work and family experience of women throughout their life span leads to two conclusions. First, it is inappropriate to give an age-categorization to women's interest in part-time work. It is true that older women may have a particular interest in continuing to work part time in later years because of their disadvantaged labor market and retirement income experience. Overall, however, the greater prevalence of part-time employment among females than males arises out of the life-long time constraints that women face performing dual roles of paid work and family and household care. Women's part-time work is not a signal of non-commitment, but of competing claims on time. The need for such schedules exists both for women in two-worker families and for single women who are family heads. Women's distinctive life experience creates added incentive for extension of part-time work scheduling with compensation equivalent to that of comparable full-time work.

At the same time, women's increased work participation also makes possible more part-time work for men. The fact that among more than three-fifths of married couples both the husband and wife are employed — up from 40 percent in 1960 — indicates the degree to which there is some continuing income even if one spouse elects to reduce working hours for a period of time.

OLDER WORKER INTEREST IN PART-TIME WORK

Preference polls, useful as a first approximation of interest in reduced-hour schedules, show that mature workers support the availability of part-time work options. A 1981 Louis Harris survey indicates that 73–79 percent of employed persons aged 55 and over had a preference for an option of working part time when they retired; more than half would prefer to do so in the same job (Chapter 5).

But interest in part-time work does not develop in a vacuum. It relates both to the influence of the work ethic and to prevailing economic conditions and social policy benefits and constraints that affect the rewards and the opportunities of work and retirement. It also relates to individual health, economic status, and life styles, and to how these factors interact with reduced-hour work schedules.

Research has demonstrated a relationship of full retirement (early or at normal retirement age) to health, economic status, and provisions of retirement programs. It is much more difficult, however, to assess what would be the level of interest in part-time work if it were more available in New Concept forms with prorated earnings and fringe benefits, guaranteeing career continuity in moving in and out of a part-time model. The pool of New Concept part-time workers would probably be larger and broader in characteristics than the present group. Some would be drawn from the economically secure, now working either full time or retired completely. Others would come from the group with low economic security or poor health who are now fully retired at early or normal retirement ages. For them, New Concept part-time work would be a feasible way to bolster income. The numbers of potential New Concept part-time workers would be greater if workers had a better understanding of the potential advantages offered by this type of work scheduling, and if colleagues and employers accepted them — like full-time employees — as a serious and committed career group. Advocates of part-time work are only gradually becoming aware of the aspects that influence preference. Current preference polls can only reflect the interest in part-time work as it exists; it cannot report what it would be if a new conception of part time was in place or/and part-time workers had the same status as full-time workers.

APATHY AND RESISTANCE TO PART-TIME WORK

Despite a strong expressed preference for various forms of part-time work, there continue to be a degree of apathy and some resistance to the introduction and acceptance of New Concept part-time work. Criticisms sometimes relate to work task coordination and smooth work flow, perceived competition of full-time with part-time work, and a lack of communication between full-time and part-time workers. When asked, older workers express a preference for part-time work, but they do not yet press strongly for its automatic inclusion as an employment option in discussions with management or in collective bargaining negotiations. Nor do they overwhelmingly elect to participate in phased retirement programs when the choice is available to them, perhaps fearing a loss of status or power, or the consequences of giving a negative signal that might be interpreted as a decrease in work commitment. Women more frequently make a choice to work part time, but they do not always give political voice to an interest in improved status for part-time work in the organizations that represent them.

Workers, union representatives, and employers are all enthusiastic about the beneficial effects of short-time compensation laws, which are, in fact, part-time programs that function in periods of employment slack, but the enthusiasm has not yet led to a movement for part-time work in other circumstances. Only a few unions give high priority to representation of part-time workers and the extension of part-time work. Union leaders tend to be skeptical about the union commitment of part-time workers. They tend to be concerned that part-time work will be used as a labor cost cutting rather than a time distributing mechanism. They worry that part-time jobs will have an adverse effect on labor standards and will constitute a competitive threat to the limited number of full-time jobs (Chapter 8). Currently, these factors weigh more heavily in policy formulation than do needs of particular groups of members or the usefulness of the issue in organizing the unorganized, many of whom are women workers. Collective bargaining clauses involving layoffs according to seniority rather than uncompensated work sharing are preferred as employment adjustment mechanisms. In social policy, emphasis is given to reducing the length of the standard workweek as a way of preserving jobs in the face of technological unemployment. Part-time work, which could be a valuable complement to such a policy, is not a high priority union goal. Employers foresee an increase in demand for part-time work, but remain uncertain about desirable forms and about its effect on the efficiency of the firm (Chapter 9). At present, part-time work has a legitimate but limited place among work schedule options.

What Are the Purposes and Forms of New Concept Part-Time Work That Influence Its Initiation? How Prevalent Is Part-Time Work for Older Workers? What Are the Findings About Part-Time Work Experience and About the Work Experience of Older Workers?

PURPOSES AND FORMS OF PART-TIME WORK

Part-time work builds on a multiple concept, its form often depending on its purpose and place of initiation (Chapters 3 and 9). Sometimes it comes into being because of a desire on the part of workers for a shorter workweek commitment when other responsibilities (home, family care, and so on), interests (school, leisure, other work), or health needs intervene. Sometimes it is initiated by employers who wish to attract older or other skilled workers, or who view the traits of some work tasks as particularly suited to such a structure, such as a job with peak loads of demand for a service. Part-time work can be a part-time job or it can be a full-time position divided as to task and/or responsibility. It can be applied in periods of full employment when skills are in short supply, or it can be well used, if carefully introduced, as a device to spread the work in periods of temporary employment retrenchment. Some part-time work applies equally well to workers of all ages; other programs are specifically designed for specific age groups, such as part-time jobs that reduce the stress of paid work during periods of child bearing and rearing or that ease the transition to retirement. Part-time work is also useful for persons who want full-time jobs but seek part-time work temporarily, while acquiring skills to raise the level of their earning capacity.

The forms of part-time work—whether standard or part of the new conception—share the quality of work hours of less than 35 a week. Standard

Old Concept part-time work is seen most commonly in particular areas of low status, low paid occupations and industries (trade, sales, and service). Fringe benefits and a potential for advancement are customarily absent. New Concept part-time forms, including regular part-time work, job sharing, work sharing under short-time compensation, and phased retirement, generally share a quality of prorated earnings equivalent to those of full-time workers and at least some fringe benefits. In phased retirement, non-work time is only sometimes compensated; the value of pensions, however, is often protected when work hours are reduced. Although still not widespread, New Concept forms can be found among individuals and groups of workers in a wide variety of occupations and industries. Overall, for working individuals, New Concept reduced-hour work provides flexibility in time allocation, some income, and the benefits of social interaction through work. For employers, initiation of a reduced-hour plan often relates to its usefulness in enhancing organizational efficiency and reducing operating costs.

Sometimes the different forms of part-time work are associated with specific purposes. Work sharing, with short-time compensation, is a major example of a program that links reduced work hours with unavoidable temporary employment retrenchment. The popularity and success of these state programs among both younger and more senior workers stem partly from the social support given by income that accompanies the reduced working hours, and partly from the careful planning and consultation that have gone on among public officials and interested private sector groups during the program's development.

A second specific purpose of part time is to attract or extend the use of skills or talents that are important to the enterprise. Part-time work, combined with phased retirement in the customary job, is used in this way. Job sharing and regular, New Concept part-time work often play a similar role. High-tech firms, in particular, have benefited from this kind of part time.

A humanitarian rationale of providing more work flexibility or easing a difficult life transition for those who are no longer able to work regular full-time schedules (for example, for health reasons) is a third reason why employers use part-time work schedules. In this case, reduced worktime relieves excessive time and energy demands and makes possible different new rhythms of interests and activities. Women's part-time work during school hours, as well as programs of phased retirement in banks and insurance companies, are illustrative of this purpose.

Researchers point also to the labor force stability sometimes sought by hiring an older part-time labor force where the turnover is very high, or where there are periodic, short-term fluctuations in demand for labor. It is not yet clear whether such hirings will become "New Concept" in their inclusion of fringe benefits.

PREVALENCE OF PART-TIME WORK

Although about 14 percent of all non-agricultural workers work part time by choice, it is not surprising that there is still little precise data to indicate the prevalence of New Concept part-time work. Government data does not distinguish between New Concept and standard Old Concept part-time schedules and rewards. The 1983 Andrus Gerontology Center survey found that one-fourth of the organizations had job sharing, one-fourth had phased retirement plans, and about two-thirds had some general permanent part-time employment. Job sharing was more frequently provided by large businesses; phased retirement was more commonly found in small firms. Among all reduced-hour employess covered by the survey, about 12 percent received the same benefits as full-time workers and 46 percent received some of the same benefits (see Chapter 3). New Concept part-time work appears to be particularly strong in white collar occupations — public employment and banking, to name two. Job sharing and regular part-time jobs are growing in another white collar area — that of the nursing profession.

EXPERIENCE OF PART-TIME WORK

The research literature on work efficiency often focuses separately on the effects of part-time workers and of older workers on enterprise experience; both are relevant to this discussion (Chapter 9). With respect to part-time work, one of the interesting lessons learned from the evaluation of the California short-time compensation system was that its success did not depend on the existence of discrete tasks or other expected occupational traits (for example, those requiring repetitive or stressful chores). In the 1980 fiscal year, almost half of short-time compensation employers, and an even higher proportion of employees, were in manufacturing; about 70 percent of all claimants were blue collar workers. In fact, the interrelatedness of production skills increased the value of retaining workers and sharing the limited worktime available. Although it is probably too early to say that *any* job is adaptable to a part-time mode — only evaluation of widespread experience can demonstrate that — the evidence does suggest the inaccuracy of the traditional notion that part-time work applies to only a limited range of low paid jobs (Chapter 9). Reduced-hour work is being successfully applied to blue collar skilled and semiskilled work and to highly professional positions, to public and private sector jobs, and to those with and without managerial and supervisory functions, if the supervisory duties are carefully defined.

The advantages of part-time structures lie partly in measurable cost savings, partly in increased employee commitment and satisfaction — as important as it is difficult to quantify — and partly in benefits and savings relative to the alternatives with which part time is compared — mandatory or early full retirement, full-time jobs, layoffs, or overtime.

Numerical data on costs are limited, but it would be wrong to conclude from this that costs and cost savings play an insignificant role in decisions related to part-time work. As in much of business planning, precise cost figures are not an essential prerequisite for thinking in cost terms. Both the initiation and structuring of part-time mechanisms are influenced by the direction and relative size of costs, as well as by their amount, when that figure can be determined.

On the basis of available cost studies, employers report that employees on reduced schedules are as productive, or even more productive, than their full-time colleagues, and that absenteeism and tardiness are less. Labor turnover costs, not a major cost saving factor for regular part-time work or job sharing, offer major benefits for firms choosing reduced hours with short-time compensation rather than layoffs. Added to these savings are the significant benefits for production efficiency and output that result from worker motivation, commitment, and satisfaction. Both the measurable and more subtle beneficial effects of part-time work can reduce costs and increase worker productivity.

There are also some additional costs attributable to part-time work. Administrative and supervisory costs are somewhat higher with part-time than with full-time work, although they are sometimes compensated for by the decrease in absenteeism that occurs. Fringe benefits that can easily be prorated offer no cost problem, but discretionary benefits are more complex. Employers are responsible for benefits in vested defined-benefit pension plans, even though the employee has long since left the firm. Health benefits, based on a per capita charge that insurance companies are loathe to prorate, present another knotty cost-add-on problem.

Several alternative approaches are being introduced to reduce employer liability in these circumstances. Sometimes firms "cash out" discretionary benefits, paying higher wages in place of a benefit. At other times, employers inaugurate a range of "cafeteria" benefits as an alternative to regular fringe benefits, whereby a percentage of wage and salary income is allocated for benefits, which are then selected by the employee based on designated benefit credits. With respect to pensions, defined-contribution plans are being offered as a substitute for defined-benefit plans. Under the new arrangements, the financial commitment of employers is limited by the contributions made. Employees who leave the firm before retirement age are paid a lump sum equivalent to the employer contribution plus interest, rather than a predetermined retirement benefit linked to the period of earlier employment. Pensions thus become a form of retirement savings, rather than accruing as group insurance. In some health plans, part-time employees now share the cost, or pay for some of the group benefits purchased. Such arrangements, while acknowledging the justification for relating benefits to productive contribution, at the same time respond to the reality that labor market attachment has become a necessary condition for health protection, for most members of society.

These alternative approaches for packaging fringe benefits represent compromise solutions. They recognize fringe benefits as a legitimate component of part-time employee compensation. On the other hand, the newer plans pay less than the amount provided as group insurance to full-time employees. The fringe benefit problem is not an easy one to resolve. In this experimental period, there is need for interchange of ideas among the insurers and employers and employees and for careful evaluation and dissemination of information about costs and benefits, so that the parties are clear about the implications of the plans they design and enroll in.

WORK EXPERIENCE OF OLDER WORKERS

If part-time work is at least as productive as full-time work, what about the productivity of an older working population? Does extending the potential work life into later years open up another source of adverse financial experience for employers? Would this extension, that would certainly mitigate the trend to early retirement, be disadvantageous to employers? There is no evidence that it would necessarily be so. A number of researchers maintain that chronological age is a poor predictor of worker productivity and that individual differences in productivity frequently overshadow the differences between age groups. There is increasing discussion about the value of using a concept of functional age to judge competence, an age that reflects intertwining effects of inheritance and environment, and which seeks to assess in measurable ways the ability of an individual, at any age, to perform the tasks required.

How Do Legislation and Social Policy Affect Part-Time Work for Older Workers? Does the Swedish Social Policy Experience with Phased Retirement Offer Any Lessons for the United States?

Federal legislation in its protective provisions relating to older and elderly workers (Chapter 7), both at work and in retirement, emphasizes equal opportunity in the labor market and partial replacement of earnings when full retirement takes place. It has given a lower planning priority to support of non-traditional work schedule arrangements, such as part-time work combined with partial retirement, and has not yet found a suitable way to respond to this particular interest of older workers in its social policy provisions.

Legislative provisions relating to social security and private pension benefits sometimes have a negative effect on part-time work. In social security, the "retirement test," after a minimum amount of earnings, currently withholds $1 of benefits for every $2 of annual earnings; this acts as a disincentive to all work, including part-time work. Under ERISA, if an employee works more than 40 hours for an employer who maintains the employee's retirement plan, or in a trade where there is a multi-employer plan, there can be a loss of private pension benefits. Similarly, the requirement of pension vesting for employees who work a minimum of half time has kept some firms from introducing part-time work and has led others to limit the annual hours that part-time employees can work. Although enacted for understandable and sometimes laudable reasons of ensuring enterprise flexibility or opening up jobs for young workers, these provisions have also resulted in limiting the part-time work that employees elect or employers provide. The ability to freeze pension benefits for employees hired after age 60 so as to limit costs of employing older workers, in an effort to encourage their being hired, similarly serves to discourage work, whether full or part time.

In an era of labor shortage, or where, as currently, social security financing would benefit from extending the time of paid labor market attachment of older workers, social policy emphasis is less on encouraging early retirement, more on providing incentives for postponing retirement. The recently enacted increased inducement to postpone retirement in the Social Security Act, as well as the increase in the age of mandatory retirement under the ADEA, both respond to this "extended employment" goal. Such provisions open up the possibility of an expanded part-time work preference in later years and in this respect support the movement for more reduced-hour work exemplified in state short-time compensation laws, part-time work embodied in the Federal Employees Part-Time Career Act, and the Federal Short-Time Compensation Law.

What is needed now is for social policy, influenced not only by the state of the economy but by the state of government finances and by demographic and economic trends, to address in a coordinated way the issues having to do with structuring more part-time jobs as a regular part of the work experience. Policy makers, in consultation with employers and union/worker representatives, must determine how best to reconcile multiple social policy goals that are sometimes at odds with each other. The governmental phased retirement program in Sweden (Chapter 3), available to workers between ages 60 and 64, provides one model of social support for phasing into retirement through part-time employment status. It merits careful study. For Swedish employees, partial pensions permit a continuation of the employment connection with some income, while reducing the stress of work hours. Employers have found advantages in facilitating needed employment adjustments and in lowering labor costs. There also appear to be favorable effects on production resulting from a greater output per work hour of part-time than full-time employees.

What Are the Growth Trends? How Does Part-Time Work Fit into the Scheme of Things? What Is Its Relation to Economic Policies and Conditions?

GROWTH TRENDS

Both the economic climate and the conceptualization of reduced-hour work options have created an environment that is conducive to an increase in demand for part-time work for older workers. There is evidence of strong interest and pockets of support for New Concept models. They are more apt to be available where full-time jobs are converted to reduced-hour work forms, often in occupations where part-time work has not before been common, rather than through an upgrading of jobs in traditional low paid part-time occupations. But although the numbers of New Concept part-time workers are still not large, there is a new sense of expectancy—an emerging consensus among federal policy makers, public sector employee groups, and large corporate firms that part-time work will grow in the near future, for all workers, and not just for those in their later years. It will undoubtedly grow more rapidly in a climate of employment expansion, especially if there is an effective organizational voice in its behalf. It will work better and be better designed in situations where there exist a cooperative working relationship and a perception of mutual benefit between the management and worker groups involved.

HOW PART-TIME WORK RELATES TO WORKER INTERESTS, WORK STRUCTURES, ECONOMIC POLICIES AND CONDITIONS

At its best, New Concept reduced-hour work is not a substitute for full-time work, but rather its complement. It offers valuable alternatives to full-time effort, for a variety of reasons and variable periods of time, over the course of a person's life, when time constraints are paramount. Mature workers are only one of several groups who benefit from its several forms. Although now a work schedule of great interest to women, as lifestyles and gender roles become more similar, it will be of increasing interest to men as well.

Nor is part time a substitute for a social policy to maintain full employment. In general, New Concept part-time work is most valuable when introduced into a full employment economy where labor skills are in short supply. It then attracts and extends available labor resources while responding to work-time preferences. But the experience with short-time compensation demonstrates that, when necessary, reduced-hour work has a broader applicability than this, providing a means for sharing of limited work in a way that prevents the creation of two separate labor categories, one fully employed and one fully unemployed.

Although part-time work has a long history in the United States, in its new conception it represents an innovative institutional structure that can apply to a wide variety of occupations. Its several forms permit a range of choices in designing reduced-hour schedules, and its success is linked to cooperative development by management and worker representatives who have an awareness of the mutual benefits that may result.

Within the larger societal economic framework (Chapter 6), although it would seem that the negative impact of inflation for those about to retire could be reduced if partial retirement were combined with continuation of job attachment in a part-time capacity, research evidence does not indicate that this has been common. That this did not happen in the recent high inflation period, despite the known effect that inflation has on income adequacy, suggests either that inflation-adjusted social security provided adequate benefits in relation to prior earnings, or that the level of dissatisfaction with the job or work environment outweighed the inflationary pull to continue in paid work. The effect of an absent third option — part-time work within the customary place of employment — cannot be measured; but had such work been available, the reported response to inflation might have been different.

The relationship of part-time work to the economic setting of unemployment presents a different picture. Because of the special circumstances of short-time compensation, such programs have been welcome and effective (Chapters 6, 7, 8, and 9). More difficult to design, but of equal importance, is a more permanent reduced-hour program, to be used as one of several measures of response to the diminished long-run labor needs that are likely to accompany technological change (Chapter 6).

Where Do We Go from Here? What Next Steps Would Advance Policy Development of a New Concept of Part-Time Work?

Where do we go from here, knowing that demographic and occupational trends support an extension of part-time work, that the preference and experience of older workers and of women indicate the considerable value that part-time work can have for them, and that benefits for the operating firm have been demonstrated as well?

There needs, first and foremost, to be increased understanding by both workers and manager/employers, and society as a whole, of what part-time work can be and can do, especially in view of the changes taking place in recent years in the conception of part-time work and how it is now being applied. Education in this area is an essential foundation for constructive and creative development of part-time structures and for generating political strength for furthering the implementation of new forms of part-time work schedules.

Second, a number of questions need to be addressed in occupational and enterprise case studies, in addition to those already dealt with in this book. Academic research and programmatic experimentation of reduced-hour plans developed cooperatively by worker and management representatives are both important. There is a need for more information about how integration of full-time and reduced-hour schedules in an enterprise affects both production and working relationships. Absolute and comparative monetary estimates of costs and benefits are still limited and rough, both with respect to alternative forms of reduced-hour work and alternative adaptive mechanisms such as overtime or layoffs. When more is known about costs and benefits, questions can be raised about how an expansion of part-time work might facilitate a more flexible schedule of production, and about possible effects of expanded part-time schedules on prices annd profits.

There are also unanswered questions about part-time workers. The literature suggests that the contribution of labor resources will be extended by more part-time options. Indeed it may. But though some workers will join the labor market or continue to work longer as a consequence of available part-time work, others may choose early partial retirement because of the attractive options. The impact of an enhanced concept of part-time work may change, but still not equally affect different occupations and industries. What will be the net effect of expanded part-time schedules on labor supply and employment and on their quality? How will the resulting changes affect income and consumer expenditures? With respect to individual workers, how will career "progress" (in any occupation) be measured and affected when the work history reflects a combination of full- and part-time work sequences? Will the part-time worker acquire status and respect and power equivalent to that of the full-time counterpart when New Concept part-time work is more prevalent?

Third, although an extension of part-time work must develop from the perceived interests of the parties involved, the federal government can do much to stimulate interest and investigation of the issue—by, for example, coordinating existing knowledge and providing guidelines and tax or other inducements to support experimentation. One useful next step would be for the government to convene a national conference representing employers, unions, policy makers, and researchers, to deal with part-time work, and the cluster of issues surrounding allocation of productive time for individuals and enterprises. Exchange of information about present status and directions of part-time work and identification of questions needing further exploration could begin a dialogue that has been too long in getting under way. Part-time work has been undervalued and the facts of its functioning often misunderstood. A national policy to foster a fuller understanding would prepare the way for the increased demand for part-time work that is sure to come.

Change is inevitable in our society, but progress is not. By responding to evolving demographic and economic trends, and designing programs with both production interest and working population preference in mind, the evolution of a new conception of part-time work could reflect both change and progress. This is an important institutional goal, affecting in one way or another almost every member of society.

References

Aaron, Henry J. 1982. *Economic Effects of Social Security.* Studies of Government Finance. Washington, D.C.: The Brookings Institution.

Aaron, Henry J., and Gary Burtless, eds. 1984. *Retirement and Economic Behavior.* Washington, D.C.: The Brookings Institution.

AFL–CIO. 1981. Statement of Executive Council on Short-Time Compensation (August 5).

_____. 1983. *The Future of Work.* A Report by the AFL–CIO Committee on the Evolution of Work (August).

Altmann, Rosalind M. 1982. "Incomes of the Early Retired." *Journal of Social Policy,* 11, no. 7 (July): 355–69.

American Management Associations. 1982. "Survey Reveals Growing Interest Among Managers in Phased Retirement." *AMA Forum* (January): 34–35. Ref. in Jondrow, Brechling, and Marcus, *Older Workers in the Market for Part Time Employment.*

Andrisani, Paul. 1977. "Effects of Health Problems on the Work Experience of Middle-aged Men." *Industrial Gerontology,* no. 2 (Spring): 97–112.

Andrisani, Paul, and Thomas Daymont. 1982. "Employment Problems and Policies for Older Workers: An Overview." (April). Mimeographed.

Appelbaum, Eileen. 1981. *Back To Work: Determinants of Women's Successful Re-entry.* Boston: Auburn House Publishing Co.

Baily, Martin N., and Arthur Okun. 1982. *The Problems of a Modern Economy,* 3rd ed., parts 1 and 2. New York: W. W. Norton.

Ball, Robert M. 1978. *Social Security Today and Tomorrow.* New York: Columbia University Press.

Bankers Life and Casualty Co. 1980. *Bankers Experience with Over-65 Workers.* Chicago.

Barfield, Richard E., and James N. Morgan. 1969. *Early Retirement: The Decision and the Experience.* Ref. in Gordus, *Leaving Early: Perspectives and Problems in Current Retirement Practice and Policy.* Ann Arbor: University of Michigan Institute of Social Research. Pp. 29–30.

Barrett, Nancy S. 1983. *The Part-Time Work Force.* Association of Part-Time Professionals, First National Conference on Employment (October).

_____. 1984. *Women as Workers.* National Conference on Women, The Economy, and Public Policy. Washington, D.C. (June 19–20).

Baruch, Grace, Rosalind Barnett, and Carol Rivers. 1984. *Lifeprints: New Patterns of Love and Work for Today's Women.* New York: New American Library.

Batten, Michael. 1981. *Toward a National Older Worker Policy.* Prepared for Senate Special Committee on Aging.

Bazzoli, G. 1984. "The Early Retirement Decision." Ph.D. dissertation, Cornell University.

Becker, Gary S. 1965. "A Theory on the Allocation of Time." *Economic Journal* 75, no. 3 (September): 493–517.

Bednarzik, Robert W. 1975. "Involuntary Part-Time Work: A Cyclical Analysis." *Monthly Labor Review* 98, no. 9 (September): 12–18.

_____. 1980. "Worksharing in the United States: Its Prevalence and Duration." *Monthly Labor Review* 103, no. 7 (July): 3–12.

_____. 1983. "Short Workweeks During Economic Downturns." *Monthly Labor Review* 106, no. 6 (June): 3–11.

Beller, Andrea H. 1982. "Occupational Segregation by Sex: Determinants and Changes." *Journal of Human Resources* 17, no. 3 (Summer): 371–91.

Beller, Andrea H., with Kee-ok Kim Han. 1984. "Occupational Sex Segregation: Prospects for the 1980s." In *Sex Segregation in the Workplace: Trends, Explanations, Remedies,* ed. Barbara F. Reskin. Washington, D.C.: National Academy Press.

Bendick, Darc, Jr., and Judith Radlinski Devine. 1981. "Workers Dislocated by Economic Change: Do They Need Federal Employment and Training Assistance?" *Seventh Annual Report of the National Commission on Employment Policy.* Washington, D.C. Pp. 175–226.

Best, Fred. 1978. "Preferences on Worktime Scheduling and Work-Leisure Trade Offs." *Monthly Labor Review* 101, no. 6 (June): 31–37.

_____. 1981. *Work Sharing: Issues, Policy Options, and Prospects.* Kalamazoo, Mich.: W. E. Upjohn Institute for Employment Research.

Best, Fred, and James Mattesich. 1980. "Short-Time Compensation Systems in California and Europe." *Monthly Labor Review* 103, no. 7 (July): 13–22.

Best, Fred, and Barry Stern. 1977. "Education, Work, and Leisure—Must They Come in That Order?" *Monthly Labor Review* 100, no. 7 (July): 3–10.

Birren, James E. 1955. "Age Changes in Skill and Learning." In *Earning Opportunities for Older Workers,* ed. Wilma Donahue. Ann Arbor: University of Michigan Press. Pp. 67–74. Ref. in Clark, Kreps, and Spengler, "Economics of Aging," p. 927.

Bixby, Lenore. 1976. "Retirement Patterns in the U.S.: Research and Policy Interaction." *Social Security Bulletin* 39, no. 8 (August): 3–19.

Bluestone, Barry, and Bennett Harrison. 1982. *The Deindustrialization of America.* New York: Basic Books.

Borzilleri, Thomas C. 1980. *In-Kind Benefit Programs and Retirement Income.* President's Commission on Pension Policy (March). Washington, D.C.

Bould, Sally. 1980. "Unemployment as a Factor in Early Retirement Decisions." *American Journal of Economics and Sociology* 39 (April): 123–26.

Bowen, William, and T. Aldrich Finegan. 1969. *The Economics of Labor Force Participation.* Princeton: Princeton University Press.

Branch, L. G. 1977. *Understanding the Health and Social Service Needs of People Over Age 65.* University of Massachusetts and Joint Center for Urban Studies, MIT and Harvard University, for Department of Health, Education, and Welfare.

Brenner, Harvey. 1982. "Assessing the Social Costs of National Unemployment Rates for the Older Population." *The Unemployment Crisis Facing Older Americans.* U.S. Select Committee on Aging, Hearings, 97th Cong. 2d sess. (October 8). Pp. 45–48.

_____. 1984. "Estimating the Effects of Economic Change on National Health and Social Well-Being." Study prepared for the use of the Subcommittee on Economic Goals and Intergovernmental Policy, Joint Economic Committee, U.S. Congress, 98th Cong. 2d sess. (June 15).

Brown, Clair Vickery. 1980. "Bringing Down the Rear: The Decline in the Relative Economic Position of Single-Mother Families." In *Women and the World of Work,* ed. Anne Hoiberg. New York: Plenum Press. Pp. 109–27.

Bureau of National Affairs. 1979. "Current Developments." *Daily Labor Report,* nos. 107, 206, 207 (October 23–25).

_____. 1981. *Daily Labor Report,* no. 102 (May 28).

Burtless, Gary. 1983. "Why Is Insured Unemployment So Low?" *Brookings Papers on Economic Activity,* vol 1. Pp. 225–49.

Cahn, Ann Foote, ed. 1977. *American Workers in a Full Employment Economy.* Subcommittee on Economic Growth and Stabilization of the Joint Economic Committee, 95th Cong. 1st sess. (September 15).

California, Health and Welfare Agency, Employment Development Department. 1982. *Shared Work Unemployment Insurance Evaluation.* Report (May).

Chollett, Deborah. 1983. *Setting Up Employee Benefit Packages: Issues and Trends.* Association of Part-Time Professionals, First National Conference on Part-Time Employment in America (October).

Clark, Robert L., ed. 1980. *Retirement Policy in an Aging Society.* Durham: Duke University Press.
Clark, Robert L., and Joseph J. Spengler. 1980. *The Economics of Individual and Population Aging.* New York: Cambridge University Press.
Clark, Robert, Juanita Kreps, and Joseph Spengler. 1978. "Economics of Aging: A Survey." *Journal of Economic Literature* 16, no. 3 (September): 919–62.
Clutterbuck, David. 1984. *Good Money: The Newsletter of Social Investing and Inventing* 2, no. 1 (January/February).
Conyers, Hon. John, Jr. (Michigan). 1983. "Reduced Workweek Legislation." *Congressional Record* (February 23): E594–95.
Cook, Alice H. 1977. "Working Women: European Experience and American Need." In *American Women Workers in a Full Employment Economy,* ed. Ann Foote Cahn. Subcommittee on Economic Growth and Stabilization of the Joint Economic Committee, 95th Cong. 1st sess. (September 15). Pp. 271–306.
Cook, Alice H., Val R. Lorwin, and Arlene Kaplan Daniels, ed. 1984. *Women and Trade Unions in Eleven Industrialized Countries.* Philadelphia: Temple University Press.
Corcoran, Mary. 1978. "Work Experience, Work Interruptions, and Wages." In *Five Thousand American Families — Patterns of Economic Progress,* vol. 6, ed. Greg J. Duncan and James N. Morgan. Ann Arbor: Institute for Social Research, University of Michigan. Pp. 47–103.
Corcoran, Mary, and Greg J. Duncan. 1978. "Work History, Labor Force Attachment, and Earnings Differences Between the Races and Sexes." *Journal of Human Resources* 14, no. 1 (Winter): 3–20.
Corcoran, Mary, Greg J. Duncan, and Michael Ponza. 1984. "Work Experience, Job Segregation, and Wages." In *Sex Segregation in the Workplace: Trends, Explanations, Remedies,* ed. Barbara F. Reskin. Washington, D.C.: National Academy of Sciences. Pp. 171–91.
Crona, Göran. 1981. "Partial Retirement in Sweden." Paper presented at the 22nd International Congress of Gerontology, Hamburg, Germany (July).
Crowley, R. W., and E. Huth. 1983. "An International Comparison of Work Sharing Programs." *Relations Industrielles* (Canada) 38, no. 3: 660–47.
Dahm, Margaret M., and Phyllis H. Fineshriber. 1979. *The Issue of Part-Time Employment.* Prepared for the National Commission on Unemployment Compensation (June).
Danziger, Sheldon, Robert Haveman, and Robert Plotnick. 1981. "How Income Transfers Affect Work, Savings, and Income Distribution." *Journal of Economic Literature* 19, no. 3 (September): 975–1028.
Danziger, Sheldon, Jacques van der Gaag, Eugene Smolensky, and Michael K. Taussig. 1984. "Implications of the Relative Economic Status of the Elderly for Transfer Policy." In *Retirement and Economic Behavior,* ed. Henry J. Aaron and Gary Burtless. Washington, D.C.: The Brookings Institution. Pp. 175–96. See also University of Wisconsin, *Focus* (Spring 1983).
Daymont, Thomas. 1983. *Worker Productivity, Employment, and Aging.* Report to Institute for Research on Educational Finance and Governance. Stanford University (January).
Daymont, Thomas, and Anne Statham. 1983. "Occupational Atypicality: Changes, Causes, and Consequences." In *Unplanned Careers: The Working Lives of Middle-Aged Women,* ed. Lois Banfill Shaw. Lexington, Mass.: Lexington Books/D.C. Heath. Pp. 61–75.
Derber, Milton. 1983. "Are We in a New Stage?" *Industrial Relations Research Association.* Proceedings of the Thirty-fifth Annual Meeting (December 1982). Pp. 1–9.
Diamond, Peter A., and Jerry A. Hausman. 1984. "The Retirement and Unemployment Behavior of Older Men." In *Retirement and Economic Behavior,* ed. Henry J. Aaron and Gary Burtless. Washington, D.C.: The Brookings Institution. Pp. 97–134.
Donahue, Wilma. 1955. *Earning Opportunities for Older Workers.* Ann Arbor: University of Michigan Press.
Douvan, Elizabeth. 1983. "Family Roles in a Twenty Year Perspective." In *The Challenge of Change: Perspectives on Family, Work, and Education,* ed. Matina Horner, Carol C. Nadelson, and Malkah T. Notman. New York: Plenum Press. Pp. 199–221.
Duffy, Martin, Evan Barrington, J. Michael Flanagan, and Lawrence Olson. 1980. *Inflation and the Elderly. Summary Report to the National Retired Teachers Association and American Association of Retired Persons.* Lexington, Mass.: Data Resources. (January).
Duncan, Greg J., Richard D. Coe, Mary E. Corcoran, Martha H. Hill, Saul D. Hoffman, and

James N. Morgan. 1984. *Years of Poverty, Years of Plenty: The Changing Economic Fortunes of American Workers and Families.* Ann Arbor: Institute for Social Research, University of Michigan.

Duncan, Greg J., with Mary E. Corcoran. 1984. "Do Women 'Deserve' to Earn Less than Men?" In *Years of Poverty, Years of Plenty: The Changing Economic Fortunes of American Workers and Families.* Ann Arbor: Institute for Social Research, University of Michigan. Pp. 153–72.

Duncan, Greg J., and James N. Morgan, eds. 1978. *Five Thousand American Families— Patterns of Economic Progress,* vol. 6. Ann Arbor: Institute for Social Research, University of Michigan.

Economic Report of the President. 1984. Transmitted to Congress, February.

Eisdorfer, Carl, and Donna Cohen. 1983. "Health and Retirement: Retirement and Health. Background and Future Directions." In *Policy Issues in Work and Retirement,* ed. Herbert S. Parnes. Kalamazoo, Mich.: W. E. Upjohn Institute for Employment Research. Pp. 57–73.

Employment and Training Report of the President. 1979. "Worktime: The Traditional Workweek and Its Alternatives." Ch. 3, pp. 75–92.

———. 1982. Program Activities in Fiscal 1981: Unemployment Insurance. Pp. 52–55.

Estey, Marten. 1981. *The Unions: Structure, Development, and Management.* New York: Harcourt Brace Jovanovich.

Federal Reserve Bank of Kansas City. 1983. *Industrial Change and Public Policy.*

Fellenius, Mats. 1984. *Partial Pension and Flexible Retirement Age—An Evaluation of the Swedish System.* Swedish National Insurance Board (March 24).

Ferber, Marianne A. 1982. "Women and Work: Issues of the 1980s." *Signs: Journal of Women in Culture and Society* 8, no. 2 (Winter): 273–95.

Fields, G. S., and O. S. Mitchell. Forthcoming. *Retirement, Pensions, and Social Security.* Cambridge: MIT Press.

Forisha, B., and B. Goldman, eds. 1980. *Outsiders on the Inside: Women and Organizations.* Englewood Cliffs, N.J.: Prentice-Hall.

Forman, Bernard I. 1982. "Gradual Retirement vs. Abrupt Termination." *Supervision* 44, no. 1 (January): 7–8.

Freeman, Richard B. Forthcoming. *Why Are Unions Faring Poorly in NLRB Representation Elections?* Cambridge, Mass.: National Bureau of Economic Research.

Freeman, Richard B., and James L. Medoff. 1984. *What Do Unions Do?* New York: Basic Books.

Fries, James. 1980. "Aging, Natural Death, and the Compression of Morbidity." *New England Journal of Medicine* 303, no. 3 (July 17): 130–35. Ref. in National Commission on Social Security, Reform, *Report,* p. 126.

Fullerton, Howard N., Jr., and John Tschetter. 1983. "The 1995 Labor Force: A Second Look." *Monthly Labor Review* 106, no. 11 (November): 3–10.

Gallup Poll. 1981. American Families—1980.

George, Jacqueline. 1984. "The Employment Effects of Technology on Women's Work." BA thesis, Wheaton College.

Ginsburg, Helen. 1982. "How Sweden Combats Unemployment Among Younger and Older Workers." *Monthly Labor Review* 105, no. 10 (October): 22–27.

———. 1983. *Full Employment and Public Policy: The United States and Sweden.* Lexington, Mass.: Lexington Books.

Ginzberg, Eli. 1982. "Early Retirement: Boon or Bane?" In *Work Decisions in the 1980s,* ed. Eli Ginzberg, et al. Boston: Auburn House Publishing Co. Pp. 77–91.

———. 1983. "The Elderly: An International Policy Perspective." *Milbank Memorial Fund Quarterly* 61, no. 3.

Ginzberg, Eli, Daniel Quinn Mills, John D. Owen, Harold L. Sheppard, and Michael Wachter, eds. 1982. *Work Decisions in the 1980s.* Boston: Auburn House Publishing Co.

Gollub, James O. 1983. *Emerging Employment Options for Older Workers: Practice and Potential.* National Commission for Employment Policy (Spring).

Gordus, Jeanne Prial, ed. 1969. *Leaving Early: Perspectives and Problems in Current Retirement Practice and Policy.* Ann Arbor: University of Michigan Institute of Social Research.

Gordus, Jeanne Prial, Paul Jarley, and Louis A. Ferman. 1981. *Plant Closings and Economic*

Dislocations. Kalamazoo, Mich.: W. E. Upjohn Institute for Employment Research.

Gordus, Jeanne Prial, and Sean P. McAlinden. 1984. *Economic Change, Physical Illness, Mental Illness, and Social Deviance.* Study prepared for the Subcommittee on Economic Goals and Intergovernmental Policy of the Joint Economic Committee, U.S. Congress. 98th Cong., 2nd sess. (June 15).

Gould, Clifford I. (Director, U.S. General Accounting Office, Federal Personnel and Compensation Division). 1982. Correspondence to Congresswoman Geraldine A. Ferraro, Chair, Subcommittee on Human Resources, Committee on Post Office and Civil Service (July 12).

Grad, Susan. 1984. "Incomes of the Aged and Nonaged, 1950–82." *Social Security Bulletin* 47, no. 6 (June): 3–17.

Grais, Bernard. 1983. *Lay-offs and Short-Time Working in Selected OECD Countries.* Paris: OECD.

Gurland, Barry, Laura Dean, Roni Gurland, and Diana Cook. 1978. "Personal Time Dependency in the Elderly of New York City: Findings from the U.S.–U.K. Cross National Geriatric Community Study." In *Dependency in the Elderly of New York City.* Community Council of Greater New York (October). Ref. in New York State, *Family Caregiving and the Elderly.*

Gustman, Alan L., and Thomas L. Steinmeier. 1982. *Partial Retirement and Wage Profiles for Older Workers.* National Bureau of Economic Research, Working Paper no. 1000.

──────. 1983a. "Minimum Hours Constraints and Retirement Behavior." *Contemporary Policy Issues,* a Supplement to *Economic Inquiry,* no. 3 (April): 77–91.

──────. 1983b. *Social Security Reform and Labor Supply.* National Bureau of Economic Research. Working paper no. 1212.

──────. 1983c. *A Structural Retirement Model.* National Bureau of Economic Research, Working Paper no. 1237.

──────. 1984. "Partial Retirement and the Analysis of Retirement Behavior." *Industrial and Labor Relations Review* 37, no. 3 (April): 403–15.

Hamermesh, Daniel. 1977. *Jobless Pay and the Economy.* Policy Studies in Employment and Welfare, no. 29. Baltimore: Johns Hopkins University Press.

──────. 1978. "Unemployment Insurance, Short-time Compensation, and the Workweek." In *Work Time and Employment,* National Commission for Manpower Policy, Special Report no. 28 (October). Pp. 231–64.

Harriman, Ann. 1982. *The Work/Leisure Trade-Off: Reduced Time for Managers and Professionals.* New York: Praeger Publishers.

Hayghe, Howard. 1981. "Husbands and Wives as Earners: An Analysis of Family Data." *Monthly Labor Review* 104, no. 2 (February): 46–59.

──────. 1983. "Married Couples: Work and Income Patterns." *Monthly Labor Review* 106, no. 12 (December): 26–29.

Hedges, Janice Neipert, and Stephen J. Gallogly. 1977. "Full and Part Time: A Review of Definitions." *Monthly Labor Review* 100, no. 3 (March): 21–28.

Hedges, Janice N., and Daniel E. Taylor. 1980. "Recent Trends in Worktime: Hours Edge Downward." *Monthly Labor Review* 103, no. 3 (March): 3–11.

Henle, Peter. 1981. *Work Sharing as an Alternative to Lay-Offs.* Washington Congressional Service, Library of Congress, 1976. Ref. in McCarthy and Rosenberg, *Work Sharing.*

Hill, Martha S., Daniel H. Hill, and James N. Morgan. 1981. *Five Thousand American Families: Patterns of Economic Progress,* vol. 9. Ann Arbor: Institute for Social Research, University of Michigan.

Hochschild, Arlie. 1983. *The Second Shift: Dual Work Families with Pre-School Children.* Conference on Women's Lives. Washington, D.C. Women's Research and Education Institute (April 20).

Hoiberg, Anne, ed. 1980. *Women and the World of Work.* New York: Plenum Press.

Holen, Arlene. 1984. "Federal Supplemental Compensation and Unemployment Insurance Recipients." *Monthly Labor Review* 107, no. 4 (April): 43–44.

Horner, Matina, Carol C. Nadelson, and Malkah T. Notman, eds. 1983. *The Challenge of Change: Perspectives on Family, Work, and Education.* New York: Plenum Press.

Hunt, H. Allan, and Timothy L. Hunt. 1983. *Human Resource Implications of Robotics.* Kalamazoo, Mich.: W. E. Upjohn Institute for Employment Research.

Hunter, Donna. 1984. "Oregon Tries the 'Workshare' Idea." In *Short-Time Compensation: A Formula for Work Sharing,* ed. Ramelle MaCoy and Martin J. Morand. New York: Pergamon Press. Pp. 95–105.

Hurd, Michael D., and John B. Shoven. 1982. *The Economic Status of the Elderly.* National Bureau of Economic Research, Working Paper no. 914.

International Labor Office. 1984. *World Labour Report.*

Ittner, Linda. 1982. "A Way to Promote Work Sharing in Lieu of Layoffs." *World of Work Report* 7, no. 212 (December): 23.

_____. 1984. "The Federal Response to Short-Time Compensation." In *Short-Time Compensation: A Formula for Work Sharing,* ed. Ramelle MaCoy and Martin J. Morand. New York: Pergamon Press. Pp. 120–35.

Jacobson, Beverly. 1980. *Young Programs for Older Workers: Case Studies in Progressive Personnel Policies.* New York: Van Nostrand Reinhold.

Jahoda, Marie. 1982. *Employment and Unemployment: A Social-Psychological Analysis.* Cambridge, England: Cambridge University Press.

Jahoda, Marie, Paul Lazarsfeld, and Hans Zeisel. 1933. *Marienthal: The Sociography of an Unemployed Community.* (Translation 1971.) Chicago: Aldine-Atherton.

Johnson, Beverly L., and Elizabeth Waldman. 1983. "Most Women Who Maintain Families Receive Poor Job Market Returns." *Monthly Labor Review* 106, no. 12 (December): 30–34.

Jondrow, James M., Frank Brechling, and Alan Marcus. 1983. *Older Workers in the Market for Part Time Employment.* National Commission for Employment Policy (Spring).

Juster, F. Thomas. Forthcoming. "A Note on Recent Changes in Time Use." In *Time, Goods, and Well Being,* ed. F. Thomas Juster and Frank Stafford. Ann Arbor: Institute for Social Research, University of Michigan.

Juster, F. Thomas, and Frank Stafford, eds. Forthcoming. *Time, Goods, and Well Being.* Ann Arbor: Institute for Social Research, University of Michigan.

Kahne, Hilda. 1975. "Economic Perspectives on the Roles of Women in the American Economy." *Journal of Economic Literature* 13, no. 4 (December): 1249–92.

_____. 1978. "Economic Research on Women and Families." *Signs: Journal of Women in Culture and Society* 3, no. 3 (Spring): 652–65.

_____. 1981. *Economic Security for Older Women: Too Little for Late in Life.* Monograph no. 1. Waltham, Mass.: National Aging Policy Center on Income Maintenance; Florence Heller Graduate School for Advanced Studies in Social Welfare. Brandeis University.

_____. Forthcoming. "Not Yet Equal: Employment Experience of Older Women and Men." *International Journal of Aging and Human Development.*

Kamerman, Sheila B. 1983. "Child Care Services: A National Picture." *Monthly Labor Review* 106, no. 12 (December): 35–39.

Kingson, Eric R. 1979. "Men Who Leave Work Before Age 62: A Study of Advantaged and Disadvantaged Very Early Labor Force Withdrawal." Ph.D. dissertation, Brandeis University. Ref. in Schulz, James H., *The Economics of Aging.* Belmont, Calif.: Wadsworth Publishing Co. P. 23.

_____. 1982. "Current Retirement Trends." In *Economics of Aging: The Future of Retirement,* ed. Malcolm H. Morrison. New York: Van Nostrand Reinhold. Pp. 61–97.

_____. 1983. *Social Security and You: What's New, What's True.* New York: World Almanac Publications.

Klein, Deborah Pisetzner. 1983. "Trends in Employment and Unemployment in Families." *Monthly Labor Review* 106, no. 12 (December): 21–25.

Lamb, Michael E., ed. 1982. *Nontraditional Families: Parenting and Child Development.* Hillsdale, N.J.: Lawrence Erlbaum Associates.

Lammers, John, and Timothy Lockwood. 1984. "The California Experiment." In *Short-Time Compensation: A Formula for Work Sharing,* ed. Ramelle MaCoy and Martin J. Morand. New York: Pergamon Press. Pp. 61–81.

Leavitt, Thomas D. 1983. *Early Retirement Incentive Programs.* A Seminar Report. National Policy Center on Aging, Brandeis University.

Lein, Laura. 1984. *Families Without Villains: American Families in an Era of Change.* Lexington, Mass.: Lexington Books/D.C. Heath.

Lein, Laura, M. Durham, M. Pratt, M. Schudson, R. Thomas, and H. Weiss. 1974. *Final Report: Work and Family Life.* National Institute of Education Project no. 3-3094. Wellesley, Mass.: Wellesley Institute for Research on Women.

Leontief, Wassily W. 1982. "The Distribution of Work and Income." *Scientific American* 247, no. 3 (September): 188–204.

_____. 1983a. *The Long-Term Impact of Technology on Employment and Unemployment.*

Symposium of the National Academy of Engineering (June): 3-7.

_____. 1983b. "Technological Advance, Economic Growth, and the Distribution of Income." *Population and Development Review* 9, no. 3 (September): 403-10.

Levin, Henry M., and Russell W. Rumberger. 1983. Stanford University. Research reported in *New York Times*, September 4, 1983.

Levitan, Sar A., and Richard S. Belous. 1977. *Shorter Hours, Shorter Weeks: Spreading the Work to Reduce Unemployment.* Baltimore: Johns Hopkins University Press.

Liem, Ramsay. 1981. "Employment and Mental Health Implications for Human Service Policy." *Policy Studies Journal* 10 (December): 350-64.

Liem, Ramsay, and Paula Rayman. 1982. "Health and Social Costs of Unemployment: Research and Policy Considerations." *American Psychologist* 37, no. 10 (October): 1116-23.

Lipsky, David B. 1970. "Interplant Transfer and Terminated Workers: A Case Study." *Industrial and Labor Relations Review* 23, no. 1 (January): 191-206.

Livesay, Harold. 1978. *Samuel Gompers and Organized Labor in America.* Boston: Little, Brown.

Lloyd, Cynthia B., ed. 1975. *Sex, Discrimination, and the Division of Labor.* New York: Columbia University Press.

Lloyd, Cynthia B., and Beth T. Niemi. 1979. *The Economics of Sex Differentials.* New York: Columbia University Press.

Long, Marion C., and Susan W. Post. 1981. *State Alternative Work Schedule Manual.* Washington, D.C.: National Council for Alternative Work Patterns, in cooperation with the National Governor's Association.

Lopata, Helen, and Joseph H. Pleck, eds. 1983. *Research in the Interweave of Social Roles, Vol. 3: Families and Jobs.* Greenwich, Conn.: JAI Press.

Lyons, Morgan. 1981. "The Older Employee as a Resource Issue for Personnel." *Personnel Journal* 60, no. 3 (March): 178-86.

MaCoy, Ramelle, and Martin J. Morand, eds. 1984a. *Short-Time Compensation: A Formula for Work Sharing.* New York: Pergamon Press.

_____. 1984b. "Short-Time Compensation: The Implications for Management." In MaCoy and Morand, *Short-Time Compensation: A Formula for Work Sharing,* Pp. 14-35.

Mallan, Lucy. 1982. "Labor Force Participation, Work Experience, and the Pay Gap Between Men and Women." *Journal of Human Resources* 17, no. 3 (Summer): 437-48.

Marshall, F. Ray, Vernon M. Briggs, and Allan G. King. 1984. *Labor Economics: Wages, Employment, Trade Unionism, and Public Policy.* 5th ed. Homewood, Ill.: Richard D. Irwin.

Masnick, George, and Mary Jo Bane. 1980. *The Nation's Families: 1960-1990.* Boston: Auburn House Publishing Co.

McCarthy, Maureen E., and Gail S. Rosenberg. 1981. *Work Sharing: Case Studies.* Kalamazoo, Mich.: W. E. Upjohn Institute for Employment Research.

McConnell, Stephen R. 1983a. "Age Discrimination in Employment." In *Policy Issues in Work and Retirement,* ed. Herbert S. Parnes. Kalamazoo, Mich.: W. E. Upjohn Institute for Employment Research. Pp. 159-96.

_____. 1983b. *Part-Time: Worker's Mandate?* Association of Part-Time Professionals, First National Conference on Part-Time Employment in America (October).

McConnell, Stephen R., Dorothy Fleischer, Carolyn Usher, and Barbara Kaplan. 1980: *Alternative Work Options for Older Workers: A Feasibility Study.* Los Angeles: The Andrus Gerontology Center.

McFarland, Ross. 1973. "The Need for Functional Age Measurements in Industrial Gerontology." *Industrial Gerontology* 19 (Fall): 1-19.

Medoff, James L. 1979. "Layoffs and Alternatives Under Trade Unions in U.S. Manufacturing." *American Economic Review* 69, no. 3 (June): 380-95.

Meier, Gretl S. 1978. *Job Sharing: A New Pattern for Quality of Work and Life.* Kalamazoo, Mich.: W. E. Upjohn Institute for Employment Research.

_____. 1982. "Professionals and Supervisors as Part Timers and Job Sharers." In *New Work Schedules in Practice: Managing Time in a Changing Society,* ed. Stanley D. Nollen. New York: Van Nostrand Reinhold. Pp. 59-68.

Meier, E. L., and E. A. Kerr. 1976. "Capabilities of Middle-Aged and Older Workers: A Survey of the Literature." *Industrial Gerontology* 3, no. 3 (Summer): 147-56.

Meisel, Harry. 1984. "The Pioneers: STC in the Federal Republic of Germany." In *Short-Time*

Compensation: A Formula for Work Sharing, ed. Ramelle MaCoy and Martin J. Morand. New York: Pergamon Press. Pp. 53–60.

Mellor, Earl F. 1984. "Investigating the Differences in Weekly Earnings of Women and Men." *Monthly Labor Review* 107, no. 6 (June): 17–28.

Mesa, Juan M. 1984. "Short-Time Working or Lay-offs? Experience from Canada and California." *International Labour Review* 123, no. 1 (January/February): 99–115.

Mincer, Jacob. 1962. "Labor Force Participation of Married Women: A Study of Labor Supply." *Aspects of Labor Economics,* National Bureau of Economic Research. Princeton: Princeton University Press. Pp. 63–105.

Mincer, Jacob, and Solomon Polacheck. 1974. "Family Investments in Human Capital: Earnings of Women." *Journal of Political Economy* 82, no. 2 (March/April): 576–608.

Moen, Phyllis. 1982a. *Family Aspects of Women's Part-Time Employment.* Final Report. Grant no. 21-25-80-12, Department of Labor, Employment Training Administration. (Sept., rev. Dec.)

_____. 1982b. "The Two-Provider Family: Problems and Potentials." In *Nontraditional Families: Parenting and Child Development,* ed. Michael E. Lamb. Hillsdale, N.J.: Lawrence Erlbaum Associates. Pp. 13–41.

Moorman, Barbara. 1982a. *Job Sharing Through Collective Bargaining.* San Francisco: New Ways to Work.

_____. 1982b. *Upgrading Part-Time Work: Why Unions Should Support Voluntary Job Sharing.* San Francisco: New Ways to Work.

Morand, Martin J., and Donald S. McPherson. 1981. *Report on Worksharing.* Indiana University of Pennsylvania, Center for Study of Labor Relations. Ref. in Bureau of National Affairs, *Daily Labor Report,* C-1.

Morgan, James N. 1981. "Antecedents and Consequences of Retirement." In *Five Thousand American Families: Patterns of Economic Progress,* ed. Martha S. Hill, Daniel H. Hill, and James N. Morgan. Ann Arbor: Institute for Social Research, University of Michigan. Pp. 207–44.

Morrison, Malcolm H. 1979. "International Developments in Retirement Flexibility." *Aging and Work* 2, no. 4 (Fall): 221–34.

_____. 1982. *Economics of Aging: The Future of Retirement.* New York: Van Nostrand Reinhold.

_____. 1983. "The Aging of the U.S. Population: Human Resource Implications." *Monthly Labor Review* 106, no. 5 (May): 13–19.

Munnell, Alicia. 1982. *The Economics of Private Pensions.* Especially Chapter 7, "Pensions in an Inflationary Environment." Washington, D.C.: The Brookings Institution. Pp. 170–98.

_____. 1983a. "Financing Options for Social Security." In *Policy Issues in Work and Retirement,* ed. Herbert S. Parnes. Kalamazoo, Mich.: W. E. Upjohn Institute for Employment Research. Pp. 179–240.

_____. 1983b. "Social Security Financing." *New England Economic Review,* Federal Reserve Bank of Boston (May/June): 46–62.

_____. 1984. "ERISA—The First Decade: Was The Legislation Consistent with Other National Goals?" *New England Economic Review,* Federal Reserve Bank of Boston (November/December): 44–63.

National Commission for Manpower Policy. 1978. *Work Time and Employment.* Special Report no. 28.

National Commission on Social Security. 1981. *Social Security in America's Future.* Final Report.

National Commission on Social Security Reform. 1983. *Report* (January).

National Council on the Aging. 1981. *Aging in the Eighties: America in Transition.* Washington, D.C.

Nemirow, Martin. 1984a. "Short-Time Compensation: Some Policy Considerations." In *Short-Time Compensation: A Formula for Work-Sharing,* ed. Ramelle MaCoy and Martin J. Morand. New York: Pergamon Press. Pp. 158–82.

_____. 1984b. "Work-Sharing Approaches: Past and Present." *Monthly Labor Review* 107, no. 9 (September): 34–39.

New York State Division of Human Rights. 1972. *Survey of State Agencies Concerning the Employment of Older Workers.* Albany: Division of Human Rights.

New York State Office for the Aging. 1983. *Family Caregiving and the Elderly.* Policy Recommendations and Research Findings. (March).

———. Forthcoming. *The Mature Worker: A Cooperative Study By New York State Government and Public Employee Unions.*

Nollen, Stanley D. 1982. *New Work Schedules in Practice: Managing Time in a Changing Society.* New York: Van Nostrand Reinhold.

———. 1983. *Employers' Response? Part-Time Employment in America.* Association of Part-Time Professionals, First National Conference on Part-Time Employment (October).

Nollen, Stanley D., Brenda Broz Eddy, and Virginia Hider Martin. 1978. *Permanent Part-Time Employment: The Manager's Perspective.* New York: Praeger Publishers.

Nollen, Stanley D., and Virginia H. Martin. 1978. *Alternative Work Schedules, Part 2: Permanent Part Time Employment.* New York: AMACOM, a division of American Management Associations.

Norwood, Janet L. 1984. *Jobs and Prices in a Recovering Economy.* U.S. Department of Labor, Bureau of Labor Statistics. Report 704.

Nusberg, Charlotte. 1980. *Flexible Retirement in Other Industrialized Countries.* International Federation on Aging (November).

Oaklander, Harold. 1982. "Workforce Reductions: United States." In *Workforce Reductions in Undertakings: Policies and Measures for the Protection of Redundant Workers in Seven Industrialized Market Economy Countries,* ed. Edward E. Yemin. Geneva: International Labour Office. Pp. 187–214.

Olmsted, Barney. 1983. "Changing Times: The Use of Reduced Work Time Options in the United States." *International Labour Review* 122, no. 4 (July–August): 479–93.

Olmsted, Barney, Suzanne Smith, and New Ways to Work Job Sharing Project. 1981. *Job Sharing: Analyzing the Cost.* San Francisco: New Ways to Work.

Olson, Lawrence, Christopher Caton, and Martin Duffy. 1981. *The Elderly and the Future Economy.* Lexington, Mass.: Lexington Books/D.C. Heath.

O'Neill, June, and Rachel Braun. 1981. *Women and the Labor Market: Survey of Issues and Policies in the U.S.* (November) Mimeographed.

Oppenheimer, Valerie Kincade. 1982. *Work and the Family: A Study in Social Demography.* New York: Academic Press.

Owen, John D. 1982. "The Economic and Social Effects of Hours Reduction." In *Work Decisions in the 1980s,* ed. Eli Ginzburg, Daniel Quinn Mills, John D. Owen, Harold L. Sheppard, and Michael L. Wachter. Boston: Auburn House Publishing Co. Pp. 107–31.

Packard, Michael D. 1982. "Retirement Options Under the Swedish National Pension System." *Social Security Bulletin* 45, no. 11 (November): 12–21.

Paris, Ellen. 1983. "It Works!" *Forbes.* (March 14).

Parnes, Herbert S., ed. 1981. *Work and Retirement: A Longitudinal Study of Men.* Cambridge: MIT Press.

Parnes, Herbert S. 1982. *Unemployment Experience of Individuals Over A Decade: Variations by Sex, Race, and Age.* Kalamazoo, Mich.: W. E. Upjohn Institute for Employment Research.

———. ed. 1983. *Policy Issues in Work and Retirement.* Kalamazoo, Mich.: W. E. Upjohn Institute for Employment Research.

Parnes, Herbert A., Arvil V. Adams, Paul J. Andrisani, Andrew I. Kohen, and Gilbert Nestel. 1975. *The Pre-Retirement Years: Five Years in the Work Lives of Middle Aged Men,* vol. 4. Washington, D.C.: U.S. Department of Labor Manpower Research Monograph No. 12.

Parnes, Herbert S., Mary G. Gagen, and Randell H. King. 1981. "Job Loss Among Long Service Workers." In *Work and Retirement: A Longitudinal Study of Men,* ed. Herbert S. Parnes. Cambridge: MIT Press.

Parnes, Herbert S., and Randy King. 1977. "Middle-Aged Job Losers." *Industrial Gerontology* 4, no. 2 (Spring): 77–95.

Parnes, Herbert S., and Lawrence Less. 1983. *From Work to Retirement: The Experience of a National Sample of Men.* Columbus: Ohio State University, Center for Human Resource Research.

Parnes, Herbert S., and Gilbert Nestel. 1981. "The Retirement Experience." In *Work and Retirement: A Longitudinal Study of Men,* ed. Herbert S. Parnes. Cambridge: MIT Press.

Paul, Carolyn E. 1983a. *A Human Resource Management Perspective on Work Alternatives for Older Workers.* Washington, D.C.: National Commission for Employment Policy.

———. 1983b. *Expanding Part-Time Work Options for Older Americans: A Feasibility Study.* Los Angeles, Calif.: Ethel Percy Andrus Gerontology Center, University of Southern California.

Perkins, Joseph. 1984. Polaroid Corporation communication (July).

Personick, Valerie A. 1983. "The Job Outlook Through 1995: Industry Output and Employment Projections." *Monthly Labor Review* 106, no. 11 (November): 24–35.

Pettersson, Marianne (Sundström). 1981. *Deltids Arbeteti Sverige* [Part-Time Work in Sweden]. Stockholm: Arbetslivscentrum.

Pleck, Joseph H. 1980. "The Work-Family Problem: Overloading the System." In *Outsiders on the Inside: Women and Organizations,* ed. B. Forisha and B. Goldman. Englewood Cliffs, N.J.: Prentice-Hall. Pp. 55–74.

———. 1983. "Husbands' Paid Work and Family Roles: Current Research Issues." *Research in the Interweave of Social Roles, vol. 3: Families and Jobs,* ed. Helen Lopata and Joseph H. Pleck. Greenwich, Conn.: JAI Press. 251–333.

Pleck, Joseph H., L. Lang, and M. Rustad. 1980. *Men's Family Work Involvement and Satisfaction.* Wellesley, Mass.: Wellesley College Center for Research on Women.

Pleck, Joseph H., Graham L. Staines, and Linda Lang. 1980. "Conflicts Between Work and Family Life." *Monthly Labor Review* 103, no. 3 (March): 29–32.

Plewes, Thomas J. 1983. *Profile of the Part-Time Worker.* Association of Part-Time Professionals. First National Conference on Part-Time Employment (October).

Polachek, Solomon W. 1975. "Discontinuous Labor Force Participation and Its Effect on Women's Market Earnings." In *Sex, Discrimination, and the Division of Labor,* ed. Cynthia Lloyd. New York: Columbia University Press. Pp. 90–122.

———. 1981. "Occupational Self-Selection: A Human Capital Approach to Sex Differences in Occupational Structure." *The Review of Economics and Statistics* 63, no. 1 (February): 60–69.

Presser, Harriet B., and Virginia S. Cain. 1983. "Shift Work Among Dual Earner Couples with Children." *Science* 219, no. 4586 (February 18): 876–79.

Quinn, Joseph F. 1975. "The Microeconomics of Early Retirement: A Cross Sectional View." Unpublished report, U.S. Department of Health, Education and Welfare (November): Ref. in Rones, "Older Men—The Choice Between Work and Retirement," 4.

———. 1980. "Retirement Patterns of Self-Employed Workers." *Retirement Policy and Future Population Aging.* Ref. in Clark, *Retirement Policy in An Aging Society.*

Quist, Gunnar, Joan Acker, and Val R. Lorwin. 1984. "Sweden." In *Women and Trade Unions in Eleven Industrialized Countries,* ed. Alice H. Cook, Val R. Lorwin, and Arlene Kaplan Daniels. Philadelphia: Temple University Press. Pp. 261–85.

Rapoport, Robert, and Rhona Rapoport. 1976. *Dual Career Families Re-examined: New Integrations of Work and Family.* New York: Harper Colophon.

Reno, Virginia. 1971. "Why Men Stop Working At or Before Age 65: Findings from the Survey of New Beneficiaries." *Social Security Bulletin* 34, no. 6 (June): 3–17.

Reskin, Barbara F., ed. 1984a. *Sex Segregation in the Work Place: Trends, Explanations, Remedies.* Washington, D.C.: National Academy Press.

———. 1984b. "Sex Segregation in the Workplace." *Gender at Work: Perspectives on Occupational Segregation and Comparable Worth.* Washington, D.C.: Women's Research and Education Institute. Pp. 1–11.

Reynolds, Lloyd G. 1984. *Labor Economics and Labor Relations.* 8th ed. Englewood Cliffs, N.J.: Prentice-Hall.

Robinson, Lawrence. 1975. "K-12 Unit Composition: An Analysis of Unit Determination Criteria and Case History." *Collective Bargaining Quarterly* 1, no. 3 (December): 80–91.

Robinson, Pauline K., and M. J. Stanford. 1983. *The Availability of Older Workers to the Labor Market: Findings and Limitations.* Los Angeles: Ethel Percy Andrus Geronotology Center, University of Southern California.

Rogers, Gayle Thompson. 1980. *Pension Coverage and Vesting Among Private Wage and Salary Workers 1979: Preliminary Estimates from the 1979 Survey of Pension Plan Coverage.* Working Paper Series No. 16, Office of Research and Statistics, Office of Policy, Social Security Administration, U.S. Department of Health, Education and Welfare.

Rones, Philip L. 1978. "Older Men: The Choice Between Work and Retirement." *Monthly Labor Review* 101, no. 11 (November): 3–10.

_____. 1980. "The Retirement Decision: A Question of Opportunity?" *Monthly Labor Review* 103, no. 11 (November): 14–17.

_____. 1982. "The Aging of the Older Population and Labor Force Participation." *Monthly Labor Review* 105, no. 9 (September): 27–28.

_____. 1983. "The Labor Market Problems of Older Workers." *Monthly Labor Review* 106, no. 5 (May): 3–12.

_____. 1984. "Recent Recessions Swell Ranks of Long-Term Unemployed." *Monthly Labor Review* 107, no. 2 (February): 25–29.

Root, Lawrence S., and Laura H. Zarrugh. 1983. *Innovative Employment Practices for Older Americans.* National Commission for Employment Policy (Spring).

Rosenberg, Gail S., and Maureen E. McCarthy. 1982. "Alternative Work Patterns and the Changing Business Environment." *New Jersey Bell Journal* 5, no. 2 (Summer): 28–37.

Runner, Diana. 1983. "Unemployment Insurance Laws: Legislative Revisions in 1982." *Monthly Labor Review* 106, no. 1 (January): 38–43.

Salisbury, Dallas L., and Deborah Chollett. 1983. Testimony on Tax Treatment of Employee Benefits. U.S. Senate Committee on Finance (June 22).

Sarris, Rosemary. 1984. *The 1981 Omnibus Reconciliation Act and Aid for Families with Dependent Children.* Ann Arbor: Institute for Social Research, University of Michigan.

Schirmer, Jennifer. 1982a. *The Limits Of Reform: Women, Capital and Welfare.* Cambridge, Mass.: Schenkman Publishing Co.

_____. 1982b. "Working Women's Marginalisation in Denmark: Traditional Assumptions and Economic Consequences of Social and Labor Market Policies." *Journal of Sociology and Social Welfare* 9, no. 7 (September): 450–62.

Schmitt, Donald G. 1984. "Postretirement Increases Under Private Pension Plans." *Monthly Labor Review* 107, no. 9 (September): 3–8.

Schorr, Alvin L., and Phyllis Moen. 1979. "The Single Parent and Public Policy." In *Work and Family: Changing Roles of Men and Women,* ed. Patricia Voydanoff (1984). Palo Alto, Calif.: Mayfield Publishing Co. Pp. 288–97.

Schroeder, Patricia. 1982. "Foreword." In *The Work/Leisure Trade-Off: Reduced Time for Managers and Professionals,* ed. Ann Harriman. New York: Praeger Publishers. Pp. ix–x.

Schulz, James H. 1978. "Private Pensions and Women." In *Women in Mid-Life: Security and Fulfillment,* U.S. House Select Committee on Aging and the Subcommittee on Retirement Income and Employment, 95th Cong. 2d sess. Washington, D.C.: USGPO (December). Pp. 205–221.

_____. 1983. "Private Pensions, Inflation, and Employment." In *Policy Issues in Work and Retirement,* ed. Herbert S. Parnes. Kalamazoo, Mich.: W. E. Upjohn Institute for Employment Research. Pp. 241–64.

_____. 1985. *The Economics of Aging.* 3rd edition. Belmont, Calif.: Wadsworth Publishing.

Schwab, Karen. 1976. "Early Labor Force Withdrawal of Men: Participants and Non-Participants, Aged 58–63." In *Almost 65: Baseline Data from the Retirement History Survey,* U.S. Department of Health, Education, and Welfare. Washington, D.C.: USGPO. Pp. 43–56.

Seligson, Michelle, Andrea Gesner, Ellen Gannett, and Wendy Gray. 1983. *School Age Child Care: A Policy Report.* Wellesley, Mass.: Wellesley College Center for Research on Women.

Shack-Marquez, Janice. 1984. "Earnings Differences Between Men and Women: An Introductory Note." *Monthly Labor Review* 107, no. 6 (June): 15–16.

Shapiro, David, and Steven H. Sandell. 1983. *Age Discrimination and Labor Market Problems of Displaced Older Male Workers.* National Commission for Employment Policy.

Shaw, Lois B. 1983a. "Does Working Part-Time Contribute to Women's Occupational Segregation?" Paper presented at Mid-West Economics Association Meeting, St. Louis, Mo. (April 9).

_____. 1983b. "Causes of Irregular Employment Patterns." In *Unplanned Careers: The Working Lives of Middle-Aged Women.* Lexington, Mass.: Lexington Books/D.C. Heath.

_____. 1983c. *Unplanned Careers: The Working Lives of Middle-Aged Women.* Lexington, Mass.: Lexington Books/D.C. Heath.

Sheppard, Harold L., and Richard E. Mantovani. 1982. *Aging in the Eighties: Part Time Employment After Retirement.* A Report for the Travelers Insurance Company by the National Council on Aging.

Sheppard, Harold L., and Sara E. Rix. 1977. *The Graying of Working America: The Coming Crisis in Retirement-Age Policy.* New York: The Free Press.

Sherman, Sally R. 1976a. "Assets on the Threshhold of Retirement." In *Almost 65: Baseline Data from the Retirement History Survey,* U.S. Department of Health, Education and Welfare. Washington, D.C.: USGPO. Pp. 69–81.

_____. 1976b. "Labor Force Status of Nonmarried Women on the Threshold of Retirement." In *Almost 65: Baseline Data from the Retirement History Survey.* U.S. Department of Health, Education and Welfare. Washington, D.C.: USGPO. Pp. 57–68.

Shkop, Yitzchak M., and Esther M. Shkop. 1982. "Job Modification as an Alternative to Retirement." *Personnel Journal* 61, no. 7 (July): 513–16.

Silvestri, George T., John M. Lukasiewicz, and Marcus Einstein. 1983. "Occupational Employment Projections Through 1995." *Monthly Labor Review* 106, no. 11 (November): 37–49.

Soldo, Beth J. 1980a. *The Dependency Squeeze on Middle-Aged Women.* Presentation to Secretary's Advisory Committee on the Rights and Responsibilities of Women. U.S. Department of Health and Human Services. Washington, D.C. (October).

_____. 1980b. "Family Caregiving and the Elderly: Prevalence and Variations." *Final Report.* Kennedy Institute, Georgetown University.

Solow, Robert M. 1975. "The Intelligent Citizen's Guide to Inflation." *The Public Interest* 28 (Winter): 30–66.

Sproat, Kezia. 1983. "How Do Families Fare when the Breadwinner Retires?" *Monthly Labor Review* 106, no. 12 (December): 40–44.

St. Louis, Robert. 1984. "Arizona, Motorola, and the STC." In *Short-Time Compensation: A Formula for Work-Sharing,* ed. Ramelle MaCoy and Martin J. Morand. New York: Pergamon Press. Pp. 82–94.

Staines, Graham L., and Joseph H. Pleck. 1983. *The Impact of Work Schedules on the Family.* Ann Arbor: Institute for Social Research, University of Michigan.

Steinberg, Ronnie, and Lois Haignere. 1984. "Separate but Equivalent: Equal Pay for Work of Comparable Worth." In *Gender at Work: Perspectives on Occupational Segregation and Comparable Worth.* Washington, D.C.: Women's Research and Education Institute. Pp. 13–26.

Stevenson, Mary Huff. 1978. "Wage Differences between Men and Women: Economic Theories." In *Women Working: Theories and Facts in Perspective,* ed. Ann H. Stromberg and Shirley Harkness. Palo Alto, Calif.: Mayfield Publishing Co. Pp. 89–107.

Stone, Julia. 1980. "Age Discrimination in Employment Act: A Review of Recent Changes." *Monthly Labor Review* 103, no. 3 (March): 32–36.

Stromberg, Ann H., and Shirley Harkness. 1978. *Women Working: Theories and Facts in Perspective.* Palo Alto, Calif.: Mayfield Publishing Co.

Summers, Lawrence H. 1983. "Comment and Discussion on Paper by Gary Burtless." *Brookings Papers on Economic Activity,* vol. 1, pp. 250–53.

Sundström, Marianne Pettersson. 1982. "Part-Time Work and Trade Union Activities Among Women." *Economic and Industrial Democracy* 3, no. 4 (November): 561–67.

Svahn, John A., and Mary Ross. 1983. "Social Security Amendments of 1983: Legislative History and Summary of Provisions." *Social Security Bulletin* 46, no. 7 (July): 3–48.

Swank, Constance. 1982. *Phased Retirement: The European Experience.* Washington, D.C.: National Council for Alternative Work Patterns.

Taeuber, Cynthia M. 1983. *America in Transition: An Aging Society.* U.S. Department of Commerce, Bureau of the Census, Current Population Reports, Special Studies, Series P-23, no. 128 (September).

Taylor, J. W. 1968. "Now, About Old Dogs/New Tricks." *Personnel Journal* 47, no. 11 (November): 786–88.

Taylor, R. N. 1975. "Age and Experience as Determinants of Managerial Information Processing and Decision Making Performance." *Academy of Management Journal,* 18, no. 1 (March): 74–81.

Terry, Sylvia Lazos. 1981. "Involuntary Part-Time Work: New Information from the CPS."

Monthly Labor Review 104, no. 2 (February): 70–74.

Thompson, Lawrence H. 1983. "The Social Security Reform Debate." *Journal of Economic Literature* 21, no. 4 (December): 1425–67.

Thurow, Lester. 1983. "Inflation." In *Dangerous Currents: The State of Economics.* New York: Random House. Pp. 50–103.

Tibbs, Dean Robert. 1984. "The Firm's Choice between Layoffs and Reduced Work Hours: A General Theory and an Application to the California Shared Work Unemployment Compensation Program." Ph.D. dissertation, University of California, Davis.

Tolley, G. S., and R. V. Burkhauser. 1977. "Integrating Social Security Into an Incomes Policy." In Tolley and Burkhauser, eds. *Income Support Policies for the Aged.* Cambridge, Mass: Ballinger Publishing Co. Ref. Clark and Spengler, *The Economics of Individual and Population Aging,* p. 96.

Treiman, David J., and Heidi Hartmann, eds. 1981. *Women, Work and Wages: Equal Pay for Jobs of Equal Value.* Washington, D.C.: National Academy Press.

U.S. Commission on Civil Rights. 1981. *Child Care and Equal Opportunity for Women.* Clearinghouse Publication 67 (June).

_____. 1983. *A Growing Crisis: Disadvantaged Women and Their Children.* Clearinghouse Publication 78 (May).

U.S. Congress, Joint Economic Committee, 98th Cong. 1st sess. 1984. *American Women: Three Decades of Change.* Hearings (November 9, 1983).

U.S. Congress. 1983. *Congressional Record* (February 23).

U.S. Congressional Budget Office. 1981. *Indexing With the Consumer Price Index: Problems and Alternatives* (June).

_____. 1982a. *Dislocated Workers: Issues and Federal Options* (July).

_____. 1982b. *Work and Retirement: Options for Continued Employment of Older Workers* (July).

U.S. Department of Commerce, Bureau of the Census. 1979. *Characteristics of the Population Below the Poverty Level.* Current Population Reports, Consumer Income, Series P-60, no. 119.

_____. 1981. *Child Support and Alimony: 1978.* Current Population Reports, Special Studies, Series P-23, no. 112 (September).

_____. 1982. *Projections of the Population of the United States: 1982–2050.* Current Population Reports, Consumer Income, Series P-25, no. 992 (October).

_____. 1983a. *Money Income of Households, Families and Persons in the United States: 1981.* Current Population Reports, Consumer Income, Series P-60, no. 137 (March).

_____. 1983b. *Characteristics of the Population Below the Poverty Level: 1981.* Current Population Reports, Consumer Income, Series P-60, no. 138 (March).

_____. 1983c. *Money Income and Poverty Status of Families and Persons in the United States: 1982.* Current Population Reports, Consumer Income Series P-60, no. 140 (July).

_____. 1983d. *American Women: Three Decades of Change. Special Demographic Analyses CDS-80-8,* Suzanne Bianchi and Daphne Spain (August).

_____. 1983e. *America in Transition: An Aging Society.* Cynthia M. Taeuber. Current Population Reports, Special Studies Series P-23, no. 128. (September).

_____. 1983f. *Child Care Arrangements of Working Mothers: June 1982.* Martin O'Connell and Carolyn C. Rogers. Current Population Reports, Special Studies Series P-23, no. 129 (November).

_____. 1984a. *Characteristics of Households and Persons Receiving Selected Noncash Benefits: 1982.* Current Population Reports, Consumer Income, Series P-60, no. 143 (January).

_____. 1984b. *Earnings in 1981 of Married-Couple Families, By Selected Characteristics of Husbands and Wives.* Current Population Reports, Special Studies, Series P-23, no. 133 (March).

_____. 1984c. *Lifetime Work Experience and Its Effect on Earnings: Retrospective Data From the 1979 Income Survey Development Program.* Joseph J. Salvo and John M. McNeil. Current Population Reports, Special Studies, Series P-23, no. 136 (June).

_____. 1984d. *Characteristics of the Population Below the Poverty Level: 1982.* Current Population Reports, Consumer Income, Series P-60, no. 144.

_____. 1984e. *Money Income and Poverty Status of Families and Persons in the U.S.: 1983.* Current Population Reports, Series P-60, no. 145 (August).

_____. Selected Dates. Current Population Reports, Series P-25.

U.S. Department of Commerce, Bureau of Economic Analysis. *Business Conditions Digest:* April 1973; May 1977; January 1983.

U.S. Department of Health and Human Services, Federal Council on Aging. 1981. *The Need for Long Term Care: Information and Issues.* DHHS Publication no. (OHDS) 81-20704. Washington, D.C.: USGPO.

U.S. Department of Health and Human Services, Public Health Service. 1982a. National Center for Health Statistics. National Health Interview Survey.

U.S. Department of Health and Human Services, Social Security Administration. 1982b. *Social Security Bulletin: Annual Statistical Supplement.*

U.S. Department of Labor. 1965. *The Older American Workers: Age Discrimination in Employment.* Report of the Secretary of Labor to the Congress. Washington, D.C.

_____. 1980. *Private Pensions and the Economic Status of the Aged.*

_____. 1981. *Studies on the Effects of Raising the Age Limit in the Age Discrimination in Employment Act.* Interim Report (December).

U.S. Department of Labor, Bureau of Labor Statistics. 1967. *Three Standards of Living for an Urban Family of Four Persons.* Bulletin No. 1570-5 (Spring).

_____. 1972. *Layoff, Recall, and Worksharing Procedures.* Bulletin 1425-13.

_____. 1979. *Characteristics of Major Bargaining Agreements, July 1, 1976.* Bulletin 2013. Ref in Oaklander, *Workforce Reductions in Undertakings.*

_____. 1980. *Handbook of Labor Statistics.* Bulletin 2070 (December).

_____. 1982a. *The Female-Male Earnings Gap: A Review of Employment and Earnings Issues.* Report 673 (September).

_____. 1982b. *Labor Force Statistics Derived from the Current Population Survey: A Databook.* Bulletin no. 2096, vol. 1 (September).

_____. 1983a. *Employee Benefits in Medium and Large Firms.* Bulletin 2176 (August).

_____. 1983b. *Handbook of Labor Statistics.* Bulletin 2175 (December).

_____. 1984a. *Employment and Earnings.* (January.)

_____. 1984b. *Jobs and Prices in a Recovering Economy.* Janet L. Norwood. Report 704 (April).

_____. 1984c. "Employee Benefits in Medium and Large Firms, 1983."

_____. 1984d. "Work Experience of the Population in 1981-82." Bulletin 2199 (June).

_____. 1984e. Supplementary Data System. Communication, June 14, 1984.

U.S. Department of Labor, Women's Bureau. 1976. *Mature Women Workers: A Profile.*

U.S. General Accounting Office. 1976. *Part-Time Employment in Federal Agencies.* Washington, D.C.: USGPO.

U.S. House of Representatives. 1978. *Women in Mid-life—Security and Fulfillment.* Select Committee on Aging and the Subcommittee on Retirement Income and Employment. 95 Cong., 2d sess. (December): 205-221.

_____. 1981. *The Early Retirement Myth: Why Men Retire Before Age 62.* A Report. Select Committee on Aging. 97th Cong., 1st sess. (October).

_____. 1982a. *An Analysis of Pension Accrual After Age 65.* Select Committee on Aging. 97th Cong., 2d sess. (May).

_____. 1982b. *The Unemployment Crisis Facing Older Americans.* Select Committee on Aging. Hearings, 97th Cong., 2d sess. (October 8): 59-76.

U.S. House of Representatives. 1983. *Demographic and Social trends: Implications for Federal Support of Dependent-Care Services for Children and the Elderly.* Select Committee on Children, Youth, and Families. 98th Cong. 1st sess. (December).

U.S. Joint Economic Committee. 1976. "Estimating the Social Costs of National Economic Policy: Implications for Mental and Physical Health and Criminal Aggression," part 1, Paper, no. 5. In *Employment: Achieving the Goals of the Employment Act of 1946, 30th Anniversary Review* (October).

U.S. Senate. 1981. *Toward a National Older Worker Policy.* Special Committee on Aging. 97th Cong., 1st sess. (September).

_____. 1982. *Aging and the Work Force: Human Resource Strategies.* An Information Paper. Special Committee on Aging. 97th Cong., 2d sess. (August). Prepared by Julia French.

U.S. White House Conference on Aging, 1981.

University of Wisconsin, Institute for Research on Poverty. 1983. *Focus* 6, no. 2 (Spring).

————. 1984. *Focus* 7, no. 1 (Winter).

Urban Institute. 1983. Policy and Research Report 13, no. 1 (Winter).

Urquhart, Michael A., and Marillyn A. Hewson. 1983. "Unemployment Continued to Rise in 1982 as Recession Deepened." *Monthly Labor Review* 106, no. 2 (February): 3–12.

Van Ginnekan, Wouter. 1984. "Employment and the Reduction of the Work Week: A Comparison of Seven European Macro-economic Models." *International Labor Review* 123, no. 1 (January/February): 35–52.

Vedder, Richard K. 1982. *Robotics and the Economy.* Staff Study prepared for the use of the Subcommittee on Monetary and Fiscal Policy of the Joint Economic Committee. 97th Cong., 2d sess. (March 26).

Voos, Paula. 1984. "Labor Union Organizing Programs 1954–1977." Ph.D. dissertation, Harvard University, May 1982. Ref. in Freeman and Medoff, *What Do Unions Do?*

Voydanoff, Patricia, ed. 1984. *Work and Family: Changing Roles of Men and Women.* Palo Alto, Calif.: Mayfield Publishing Co.

Vroom, V. H., and B. Pahl. 1971. "Relationship Between Age and Risk Taking Among Managers." *Journal of Applied Psychology* 55, no. 5 (October): 399–405.

Wachtel, Howard M. 1984. *Labor and the Economy.* New York: Academic Press.

Wachter, Michael L., and William L. Wascher. 1983. "Labor Market Policies in Response to Structural Changes in Labor Demand." *Industrial Change and Public Policy.* Kansas City: Federal Reserve Bank of Kansas City. Pp. 177–215.

Waldman, Elizabeth. 1983. "Labor Force Statistics from a Family Perspective." *Monthly Labor Review* 106, no. 12 (December): 16–20.

Welford, Alan T. 1958. *Aging and Human Skill.* London: Oxford University Press. Ref. in Clark, Kreps, and Spengler, "Economics of Aging."

Wertheimer, Barbara Mayer. 1984. "The United States of America." In *Women in Trade Unions in Eleven Industrialized Countries,* ed. Alice H. Cook, Val R. Lorwin, and Arlene Kaplan Daniels. Philadephia: Temple University Press. Pp. 286–311.

Whittaker, William G. 1979. Background information on H.R. 1784: *A Proposal to Reduce the Hours of Work, To Provide for Double Pay for Overtime, and to Eliminate Mandatory Overtime.* Library of Congress, Congressional Service (October).

————. 1980. *Federal Legislative Interest in Alternative Patterns of Work: An Overview.* Congressional Research Service, Library of Congress. Report no. 80-66E. (March 31).

Wieczorek-Zeul, Heidemarie. 1983. *Statement of the Enquiry Commission of the European Parliament on the Situation of Women in Europe.* Memorandum of the European Parliament Concerning the Re-Structuring and Shortening of Working Time (April).

Winston, Gordon C. 1982. *The Timing of Economic Activities.* New York: Cambridge University Press.

Women's Research and Education Institute. 1984. *Gender at Work: Perspectives on Occupational Segregation and Comparable Worth.* Washington, D.C.

Work in America Institute. 1981. *New Work Schedules for a Changing Society.* New York: Work in America Institute.

Yemin, Edward, ed. 1982. *Workforce Reductions in Undertakings: Policies and Measures for the Protection of Redundant Workers in Seven Industrialized Market Economy Countries.* Geneva: International Labour Office.

Yohalem, Alice M., ed. 1980. *Women Returning to Work: Policies and Progress in Five Countries.* Totowa, N.J.: Allanheld, Osmun.

Zalusky, John. 1983. *Part-Time Work and Unions.* Association of Part-Time Professionals, First National Conference on Part-Time Employment (October).

Index

Absenteeism
  age and, 140
  in cost-benefit analysis of part-time work,
    134–36, 154
Affirmative action, occupational segregation
    and, 49
Age Discrimination in Employment Act
    (ADEA), 6, 10, 13, 97–98
American Federation of Labor–Congress of
    Industrial Organizations (AFL-CIO)
  short-time compensation and, 122
  workweek length and, 121–22
American Federation of State, County, and
    Municipal Employees (AFSCME), 115,
    123
Andrus Gerontology Center, 38, 95, 142, 153
Arizona, 35, 102

BancOhio, 32
Bankers Life and Casualty Company, 94
Barrington, Evan, 12
Bednarzik, Robert W., 118
Blacks
  early retirement among, 72
  female heads of households among, 54, 55,
    57
  work discontinuities among, 51–52
Brenner, Harvey, 84

California, 35
  reduced-schedule programs in, 32, 86,
    122–23, 136, 137, 153
  work sharing in, 102–4, 105, 130–31
Child care, 57–58
Coalition of Labor Union Women (CLUW),
    116
Consumer Price Index (CPI), 77
Corcoran, Mary, 51
Cost-benefit analysis, 153–54

absenteeism in, 134–36, 154
administrative and supervisory costs, 137,
    154
fringe benefits in, 7, 137–39
labor turnover in, 7, 136–37, 154
productivity in, 7, 134, 154

Danziger, Sheldon, 67
Daymont, Thomas, 141
Demographic trends
  growth in number of older workers, 2, 4, 5,
    11–12, 148
  increase in number of working women, 1, 4,
    148
  influence on labor force trends, 14–16,
    148–49
  labor force participation rates, 16–19, 148
  trade unions and, 113
Derber, Milton, 113
Disability pension plans, Swedish, 38–39, 40
Divorce, female heads of household and, 54
Duffy, Martin, 12

Early retirement
  economic considerations in, 14, 18, 72–73,
    155–56
  health status and, 72–73
  of men versus women, 93–94
  social security benefits and, 80, 82, 93–94
  trends for, 14, 18, 20
Earnings
  of men versus women, 45–46, 47, 49, 52, 54
  of older persons, 12–13, 47, 49, 67–68,
    77–78, 83
  of part-time versus full-time employees,
    30–31
  social security test of, 95–96, 155
  work discontinuity impact on, 52
Economic considerations
  in early retirement, 14, 18, 72–73, 155–56